Better Homes and Gar...

HOMEMA
IN NO TIM

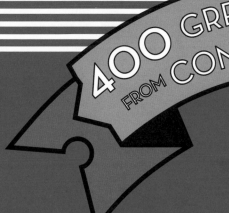

400 GREAT-TASTING RECIPES FROM CONVENIENCE FOODS

Meredith® Books
Des Moines, Iowa

Better Home and Gardens® *Homemade in No Time*
Editors: Jan Miller, Victoria Forlini
Contributing Editor: Kristi Thomas
Writer: Marge Perry
Senior Associate Design Director: Doug Samuelson
Graphic Designer: Joline Rivera
Copy Chief: Terri Fredrickson
Publishing Operations Manager: Karen Schirm
Managers, Book Production: Pam Kvitne, Marjorie J. Schenkelberg, Rick von Holdt, Mark Weaver
Contributing Copy Editor: Karen Fraley
Contributing Proofreaders: Gretchen Kauffman, Susan J. Kling, Jim Roberts
Illustrator: Daniel Pelavin
Indexer: Kathleen Poole
Editorial Assistants: Cheryl Eckert, Karen McFadden
Edit and Design Production Coordinator: Mary Lee Gavin
Test Kitchen Director: Lynn Blanchard
Test Kitchen Product Supervisor: Jill Moberly
Test Kitchen Home Economists: Marilyn Cornelius; Juliana Hale; Laura Harms, R.D.; Jennifer Kalinowski, R.D.;
    Maryellyn Krantz; Jill Moberly; Dianna Nolin; Colleen Weeden; Lori Wilson; Charles Worthington

Meredith® **Books**
Editor in Chief: Linda Raglan Cunningham
Design Director: Matt Strelecki
Managing Editor: Gregory H. Kayko
Executive Editor: Jennifer Dorland Darling

Publisher: James D. Blume
Executive Director, Marketing: Jeffrey Myers
Executive Director, New Business Development: Todd M. Davis
Executive Director, Sales: Ken Zagor
Director, Operations: George A. Susral
Director, Production: Douglas M. Johnston
Business Director: Jim Leonard

Vice President and General Manager: Douglas J. Guendel

Better Homes and Gardens® **Magazine**
Editor in Chief: Karol DeWulf Nickell
Deputy Editor, Food and Entertaining: Nancy Hopkins

Meredith Publishing Group
President, Publishing Group: Stephen M. Lacy
Vice President-Publishing Director: Bob Mate

Meredith Corporation
Chairman and Chief Executive Officer: William T. Kerr

Chairman of the Executive Committee: E. T. Meredith III

All of us at Better Homes and Gardens® Books are dedicated to providing you with the information and ideas you need to
create delicious foods. We welcome your comments and suggestions. Write to us at: Better Homes and Gardens Books,
Cookbook Editorial Department, 1716 Locust St., Des Moines, IA 50309-3023.

If you would like to purchase any of our cooking, crafts, gardening, home improvement,
or home decorating and design books, check wherever quality books are sold.
Or visit us at: bhgbooks.com

Our Better Homes and Gardens® Test Kitchen seal assures you that every recipe in *Homemade In No Time* has been tested in the Better Homes and Gardens® Test Kitchen. This means that each recipe is practical and reliable, and meets our high standards of taste appeal. We guarantee your satisfaction with this book for as long as you own it.

CONTENTS

SCRATCH BASICS

Have you learned the indispensable skill of speed scratch cooking? It's simple: Use convenience products in smart combinations with wholesome fresh foods to make great tasting meals—in a fraction of the time.

Half the battle is won with good meal planning and a well-stocked pantry. Meal planning takes only a few minutes each week. As for stocking your pantry, by no means should this entail going through your cupboards with a pen and paper in hand. A much simpler, and painless, solution exists.

Your once-a-week shopping expedition can be streamlined as well, so you don't spend all day Sunday at the grocery store. Once you're home, storing those ingredients in a simplified, organized way saves you time all week long.

It's also important to take stock of your kitchen equipment. Do you have the basic tools needed to get dinner on the table quickly? Are they accessible? Look around your kitchen and ask yourself if the items you leave out on your counter are things you use nearly every day. If not, put them in a cupboard.

Throughout this section, you'll learn useful, timesaving ideas, including tricks to ensure as little cleanup as possible, how to find shortcut ingredients that don't taste like processed or fast food, how to organize your preparation work space, and how to plan your preparation tasks for maximum efficiency—and a minimum amount of time.

Some of the tips, tricks, and techniques might save you only seconds; others can cut hours from the time you devote each week to meal preparation.

Meal Planning

Surveys show that one of the biggest obstacles to getting dinner on the table is simply figuring out what to cook. By 4 p.m. on most weekdays, many cooks still haven't decided what to make for dinner that evening. After a long, tiring day, dinner could result from one of three choices: 1. Making one of your old reliables—the three to four dishes you serve all the time. 2. Picking up take-out on the way home. 3. Doing battle with the long lines at the grocery store. There is a better way!

Try the following method just once and you'll be hooked.

Play the Slots

Think about the five weeknights as slots you have to fill. If you value variety in your diet, that means each week might include one chicken, one pork, one fish, one beef, and one meatless meal. Or if your family prefers to eat fish twice a week, think of your slots that way. Now pick recipes from each chapter. If you know your schedule is going to be hectic, plan to cook a double batch of a favorite dish and freeze it, or make something that is exceptionally quick to cook. Most nights, assume dinner preparation will take between 15 and 45 minutes.

The Smart List

Make your shopping list do some of the work for you. By compiling the list into sections based on how the grocery store is organized, you'll be in and out of the market much faster. You won't get to the dairy aisle and have to backtrack because you didn't notice "lemons" scribbled at the bottom of your list.

Divide your grocery list into six sections. Label the sections with the following headings:

Meat, Fish, and Poultry

Produce

Dairy

Shelf Items

Freezer Items

Cleaning and Household Items

Every week, use this format to make the list. As you run out of items, write them down under the appropriate heading. When planning your meals for the week, you can easily run through the recipes and fill in the ingredients under the appropriate headings. This takes no more time than writing the list in random order, and it saves substantial time in the supermarket.

Add to the list on an ongoing basis to keep your pantry in good shape. It's simple to do. Just keep the list in a readily accessible spot in the kitchen, and every time you notice something is getting low, or used up, jot it down. This takes less than 15 seconds—and saves a lot of trouble later!

Planning Ahead: Cook Once to Eat Twice

Double Batching: One of the best ways to get a homemade meal on the table in no time is to pull it, fully cooked, out of the freezer. Some dishes lend themselves to freezing and reheating, including slow-braised meats and stews and many casseroles. Why make just enough for one meal? Preparing a double batch of dinner is often little extra work, yet it yields twice the servings. After the second batch cools completely, wrap it well to freeze. Decide if it is more useful to freeze in single, small, or family-sized portions, then label with the name of the dish, how many people it will feed, and the date.

Tweaking: Some leftovers make great, entirely new meals. A roast pork tenderloin can become hot Cuban sandwiches the second night, and chili can be rewarmed with additional tomato sauce and tossed with pasta, broccoli florets, and shredded cheddar cheese for a great Southwestern Pasta dinner.

Reconfiguring: You can also start with a basic ingredient, then take it in different directions to make two distinct meals. Buy twice as much ground beef as you need for tonight's chili. Cook all the beef together, then cover the unused portion tightly and refrigerate. In a couple of days, you'll throw together Hamburger Stroganoff in no time.

Pantry Ingredients and Organization

A wisely stocked, organized pantry can make all the difference in the length of time it takes to get a meal on the table. Remember the term pantry refers to the combination of your cupboard (shelf items), freezer, and longer-lasting refrigerator items.

Fill all three with smart foods—foods that deliver a lot of flavor, texture, and nutrition with minimal effort.

Your pantry can provide all kinds of timesavers. At the most basic level, canned and frozen fruits and vegetables are often great convenience items—and at no cost in flavor, texture, or nutrition. When certain fruits and vegetables are out of season, canned and frozen versions provide excellent, easy-to-use substitutes. Think, for example, about a recipe calling for chopped tomatoes. If you have to wash, core, and chop several Roma tomatoes, it will take you more time than simply opening a can. For some recipes, fresh tomatoes are essential, but for many others, canned tomatoes are actually better. Similarly,

frozen peach slices are ready-to-use, which means they can go directly from the bag into your recipe—eliminating the need for blanching, peeling, and slicing.

To build your pantry, start with the essentials—the staples it takes to make many of your meals. These ingredients, such as flour, sugar, oils, and salt, must be replenished when you run low.

Shortcut ingredients, foods that minimize preparation steps, are a boon to the time-pressed cook. Shredded cheese, bottled minced garlic, and frozen, peeled, and deveined shrimp are good examples of foods that already have some of the preparation steps completed. These ingredients may not be called for in shortcut form in a recipe, but can be substituted.

In many of the recipes in this book, you'll see an ingredient listed that is actually a partially prepared food when you buy it. Biscuit mix, brownie mix, shredded beef in barbecue sauce, bottled marinara sauce, and many other products that combine ingredients that are partially cooked and/or can be used right out of the box or can are convenience items.

Begin with the following items to build your own ideal pantry. Skim through the list and check the ingredients you want.

HOW TO STOCK YOUR PANTRY

Dry Storage

Canned beans: Most are drained and rinsed before using and do not have to be cooked. Add to salads for instant protein; use whole or pureed for hearty soups; toss with a grain for a nutritious meatless meal; or puree into a nearly instant dip for vegetables and chips. Choose from black, Great Northern, kidney, pinto, garbanzo, and others.

Canned refried beans: Use in Mexican-style dishes such as enchiladas, burritos, quesadillas, and more or as the basis for dip to serve with tortilla chips.

Canned soups and broths: Use to form an instant, flavorful foundation for casseroles or as the base for a braising liquid or sauce. Canned broths (chicken, beef, vegetable, and clam juice) give flavor to soups, sauces, and braises and serve as a mild flavor base. Convenient dry bouillons are available in beef, chicken, and vegetable flavors for an inexpensive soup base.

Canned fish: Mix canned tuna and salmon with mayonnaise for cold salads or bake inside tomatoes or small zucchini; toss with pasta, cheese, and vegetables; combine with cream cheese and seasonings for an instant party appetizer. Canned minced clams or canned crab are great for chowders and pasta.

Grains and starch: Many grains are available partially cooked (parboiled) and can be ready in less than 15 minutes.

*Rice: Quick-cooking brown and white rices are available in two forms: parboiled and boil-in-a-bag. In addition, basmati rice cooks in 15 minutes. Many flavored rices are already seasoned.

*Pasta and noodles: Some pasta and noodle shapes can be ready in less than 7 minutes, including fine egg noodles, elbows, angel hair, and vermicelli; most dried shapes boil for less than 15 minutes. Some Asian-style noodles, including Chinese curly noodles, cook in less than 5 minutes.

*Couscous: This precooked grain is ready in less than 15 minutes.

*Less common grains, which are available at many grocery stores and can be cooked in 15 minutes or less, include quick-cooking barley, bulgur, and quinoa.

*Instant polenta, spaetzle, and mashed potato flakes can be prepared in minutes.

Oils: Many types add subtle flavor.

*Sesame and peanut oils add flavor to Asian dishes.

*Extra-virgin olive oil adds Mediterranean flavor. Olive oil is mildly flavorful and good for sautéing, especially in many Mediterranean and Middle Eastern dishes.

*Canola oil has no flavor and is a good choice for most sautéing and frying.

Vinegars: Many types of vinegars are available, including flavored varieties.

*Red wine vinegar is the most basic vinegar to keep on hand. It is used for Italian salad dressing, as well as many other recipes.

*Apple cider vinegar is used in many recipes, particularly when there is fruit in the recipe.

*Balsamic vinegar adds a sweet depth and is used in dressings, sauces, and glazes.

*Rice vinegar is a sweet Asian vinegar used in sauces and dressings. It is much less acidic than most other vinegars.

Condiments, marinades, and sauces: While hundreds of specialty sauces and marinades are available in the market, this section focuses on the most common and widely available ones. Bottled sauces like these can turn a simple piece of chicken, steak, or fish into a great meal with very little effort.

Barbecue sauce	Hot sauce and/or Tabasco
Bottled marinara and Alfredo pasta sauces	Mustards (Dijon, brown, and yellow)
Bottled pesto	Salad dressings
Catsup	Salsa
Chutney	Soy sauce
Dry gravy mix	Teriyaki sauce
Enchilada sauce	Worcestershire sauce
Hoisin sauce	

Miscellaneous shelf items: This section includes a whole gamut of food products. Prepare your own list to round out your pantry. Here are some essentials.

Dry breadcrumbs (plain or seasoned)	Jelly, jam, preserves, marmalade
Coconut milk	Maple syrup
Cornmeal	Molasses
Crackers	Nuts (almonds, pecans, and walnuts)
Honey	Peanut butter

Canned and bottled vegetables and fruits: This section of your kitchen can help save you in a pinch. A quick side dish or last-minute flavor addition can be plucked from your pantry in a shelf-stable can or jar.

Artichoke hearts	Pitted olives and olive paste (tapenade)
Capers	Roasted red sweet peppers
Chile peppers	Tart cherries
Corn	Tomato products (whole Roma tomatoes, diced tomatoes, tomato paste, tomato sauce, and sun-dried tomatoes)
Mandarin oranges	
Mushrooms	
Pineapple	Water chestnuts

Dried fruits: These are as useful in making main courses and side dishes as they are in desserts. Choose from cranberries, raisins, cherries, apricots, dates, dried plums, and peaches.

Herbs, spices, dry seasoning mixes: When you need a flavor boost, these essentials are indispensable.

Allspice	Garlic powder
Basil	Ground cumin
Black pepper	Ground ginger
Blackened or Cajun seasoning	Italian seasoning mix
Caraway seeds	Mustard powder
Chili powder	Nutmeg
Chinese five-spice powder	Onion powder
Chipotle chili powder	Oregano
Cinnamon	Paprika
Cloves	Rosemary
Coriander	Sage
Curry powder	Taco, fajita, and burrito mixes
Dried minced onion	Tarragon
Fennel seeds	Thyme

Cooking essentials: Many of the essential ingredients for everyday cooking are shown in other lists. Here are a few more necessities.

All-purpose flour	Salt
Bottled minced garlic	Sugar (granulated, powdered, and brown)
Bottled minced ginger	
Cornstarch	

Baking essentials: For a dessert in a hurry or a few quick muffins, this list will keep you prepared.

Baking soda	Evaporated milk
Baking powder	Flaked coconut
Biscuit mix	Instant pudding mix
Brownie mix	Muffin mix
Buttermilk powder	Shortening
Cake mix	Sweetened condensed milk
Chocolate syrup or sauce	

Freezer Storage

The size of your freezer will dictate how many items on the list to keep on hand.

Meat, Poultry & Seafood

Bacon	Roasted chicken breast in pieces
Cooked, diced leftover beef and/or poultry	Scallops
Fish fillets	Breads, starches, grains
Ground beef	Bread dough
Ground turkey	Dinner rolls
Individually frozen boneless chicken cutlets	English muffins
Peeled uncooked shrimp	Pastry tart shells
Pork chops, bone-in and boneless, individually frozen	Piecrust
Precooked sausage links	Pizza crust
Ravioli, stuffed shells, tortellini	Puff pastry
	Sandwich bread

Vegetables & Fruits:

Artichoke hearts	Pearl onions
Blueberries	Plain hash brown potatoes
Chopped onions	Sliced peaches
Corn kernels	Spinach
Lima beans	Strawberries in light syrup
Mixed vegetables	Whole strawberries
Peas	

Desserts & Sweet

Ice cream	Butter
Piecrust	Egg substitute
Pound cake	Grated Parmesan cheese
Whipped nondairy topping	Shredded cheeses (cheddar, mozzarella and/or Monterrey Jack)
Dairy	

Refrigerator Storage

While it often seems the primary function of the refrigerator is to store the most perishable foods, it also serves as the keeper for the open bottles and jars you use only occasionally. Some foods will only keep for a certain amount of time, so dispose of them when appropriate.

Buttermilk	Lemons
Butter or margarine	Limes
Carrots (peeled baby carrots)	Precooked polenta
Celery	Peeled, cut potatoes (sold in bags in the refrigerated case)
Cheeses (such as mozzarella, grated Parmesan, blue cheese, and cheddar)	Ready-to-use pizza dough
Cream cheese	Tubes of bread and biscuit dough

HOW TO ORGANIZE YOUR PANTRY

Now that you have this great list of items to keep on hand, what do you do with them? After all, you won't use them all up in one week, and if you don't store them in some organized way, you'll forget they're there.

YOUR FREEZER: NO MORE U.F.O.S

If you're like most people, there's been more than one occasion on which you've discovered a U.F.O. (Unidentified Frozen Object) buried in your freezer. U.F.O.s exist because you're in a hurry and sometimes wrap something and throw it in the freezer. Day after day, you grab the packages that require no guesswork, until eventually, those unidentifiable containers have been shoved to the very back of the freezer.

To avoid this waste and frustration, follow these simple steps to keep an organized freezer. Whether you have a top, bottom, or side-by-side freezer, the same guidelines apply to help make short work of keeping your freezer contents accessible.

1. Wrap and Label
*Start by marking a 2- to 3-inch piece of masking tape with a brief description of the package contents and the date. The label might read: "Chicken breast on the bone 10/29/04" or "Sliced cooked brisket, 12/01/04."

*Wrap the food airtight in plastic wrap, making sure you form a package that is flat on the bottom.

*Place the masking tape label along one edge—the edge that will face you when you open the freezer door.

*If the package is small, slip it into a resealable plastic bag, perhaps combined with similar items, all with labels facing out.

2. Divide and Conquer
Think of your freezer, no matter how large or small, as having sections. Each food belongs in a specific section: chicken, lamb, beef, pork, seafood, fruits, and vegetables, heat-and-eat foods, dairy, desserts, breads, grains, and so on. Designate a section in the freezer to each kind of food. You might want to group similar items together in containers.

REFRIGERATOR MANAGEMENT: MUSTARDS UNITE!

Think how much easier it would be to find things in the fridge if similar types of food were always grouped together—and on the same shelf. Say, for example, you have a jar of Dijon mustard and one of yellow mustard. If they were always on the door, one shelf down, it would take you no time to pull them out of the fridge. If all your condiments—olives, capers, pickles, pickled jalapeños, etc.—are grouped together in the fridge, there's no time wasted rummaging through shelves. Similarly, put all sandwich spreadables—mayonnaise, mustard, and catsup—together and near the other condiments. Now not only will you be able to find what you need when you need it—so will the rest of your family!

Many shops that carry home organization products sell clear plastic lazy Susan trays designed specifically for the refrigerator. They're a great way of making all those little jars accessible, although they use space a little less efficiently.

Designate certain areas of the refrigerator for specific foods. Start by assigning the tallest areas for beverages. Make an area on the bottom shelf for raw meats. Keep raw meat on the bottom shelf so that if the package leaks, the uncooked fluids won't come into contact with any ready-to-eat foods, possibly causing illness. Keep all dairy, such as cottage cheese, yogurt, sour cream, and cheese together. Keep egg cartons against the wall in the refrigerator to minimize the chance of crushing or knocking off the shelf. All leftovers should be grouped together on a shelf and all vegetables in the crisper drawer. Always use the same spot for each of your food groups.

Assembling ingredients for dinner is much faster when you know exactly where everything is. It also makes it much easier to enlist the help of other household members.

TAKING CONTROL, ONE SHELF & DRAWER AT A TIME

If you stand in the middle of your kitchen and think about all the drawers and cupboards jammed with boxes and cans and bottles, the idea of organizing them might seem overwhelming. Just pick one place to get started. Put your garbage pail next to the cupboard or drawer and simply throw out any food that has been there for more than 2 months without being touched. It is amazing how much space these never-gonna-use items, such as open cookie containers and cereal nobody likes, take up.

The most important rule when organizing your cupboards and drawers is to keep all items visible. In order to do this:

* Face all package labels forward

* Stagger heights: Put tall foods in back or use shelf steps, available at housewares shops, to create different heights.

* Group similar items: For example, keep all the starches together so that pasta, couscous, and rice are in the same place.

* Use clear plastic containers to hold small or awkwardly shaped objects or to keep groups together. That way, if you need to get something out from behind them, you simply lift out one container, rather than several small bags or bottles.

Organize your pantry by the way you use ingredients. Keep pasta sauces near pasta and rice vinegar near soy sauce. Honey might be near the tea, which may nestle against cocoa.

Outfit your cupboards to maximize the visibility of their contents. If you keep your oils and vinegars in a wall cabinet, for example, place the bottles on a lazy Susan (with the labels facing out). You'll be able to see and reach all the bottles, rather than having some get buried in the back.

Similarly, a lazy Susan is ideal for holding alphabetized herb and spice jars. Keeping the spices alphabetized is a timesaver.

KITCHEN EQUIPMENT

Where do you do most of your preparation in the kitchen? Most likely it is within a step or two of the sink and/or stove. The drawers and cupboards closest to your usual work space should hold the kitchen equipment you use most often. For most weeknight meals, a basic equipment list includes:

Paring knife	**Large spoons**
Chef's knife (8 to 10 inches)	**Wooden spoons**
Kitchen shears	**Can opener**
Mixing bowls	**Whisk**
2 skillets (1 large, 1 small)	**2 or more cutting boards**
2 saucepans (1 large, 1 small)	**Strainer**
1 soup pot	**Colander**
Baking dish	**Instant-read meat thermometer**
Broiler pan	**Measuring cups and spoons**
Spatulas	

Store these items closest to your workspace. It is convenient to keep the utensils in a canister tucked back under the overhead cabinets, but still well within reach. Knives can go in a divided drawer or knife block. Avoid storing your most frequently used skillets and pots in a big stack, if possible, which makes them a hassle to pull out every night. Try to limit stacks for those items to three pans, even if it means making higher stacks of less often used equipment.

Other appliances, gadgets, and utensils help make weeknight cooking easier. Additional helpful tools include:

Microplane or similar grater: Shaped like a ruler, these super-sharp graters are easy to manage and ideal for grating cheese, citrus peel, and chocolate.

Food processor: If you have the room, this appliance makes prep work easier. Use it to puree soups, chop and mince vegetables, mix dough, and more.

Handheld blender: Don't bother transferring soup ingredients to a traditional blender. A handheld blender lets you puree right in the pot—which saves you time and cleanup.

Vegetable peeler: Be sure your straight-edge vegetable peeler is sharp to make short work of scraping carrots and potatoes. Also consider a julienne peeler, which gives you attractive thin julienne strips without all the knife work.

Knife sharpener or steel: Sharp knives cut better and cause far fewer accidents than dull knives. Whether you choose an electric sharpener, steel, or stone, be sure to keep your knives as sharp as possible.

The best way to organize your kitchen so that your physical space contributes to the speed and efficiency with which you can get a meal on the table is to edit. When you look around at the counters, do you use all the visible objects on a regular basis? If you don't use an item several times a week, put it in a cupboard. Tuck items out of sight if they don't regularly help you prepare meals.

HOW TO COOK FASTER AND MORE EFFICIENTLY

To get faster and more efficient in the kitchen, all you have to do is take more time to prepare before you begin cooking. You can save time—and headaches—by following these simple steps:

1. Think through the preparation of the side dishes before you get started. Will the rice take longer to cook than the main dish? Do you need to set a big pot of water to boil for pasta? Start these before you begin cooking the main course. Now is the time to figure out when you should begin cooking the vegetable.

2. Read the recipe all the way through first. You don't want to be halfway done making a dish before realizing it has to marinate overnight, calls for an ingredient you don't have, or requires an unfamiliar cooking technique.

3. Assemble all your ingredients on the counter. Don't cut or dice or open packages yet—just put them all out, following the order of the list in the recipe. It's a good way to make sure you have everything, and it saves time while cooking.

4. Make each ingredient fit the description on the recipe ingredients list. If the ingredients call for 1/2 cup snipped parsley, now is the time to clean, snip, and measure.

When it's time to begin combining ingredients and cooking, organize your work space.

*Place unused ingredients on one side of your board or bowl. As you use each ingredient—add 1/2 teaspoon of salt to the bowl, for example—move the salt container to the other side.

This way, if the phone rings or you get distracted, you'll know which ingredients have been used.

*Try to work with all your vegetables and other nonmeat ingredients on the cutting board first, then with the meat. That way, you don't have to worry about scrubbing down the board in between. Never go from working with raw meat to vegetables without cleaning the board thoroughly in between.

*Place used utensils in the sink as you go.

Make your cleanup easier: after the rush of getting dinner on the table, no one likes to face scouring a big pile of pots. Here are some shortcuts to keep in mind:

*Not everything is best stirred or tossed with a utensil. Sometimes, hands do a better job. Think about tossing ground beef and seasonings. Salad ingredients get more evenly distributed if you use your hands. If you are concerned about cleanliness, purchase inexpensive plastic kitchen gloves.

*Coat measuring cups and spoons with nonstick cooking spray before measuring honey, molasses, peanut butter, or any other sticky ingredient. Your ingredients will slide right out.

*Line the broiler pan with foil and coat the broiler rack with cooking spray to keep juices and fat from scorching the surface.

*For one less bowl to clean, use resealable plastic bags for coating meat with flour or for marinating.

Good meal planning, a well-organized pantry filled with smart foods, and a kitchen laid out to function the way you work pave the way to preparing meals faster and more efficiently. The collection of great-tasting recipes on the following pages is all you need to create wonderful homemade meals in no time.

APPETIZERS & SNACKS

FETA CHEESE BALL

Prep: 15 minutes

Chill: 5 hours

Makes: about 1¾ cups

1   8-ounce package cream cheese

4   ounces feta cheese, crumbled (1 cup)

⅓   cup finely chopped ripe olives

3   tablespoons thinly sliced green onions

1   tablespoon snipped fresh basil or 1 teaspoon dried basil, crushed

     Lettuce leaves

     Chopped or sliced ripe olives (optional)

     Assorted crackers

1 In a food processor bowl or a medium mixing bowl combine cheeses. Cover and process or beat with electric mixer on medium speed until nearly smooth. Stir in the ⅓ cup olives, the green onions, and basil.

2 Cover and chill about 1 hour or until slightly stiffened. Form mixture into a ball.

3 Wrap and chill about 4 hours or until firm.

4 Place on lettuce-lined serving plate. If desired, garnish with additional olives. Serve with crackers.

Make-Ahead Directions: Prepare as directed through step 2. Wrap and chill up to 24 hours. Serve as directed in step 4.

Nutrition Facts per 2 tablespoons spread: 82 cal., 8 g total fat (5 g sat. fat), 25 mg chol., 165 mg sodium, 1 g carbo., 0 g fiber, 2 g pro.

BLUE CHEESE WALNUT SPREAD

Start to Finish:

10 minutes

· ·

Makes: 1 cup spread

1	3-ounce package cream cheese, softened
2	ounces blue cheese, crumbled
¼	cup dairy sour cream
½	teaspoon Worcestershire sauce
¼	cup chopped walnuts, toasted
1	tablespoon snipped fresh chives
	Assorted crackers, apple slices, and/or pear slices

1 In a small bowl stir together cream cheese, blue cheese, sour cream, and Worcestershire sauce. Stir in toasted walnuts and snipped chives. Serve with assorted crackers.

Nutrition Facts per 2 tablespoons spread: 100 cal., 9 g total fat (5 g sat. fat), 20 mg chol., 138 mg sodium, 1 g carbo., 0 g fiber, 3 g pro.

SPANISH OLIVE SPREAD

Prep: **15** minutes
Chill: **4** to **24** hours

Makes: about 20 servings

1½   cups finely shredded Swiss cheese (6 ounces)

1   3-ounce jar pimiento-stuffed green olives, drained and chopped

½   cup mayonnaise or salad dressing

     Assorted crackers

1 In a medium bowl stir together Swiss cheese and olives. Stir in mayonnaise. Cover and chill for at least 4 hours or up to 24 hours.

2 Before serving, gently stir mixture. Serve with crackers.

Nutrition Facts per serving: 76 cal., 7 g total fat (2 g sat. fat), 10 mg chol., 140 mg sodium, 0 g carbo., 0 g fiber, 2 g pro.

SMOKED FISH SPREAD

Prep: 10 minutes
Chill: 4 to **24** hours

Makes: about 1 cup

6	ounces smoked skinless, boneless whitefish
2	tablespoons mayonnaise or salad dressing
½	of an 8-ounce package cream cheese, softened
2	tablespoons Dijon-style mustard
¼	teaspoon ground white pepper
	Assorted crackers

1 Using a fork, finely flake the fish. (Or place fish in a food processor bowl. Cover and process with several on/off turns until fish is finely chopped.) Set aside.

2 In a medium bowl gradually stir mayonnaise into the softened cream cheese. Stir in the mustard and white pepper. Fold in the fish.

3 Cover and chill for at least 4 hours or up to 24 hours. To serve, spread on crackers.

Nutrition Facts per tablespoon spread: 52 cal., 4 g total fat (2 g sat. fat), 17 mg chol., 160 mg sodium, 0 g carbo., 0 g fiber, 3 g pro.

GARBANZO BEAN DIP

Makes: about 1¾ cups

1	15-ounce can garbanzo beans (chickpeas), rinsed and drained
½	cup plain yogurt
¼	cup bottled buttermilk salad dressing
2	tablespoons seasoned fine dry bread crumbs
2	teaspoons lemon juice
½	teaspoon crushed red pepper
2	tablespoons chopped pitted ripe olives
	Assorted crackers or vegetable dippers

1 In a food processor bowl or blender container combine garbanzo beans, yogurt, salad dressing, bread crumbs, lemon juice, and crushed red pepper. Cover and process or blend until smooth. Stir in olives. If desired, cover and chill for 1 hour before serving. Serve with crackers or vegetable dippers.

Make-Ahead Directions: Prepare as directed, except cover and chill for up to 24 hours.

Nutrition Facts per 2 tablespoons dip: 82 cal., 3 g total fat (1 g sat. fat), 2 mg chol., 198 mg sodium, 10 g carbo., 2 g fiber, 2 g pro.

PRALINE-TOPPED BRIE

Prep: 10 minutes
Bake: 15 minutes

Oven: 350°F
Makes: 10 to 12 appetizer servings

1   13- to 15-ounce round Brie or Camembert cheese
½   cup orange marmalade
2   tablespoons packed brown sugar
⅓   cup coarsely chopped pecans, toasted
    Baguette slices, toasted, and/or assorted plain crackers

1 Preheat oven to 350°. Place the round of cheese in a shallow ovenproof serving dish or pie plate. In a small bowl stir together orange marmalade and brown sugar. Spread on top of cheese. Sprinkle with toasted pecans.

2 Bake in preheated oven about 15 minutes for smaller round, about 20 minutes for larger round, or until cheese is slightly softened and topping is bubbly. Serve with baguette slices and/or crackers.

Nutrition Facts per serving of cheese: 198 cal., 13 g total fat (7 g sat. fat), 37 mg chol., 242 mg sodium, 14 g carbo., 0 g fiber, 8 g pro.

HOT CRAB SPREAD

Start to Finish:

15 minutes

Makes: about 1 cup

½ of an 8-ounce tub cream cheese with garden vegetables

1 6- to 6½-ounce can crabmeat, drained, flaked, and cartilage removed

2 tablespoons sliced green onion

1 teaspoon lemon juice

½ teaspoon dried dill

Several dashes bottled hot pepper sauce

Assorted crackers

1 In a small saucepan heat cream cheese over medium-low heat until softened. Stir in crabmeat, green onion, lemon juice, dill, and hot pepper sauce. Cook and stir for 3 to 4 minutes more or until heated through. Serve warm with crackers.

Nutrition Facts per 2 tablespoons spread: 72 cal., 5 g total fat (3 g sat. fat), 31 mg chol., 151 mg sodium, 1 g carbo., 0 g fiber, 5 g pro.

HOT ARTICHOKE & ROASTED PEPPER PARMESAN CHEESE DIP

Prep: **15** minutes

Bake: **25** minutes

....

Oven: 350°F

Makes: about 3¾ cups
(12 servings)

1   8-ounce package cream cheese, softened

1   cup shredded Parmesan or Asiago cheese (4 ounces)

1   teaspoon bottled minced garlic (2 cloves)

1   13- to 14-ounce can artichoke hearts, drained

1   cup bottled roasted red sweet peppers, drained

1   cup sliced fresh mushrooms

½   cup sliced green onions

Thinly sliced French bread, toasted, or toasted pita wedges

Chopped bottled roasted red sweet peppers (optional)

Fresh parsley (optional)

1 Preheat oven to 350°. In a food processor combine cream cheese, Parmesan cheese, and garlic. Cover and process until well mixed. Add drained artichoke hearts, the 1 cup roasted peppers, the mushrooms, and green onions. Cover and process with on/off turns until finely chopped.

2 Transfer mixture to an 8-inch quiche dish or 9-inch pie plate, spreading evenly.

3 Bake, covered, in preheated oven about 25 minutes or until heated through. Serve warm with thinly sliced French bread. If desired, garnish with additional roasted pepper and parsley.

Mixer Method: In a medium mixing bowl beat cream cheese, Parmesan cheese, and garlic (2 cloves) with an electric mixer on medium to high speed until well mixed. Finely chop drained artichoke hearts, the 1 cup roasted peppers, the mushrooms, and green onions. Stir into beaten cheese mixture. Spoon into quiche dish or pie plate; bake as directed in step 3.

Microwave Directions: Prepare as directed through step 2, making sure to use a microwave-safe quiche dish or pie plate. Microwave on 70% (medium-high) power for 6 to 8 minutes or until heated through, stirring the dip and turning the dish halfway through cooking time.

Nutrition Facts per serving: 126 cal., 10 g total fat (7 g sat. fat), 31 mg chol., 271 mg sodium, 4 g carbo., 2 g fiber, 5 g pro.

EASY JALAPEÑO SALSA

Start to Finish:

10 minutes

. . . .

Makes: about 1½ cups

¼   cup coarsely chopped onion

1   to 2 fresh jalapeño chile peppers, seeded and coarsely chopped*

¼   cup snipped fresh cilantro

1   14½-ounce can Italian-style stewed tomatoes, drained

¼   teaspoon salt

     Tortilla chips

1 In a blender or food processor combine onion, jalapeño peppers, and cilantro. Cover and blend or process for 2 to 3 pulses. Add drained tomatoes and salt. Cover and blend or process for 1 to 2 pulses more or until salsa reaches desired consistency. Serve with tortilla chips.

Make-Ahead Directions: Prepare as directed. Cover and chill for up to 24 hours.

*Note: Because chile peppers contain volatile oils that can burn your skin and eyes, avoid direct contact with them as much as possible. When working with chile peppers, wear plastic or rubber gloves. If your bare hands do touch the peppers, wash your hands and nails well with soap and warm water.

Nutrition Facts per ¼ cup salsa: 24 cal., 0 g total fat (0 g sat. fat), 0 mg chol., 229 mg sodium, 5 g carbo., 1 g fiber, 1 g pro.

SMOKY CHIPOTLE FONDUE

Start to Finish:

15 minutes

Makes: about 1 cup

8   ounces American cheese, cubed

2   tablespoons dry white wine

2   teaspoons Dijon-style mustard

½   teaspoon Worcestershire sauce

1   to 2 canned chipotle chile peppers in adobo sauce, chopped*

2   to 4 tablespoons milk

Crusty French bread cubes or tortilla chips

1 In a heavy, medium saucepan combine American cheese, white wine, mustard, Worcestershire sauce, and chipotle peppers. Cook and stir over medium-low heat until melted and smooth. Stir in enough of the milk to reach desired consistency. Transfer to a fondue pot; keep warm over a fondue burner.

2 Serve fondue immediately with bread cubes. If the fondue mixture thickens, stir in some additional milk.

*Note: Because chile peppers contain volatile oils that can burn your skin and eyes, avoid direct contact with them as much as possible. When working with chile peppers, wear plastic or rubber gloves. If your bare hands do touch the peppers, wash your hands and nails well with soap and warm water.

Nutrition Facts per 2 tablespoons fondue: 114 cal., 9 g total fat (6 g sat. fat), 27 mg chol., 427 mg sodium, 1 g carbo., 0 g fiber, 6 g pro.

COCONUT SHRIMP WITH MANGO GINGER DIP

Prep: 15 minutes
Bake: 10 minutes

. . . .

Oven: 400°F
Makes: 10 appetizer servings

1	pound fresh or frozen peeled and deveined shrimp
1	cup flaked coconut, toasted and chopped
1/2	cup seasoned fine dry bread crumbs
3/4	teaspoon curry powder
2	slightly beaten egg whites
	Nonstick cooking spray
1/2	cup mango chutney
1/4	cup orange juice
1/4	teaspoon ground ginger

1 Thaw shrimp, if frozen. Rinse shrimp; pat dry with paper towels.

2 Preheat oven to 400°. Grease a 15×10×1-inch baking pan; set aside. In a shallow bowl combine coconut, bread crumbs, and curry powder. Place egg whites in another small shallow bowl. Dip shrimp into the egg whites; dip into the coconut mixture, pressing the mixture firmly onto the shrimp. Place on prepared baking pan. Coat shrimp with cooking spray.

3 Bake in preheated oven for about 10 minutes or until shrimp turn opaque. Meanwhile, in a small bowl combine chutney, orange juice, and ginger. Serve with shrimp.

Nutrition Facts per serving: 175 cal., 5 g total fat (4 g sat. fat), 69 mg chol., 287 mg sodium, 21 g carbo., 2 g fiber, 12 g pro.

DATE-SAUSAGE BITES

Prep: 20 minutes
Bake: 20 minutes

. . . .

Oven: 400°F
Makes: about 27 pieces

½   of a 17.3-ounce package frozen puff pastry (1 sheet)

6   ounces maple-flavored bulk pork sausage or regular bulk pork sausage

½   cup pitted chopped dates

½   teaspoon garlic powder

¼   teaspoon dried sage or oregano, crushed

⅛   teaspoon crushed red pepper

⅛   teaspoon black pepper

1 Let puff pastry stand at room temperature for 20 to 30 minutes or just until thawed. Preheat oven to 400°. Carefully unfold puff pastry. Cut along folds, making 3 rectangles; set aside.

2 For filling, in a small bowl combine sausage, dates, garlic powder, sage, red pepper, and black pepper. Spread about ¼ cup of the filling lengthwise down half of each pastry rectangle to within ½ inch of one long edge. Fold the other long edge of the pastry over meat mixture; pinch edges to seal.

3 Cut filled pastries into 1-inch pieces. Place the pieces on an ungreased 15×10×1-inch baking pan.

4 Bake in preheated oven about 20 minutes or until golden. Serve warm.

Make-Ahead Directions: Prepare as directed through step 2. Cover; chill for up to 2 hours. Continue as directed in steps 3 and 4.

Nutrition Facts per piece: 75 cal., 5 g total fat (1 g sat. fat), 4 mg chol., 76 mg sodium, 6 g carbo., 0 g fiber, 1 g pro.

SWEET, HOT & SOUR MEATBALLS

Prep: 5 minutes
Bake: 20 minutes

Oven: 350°F
Makes: 10 servings

1	16-ounce package frozen cooked meatballs (32)
⅓	cup apple jelly
3	tablespoons spicy brown mustard
3	tablespoons whiskey or apple juice
½	teaspoon Worcestershire sauce
	Few dashes bottled hot pepper sauce

1 Preheat oven to 350°. Place meatballs in a single layer in a shallow baking pan. Bake, uncovered, in preheated oven about 20 minutes or until heated through (160°F).

2 Meanwhile, in a large saucepan stir together apple jelly, mustard, whiskey, Worcestershire sauce, and hot pepper sauce. Cook and stir over medium heat until jelly melts and mixture bubbles. Using a slotted spoon, transfer meatballs from baking pan to saucepan with jelly mixture; stir gently to coat. Return to boiling; reduce heat. Simmer, uncovered, for 3 to 5 minutes or until sauce thickens, stirring occasionally.

Nutrition Facts per serving: 182 cal., 12 g total fat (5 g sat. fat), 16 mg chol., 436 mg sodium, 10 g carbo., 1 g fiber, 6 g pro.

BUFFALO CHICKEN WINGS

Prep: 15 minutes
Bake: 1 hour

. . . .

Oven: 350°F
Makes: 10 servings

1   2- to 2 ½-pound bag frozen chicken wing pieces
1   1.75-ounce package Buffalo chicken wing seasoning mix with cooking bag
1   8-ounce carton dairy sour cream ranch dip
½   cup crumbled blue cheese (2 ounces)
2   tablespoons milk
    Celery sticks

1 Preheat oven to 350°. Place frozen wing pieces in cooking bag. Add seasoning and shake to coat. Close bag with nylon tie. Place bag in a shallow baking pan and arrange pieces in a single layer. Cut 2 slits in the top of the bag to allow steam to escape. Bake in preheated oven about 1 hour or until chicken pieces are tender and no longer pink, carefully cutting bag open to check doneness.

2 Meanwhile, in a small bowl combine the ranch dip, blue cheese, and milk. Cover and chill until serving time.

3 Place wings in a serving dish, spooning some of the cooking liquid over wings to moisten (discard remaining cooking liquid). Serve wings with blue cheese mixture and celery sticks.

Nutrition Facts per serving: 269 cal., 20 g total fat (7 g sat. fat), 114 mg chol., 735 mg sodium, 4 g carbo., 1 g fiber, 18 g pro.

HAM- &-CHEESE CRESCENT SNACKS

Prep: **15** minutes
Bake: **18** minutes

. . . .

Oven: 375°F
Makes: 12 servings

1	8-ounce package (8) refrigerated crescent rolls
2	tablespoons butter or margarine, softened
1	to 2 teaspoons yellow mustard
1	cup cubed cooked ham
⅓	cup chopped onion
⅓	cup chopped green sweet pepper
1	cup shredded cheddar or American cheese (4 ounces)

1 Preheat oven to 375°. Unroll crescent roll dough onto an ungreased baking sheet. Pat or roll dough to a 13×9-inch rectangle. Crimp edges of the dough.

2 In a small bowl combine butter and mustard; stir until smooth. Spread evenly over dough. Top with ham, onion, and sweet pepper. Sprinkle with cheese.

3 Bake in preheated oven for 18 to 20 minutes or until edges are golden and cheese is melted. Serve warm.

Make-Ahead Directions: Prepare as directed through step 2. Cover and chill for up to 2 hours. Bake as directed in step 3.

Nutrition Facts per serving: 146 cal., 10 g total fat (4 g sat. fat), 22 mg chol., 386 mg sodium, 8 g carbo., 0 g fiber, 6 g pro.

SPINACH-STUFFED MUSHROOMS

Prep: 30 minutes
Bake: 15 minutes

. . . .

Oven: 350°F
Makes: 12 servings

1	12-ounce package frozen spinach soufflé, thawed*
¼	cup seasoned fine dry bread crumbs
½	teaspoon dried oregano, crushed
24	large fresh mushrooms (1½ to 2 inches in diameter)
2	tablespoons grated Parmesan cheese

1 Preheat oven to 350°. Remove thawed soufflé from package. In a small saucepan stir together thawed soufflé, bread crumbs, and oregano. Cook and stir spinach mixture over medium-low heat about 10 minutes or until heated through.

2 Meanwhile, wash and drain the mushrooms. Remove stems and discard; reserve caps.

3 Fill mushroom caps with spinach mixture. Sprinkle with Parmesan cheese. Place in a 15×10×1-inch baking pan. Bake, covered, in preheated oven for 15 to 20 minutes or until heated through.

***Note:** To thaw frozen spinach soufflé, place package in a plastic bag; seal tightly. Place plastic bag in a bowl of hot water for 15 minutes, changing water twice. Remove thawed soufflé from package.

Nutrition Facts per serving: 54 cal., 3 g total fat (1 g sat. fat), 22 mg chol., 196 mg sodium, 5 g carbo., 1 g fiber, 3 g pro.

CUCUMBER-CHEESE BITES

Start to Finish:

20 minutes

Makes: 20 appetizer servings

2   medium cucumbers

1/2   cup flavored cheese spread (such as Boursin)

      Assorted toppers (such as snipped fresh chives, crumbled crisp-cooked bacon, finely chopped hard-cooked eggs, quartered cherry tomatoes, and/or sliced green onions)

1 If desired, using a vegetable peeler or zester, remove a few lengthwise strips of peel from cucumbers. Slice cucumbers 1/2 inch thick. Spread a small amount of the cheese spread onto each cucumber slice; sprinkle with assorted toppers.

Make-Ahead Directions: Prepare as directed. Cover with plastic wrap. Chill for up to 4 hours before serving.

Nutrition Facts per serving: 15 cal., 1 g total fat (1 g sat. fat), 0 mg chol., 17 mg sodium, 1 g carbo., 0 g fiber, 0 g pro.

ITALIAN CHEESE CUPS

Prep: 15 minutes
Bake: 10 minutes

Oven: 350°F
Makes: 30 appetizer servings

2 2.1-ounce (15 count) packages 1³⁄₄-inch baked miniature phyllo shells

¹⁄₂ cup oil-packed dried tomatoes, drained and finely chopped

4 ounces fresh mozzarella cheese, cut into 30 pieces

3 tablespoons refrigerated pesto

1 Preheat oven to 350°. Place phyllo shells on a large baking sheet. Place ¹⁄₄ teaspoon of the finely chopped dried tomato in the bottom of each shell. Top tomato in each shell with a piece of mozzarella and about ¹⁄₄ teaspoon of the pesto.

2 Bake in the preheated oven about 10 minutes or until cheese is melted. Serve warm.

Nutrition Facts per serving: 47 cal., 3 g total fat (0 g sat. fat), 2 mg chol., 44 mg sodium, 3 g carbo., 0 g fiber, 2 g pro.

HORSERADISH-RADISH SANDWICHES

Prep: 45 minutes

Bake: 10 minutes per batch

. . . .

Oven: 375°F

Makes: 16 appetizer servings

⅔ cups herbed goat cheese (chèvre) or two 5-ounce containers semi soft cheese with garlic and herbs

1 tablespoon finely chopped green onion

3 to 4 teaspoons hot-style prepared horseradish

½ of 17.3-ounce package frozen puff pastry (1 sheet), thawed

 Milk

 Coarse salt (optional)

1 small English cucumber, very thinly sliced

5 radishes, very thinly sliced

1 In a medium bowl combine cheese, green onion, and horseradish. Cover and chill until ready to use.

2 Preheat oven to 375°. Unfold pastry sheet on a lightly floured surface. With the tines of a fork, generously prick the pastry. Cut pastry into 16 squares. Transfer squares to an ungreased baking sheet. Brush pastry lightly with milk. If desired, sprinkle with coarse salt.

3 Bake in preheated oven for 10 to 12 minutes or until golden. Cool on a wire rack.

4 To assemble, use a knife to split the baked pastries horizontally. Spread about 1 teaspoon of the cheese mixture on the cut side of each bottom pastry. Top with several cucumber slices and radish slices. Spread the cut side of each top pastry with about 1 teaspoon of the cheese mixture. Place, spread sides down, on top of radish slices.

Nutrition Facts per serving: 94 cal., 7 g total fat (1 g sat. fat), 4 mg chol., 94 mg sodium, 6 g carbo., 0 g fiber, 2 g pro.

CHEESE PUFFS

Prep: 30 minutes
Bake: 12 minutes

. . . .

Oven: 400°F
Makes: 32 puffs

1 3-ounce package cream cheese, softened

1 egg yolk

1 teaspoon lemon juice

1 teaspoon snipped fresh chives

   Dash black pepper

½ cup shredded white cheddar cheese (2 ounces)

2 slices bacon, crisp-cooked, drained, and crumbled

1 17.3-ounce package frozen puff pastry (2 sheets), thawed

   Milk

1 Preheat oven to 400°. For filling, in a small mixing bowl combine cream cheese, egg yolk, lemon juice, chives, and pepper; beat with an electric mixer on medium speed until nearly smooth. Stir in cheddar cheese and bacon.

2 On a lightly floured surface, roll 1 of the pastry sheets to a 12-inch square. Cut into sixteen 3-inch squares. Top each square with about 1 teaspoon of the filling. Brush edges of each square with milk. Fold each square in half diagonally. Seal edges by pressing with tines of a fork or fingers. Place on an ungreased baking sheet. Repeat with remaining pastry sheet and filling.

3 Bake in preheated oven for 12 to 15 minutes or until golden.

Make-Ahead Directions: Prepare as directed through step 2. Cover and chill for up to 4 hours. Bake as directed in step 3.

Nutrition Facts per puff: 87 cal., 7 g total fat (1 g sat. fat), 12 mg chol., 83 mg sodium, 6 g carbo., 0 g fiber, 1 g pro.

PIZZAZZY LITTLE PIZZETTAS

Prep: 25 minutes
Bake: 9 minutes

. . . .

Oven: 425°F
Makes: 6 pizzettas

1 10-ounce package refrigerated pizza dough (for 1 crust)
   Desired toppings (see below)

1 Preheat oven to 425°. Lightly grease a large baking sheet; set aside.

2 Unroll the pizza dough onto a lightly floured surface. Using a lightly floured rolling pin, roll dough into a $13\frac{1}{2}\times9$-inch rectangle. Cut dough into six $4\frac{1}{2}$-inch squares. Place squares about 1 inch apart on the prepared baking sheet. Add a decorative edge to each pizza by using the tines of a fork or crimping the dough with your fingers.

3 Prebake the dough squares in preheated oven for 4 to 5 minutes or until lightly browned. Top as suggested below or as desired. Bake for 5 to 6 minutes more or until toppings are heated through.

Smoked Chicken & Roasted Pepper Pizzettas: For each pizzetta, spread 1 tablespoon cream cheese with chives on prebaked crust to within $\frac{1}{2}$ inch of edges. Top with 2 tablespoons chopped smoked chicken, 1 tablespoon thinly sliced bottled roasted red sweet pepper and 1 teaspoon snipped fresh basil. Sprinkle with 2 tablespoons shredded Gouda cheese.

Nutrition Facts per pizzetta: 155 cal., 4 g total fat (2 g sat. fat), 11 mg chol., 333 mg sodium, 22 g carbo., 1 fiber, 6 g pro.

CAJUN PEANUTS

Prep: 10 minutes
Bake: 12 minutes

. . . .

Oven: 350°F
Makes: 2¼ cups (eight ¼-cup servings)

1 egg white
4 teaspoons salt-free Cajun seasoning
⅛ teaspoon cayenne pepper
2¼ cups honey-roasted peanuts (12 ounces)

1 Preheat oven to 350°. Line a 15×10×1-inch baking pan with foil; grease foil. Set aside.

2 In a medium bowl beat egg white until frothy. Stir in Cajun seasoning and cayenne pepper. Add peanuts; toss to coat. Spread peanuts in a single layer on prepared baking pan.

3 Bake in preheated oven for 12 minutes, stirring once halfway through baking. Cool completely. Break up any large clusters of nuts.

Nutrition Facts per ¼-cup serving: 182 cal., 16 g total fat (3 g sat. fat), 0 mg chol., 142 mg sodium, 8 g carbo., 1 g fiber, 7 g pro.

MEXICAN SNACK MIX

Prep: 10 minutes
Bake: 30 minutes

Oven: 300°F
Makes: 10 cups

6	cups bite-size corn or rice square cereal
2	cups pretzel knots
2	cups sesame and cheese snack sticks
1	cup hot and spicy peanuts or salted peanuts
½	cup butter or margarine
1	tablespoon bottled hot pepper sauce (optional)
2	teaspoons Mexican seasoning

1 Preheat oven to 300°. In a large roasting pan combine cereal, pretzels, snack sticks, and peanuts.

2 In a small saucepan heat and stir butter, hot pepper sauce (if desired), and Mexican seasoning over low heat until butter is melted. Drizzle butter mixture over cereal mixture, tossing to coat.

3 Bake, uncovered, in preheated oven for 30 minutes, stirring twice. Spread mixture out onto a large piece of foil to cool. Store mixture in an airtight container for up to 1 week.

Nutrition Facts per ½-cup serving: 171 cal., 10 g total fat (4 g sat. fat), 13 mg chol., 316 mg sodium, 17 g carbo., 1 g fiber, 4 g pro.

WHITE CHOCOLATE PARTY MIX

Makes: 20 servings

4	cups tiny pretzels
2½	cups round toasted oat cereal
2½	cups bite-size corn square cereal
1	cup salted peanuts
1	cup candy-coated milk chocolate pieces (8 ounces)
2	cups white baking pieces (12 ounces)
1	tablespoon shortening

1 Line a 15×10×1-inch baking pan with waxed paper; set aside. In a large bowl combine pretzels, oat cereal, corn square cereal, peanuts, and milk chocolate pieces; set aside.

2 In a microwave-safe medium bowl combine white baking pieces and shortening; microwave on 100% (high) power for 1 to 2 minutes or until baking pieces are melted, stirring every minute until smooth. Pour over cereal mixture; mix well.

3 Spread onto prepared baking pan. Cool completely; break apart. Store in an airtight container.

Nutrition Facts per serving: 290 cal., 13 g total fat (8 g sat. fat), 1 mg chol., 284 mg sodium, 36 g carbo., 2 g fiber, 3 g pro.

BREAKFAST & BRUNCH

BRUNCH TURNOVERS

Prep: 30 minutes
Bake: 12 minutes

Oven: 400°F
Makes: 9 turnovers

1	10-ounce package refrigerated pizza dough (for 1 crust)
¼	cup orange marmalade
¾	cup chopped Canadian-style bacon or cooked ham
¾	cup shredded Swiss cheese (3 ounces)
¼	cup thinly sliced green onions
	Freshly ground black pepper
	Milk
	Poppy seeds and/or sesame seeds

1 Preheat oven to 400°. Line a baking sheet with foil; grease foil. Set aside. Unroll pizza dough onto a lightly floured surface. Roll pizza dough into a 12-inch square. Spread orange marmalade evenly over dough. Cut dough into nine 4-inch squares.

2 For filling, in a medium bowl stir together the Canadian-style bacon, cheese, and green onions. Place about 3 tablespoons of the filling on each dough square. Sprinkle each lightly with pepper. Fold a corner of each dough square over filling to opposite corner. Use the tines of a fork to seal edges. Prick tops of turnovers with fork.

3 Place turnovers on prepared baking sheet. Brush with milk and sprinkle with poppy and/or sesame seeds. Bake in preheated oven for 12 to 15 minutes or until golden (filling will leak out slightly). Serve warm.

Nutrition Facts per turnover: 149 cal., 5 g total fat (2 g sat. fat), 16 mg chol., 326 mg sodium, 18 g carbo., 1 g fiber, 8 g pro.

HEARTY SCRAMBLED EGGS

Start to Finish:

15 minutes

. . . .

Makes: 4 servings

2	tablespoons butter or margarine
1	cup loose-pack frozen diced hash brown potatoes with onion and peppers
1	4-ounce can (drained weight) mushroom stems and pieces, drained
¼	teaspoon black pepper
⅛	teaspoon ground sage
8	eggs
⅓	cup milk
1	10-ounce can chunk-style ham, drained and flaked

1 In a large skillet melt butter over medium-high heat. Add hash brown potatoes, mushrooms, pepper, and sage; cook for 2 minutes. Reduce heat to medium. Cook about 3 minutes more or until potatoes are tender, stirring occasionally.

2 Meanwhile, in a bowl beat together eggs and milk. Stir in ham. Stir ham mixture into potato mixture in skillet.

3 Cook, without stirring, until the egg mixture begins to set on the bottom and around the edge. With a large spoon or spatula, lift and fold the partially cooked egg mixture so uncooked portion flows underneath. Continue cooking over medium heat about 4 minutes or until eggs are cooked through but are still glossy and moist. Remove from heat immediately.

Nutrition Facts per serving: 365 cal., 25 g total fat (10 g sat. fat), 482 mg chol., 1,098 mg sodium, 10 g carbo., 1 g fiber, 26 g pro.

KNIFE-&-FORK BREAKFAST BURRITO

Start to Finish:
25 minutes

. . . .

Makes: 4 servings

1	cup canned black beans, rinsed and drained
1/3	cup bottled chunky salsa
4	eggs
2	tablespoons milk
1/4	teaspoon black pepper
1/8	teaspoon salt
	Nonstick cooking spray or cooking oil
1	medium tomato, thinly sliced
1/2	cup crumbled queso fresco or shredded Monterey Jack cheese (2 ounces)
1/4	cup dairy sour cream
4	teaspoons snipped fresh mint
	Bottled chunky salsa (optional)

1 In a small saucepan mash the beans slightly. Stir in the 1/3 cup salsa. Heat through over low heat. Cover and keep warm while making egg "tortillas."

2 In a medium bowl beat eggs with a whisk; whisk in milk, pepper, and salt. Coat an unheated 10-inch nonstick omelet pan (or skillet with flared sides) with cooking spray. Preheat pan over medium heat until a drop of water sizzles.

3 For each egg "tortilla," pour about 1/4 cup of the egg mixture into the pan. Lift and tilt pan to spread egg mixture over bottom. Return to heat. Cook for 1 1/2 to 2 minutes or until lightly browned on bottom (do not turn).

4 Loosen edges of the egg "tortilla" with spatula; carefully slide out onto a serving plate, browned side down. On one half of the "tortilla," spread one-fourth of the bean-salsa mixture. Top with some of the tomato and cheese. Fold in half and into half again to form the burrito. Keep warm while preparing remaining tortillas and assembling remaining burritos. Top with sour cream, remaining cheese, and mint. If desired, serve with additional salsa.

Nutrition Facts per serving: 179 cal., 9 g total fat (4 g sat. fat), 223 mg chol., 389 mg sodium, 14 g carbo., 4 g fiber, 14 g pro.

WARM-YOU-UP SAUSAGE ROLL

Prep: **25** minutes
Bake: **15** minutes

Oven: 375°F
Makes: 6 servings

1   pound bulk pork sausage or 8 ounces bulk pork sausage plus 8 ounces bulk Italian sausage

³/₄   cup chopped red, orange, and/or yellow sweet pepper

¹/₂   cup chopped onion

1   3-ounce package cream cheese, cubed

1   8-ounce package (8) refrigerated crescent rolls

1 Preheat oven to 375°. In a large skillet cook sausage, sweet pepper, and onion until meat is brown and onion is tender. Drain off fat. Add cubed cream cheese, stirring with a wooden spoon until cream cheese is melted and mixture is well mixed. Keep warm.

2 Grease a baking sheet. Unroll the crescent roll dough onto prepared baking sheet. Carefully pinch together the perforations and press the dough into a 13×9-inch rectangle. Spoon the sausage mixture lengthwise down the center of the dough, making a 3-inch-wide strip.

3 On both long sides of dough rectangle, make 2¹/₂-inch cuts from edge toward center, spacing the cuts 1 inch apart. Starting at one end and alternating from side to side, fold and twist the dough strips at an angle over the filling, giving pastry a ladderlike appearance.

4 Bake in preheated oven for 15 to 18 minutes or until golden. Serve warm.

Nutrition Facts per serving: 509 cal., 43 g total fat (15 g sat. fat), 67 mg chol., 855 mg sodium, 18 g carbo., 1 g fiber, 13 g pro.

TEX-MEX BREAKFAST PIZZA

Prep: 25 minutes
Bake: 8 minutes

Oven: 375°F
Makes: 8 servings

Nonstick cooking spray

1½ cups loose-pack frozen diced hash brown potatoes, thawed

2 green onions, sliced

1 to 2 canned jalapeño chile peppers or canned whole green chile peppers, drained, seeded, and chopped*

½ teaspoon bottled minced garlic (1 clove)

¼ teaspoon ground cumin

1 cup refrigerated or frozen egg product, thawed

¼ cup fat-free milk

1 tablespoon snipped fresh cilantro

1 16-ounce Italian bread shell (Boboli)

½ cup shredded reduced-fat Monterey Jack cheese (2 ounces)

1 small tomato, seeded and chopped

1 Preheat oven to 375°. Coat an unheated large skillet with cooking spray. Preheat over medium heat. Add potatoes, green onions, chile peppers, garlic, and cumin. Cook and stir about 3 minutes or until the vegetables are tender.

2 In a small bowl stir together egg product, milk, and cilantro; add to potato mixture in skillet. Cook, without stirring, until mixture begins to set on the bottom and around the edge. Using a spatula, lift and fold the partially cooked mixture so uncooked portion flows underneath. Continue cooking and folding until egg product is cooked through but is still glossy and moist. Remove from heat.

3 To assemble pizza, place the bread shell on a large baking sheet or a 12-inch pizza pan. Sprinkle half of the cheese over the shell. Top with egg mixture, tomato, and the remaining cheese.

4 Bake in preheated oven for 8 to 10 minutes or until cheese is melted. Cut into wedges to serve.

***Note:** Because chile peppers contain volatile oils that can burn your skin and eyes, avoid direct contact with them as much as possible. When working with chile peppers, wear plastic or rubber gloves. If your bare hands do touch the peppers, wash your hands and nails well with soap and warm water.

Nutrition Facts per serving: 235 cal., 6 g total fat (1 g sat. fat), 8 mg chol., 424 mg sodium, 33 g carbo., 2 g fiber, 14 g pro.

EGG CASSEROLE WITH CAJUN SAUCE

Prep: 20 minutes
Bake: 40 minutes

. . . .

Oven: 325°F
Makes: 6 servings

2	cups plain croutons
1	cup shredded Monterey Jack cheese (4 ounces)
4	eggs
2	cups milk
1	teaspoon yellow mustard
	Dash black pepper
1	recipe Cajun Sauce

1 Preheat oven to 325°. Grease a 2-quart square baking dish. In prepared baking dish combine croutons and cheese; set aside.

2 In a medium bowl whisk together eggs, milk, mustard, and pepper. Pour egg mixture over croutons and cheese in baking dish.

3 Bake in preheated oven about 40 minutes or until knife inserted near center comes out clean.

4 Meanwhile, prepare Cajun Sauce. Let casserole stand for 10 minutes before serving. Serve with Cajun Sauce.

Cajun Sauce: In a medium saucepan combine one $14^1/_2$-ounce can diced tomatoes with green pepper and onion, undrained; 1 teaspoon Cajun seasoning; 1 teaspoon sugar; and dash black pepper. Bring to boiling; reduce heat. Simmer, uncovered, about 10 minutes or until mixture is slightly thickened and reduced to $1^1/_4$ cups. Stir in $^1/_4$ cup sliced pimiento-stuffed green olives; heat through. Makes $1^1/_2$ cups.

Nutrition Facts per serving: 234 cal., 12 g total fat (6 g sat. fat), 165 mg chol., 588 mg sodium, 18 g carbo., 1 g fiber, 13 g pro.

CHEESY SEAFOOD STRATA

Prep: 20 minutes
Bake: 45 minutes

Oven: 350°F
Makes: 4 servings

8	¾-inch slices French bread (about 6 ounces)
1	5-ounce container semisoft cheese with garlic and herbs
1	6- or 8-ounce package flake-style imitation crabmeat
½	cup loose-pack frozen peas
1	cup shredded cheddar cheese (4 ounces)
4	eggs
2	cups milk
¼	teaspoon black pepper

1 Lightly grease a 2-quart square baking dish; set aside. Spread 1 side of each bread slice with semisoft cheese. Place 4 of the slices, spread sides up, in prepared baking dish. Sprinkle with crabmeat and peas. Sprinkle with half of the cheddar cheese. Top with remaining 4 bread slices, spread sides up. Sprinkle with remaining cheddar cheese.

2 In a medium bowl beat eggs with a whisk. Whisk in milk and pepper; pour over bread. Press bread slices lightly with the back of a large spoon to coat with egg mixture. Cover and chill for at least 2 hours or up to 24 hours.

3 Preheat oven to 350°. Bake strata, covered loosely with foil, in preheated oven for 25 minutes. Uncover and bake for 20 to 25 minutes more or until a knife inserted near the center comes out clean. Let stand for 10 minutes before serving.

Nutrition Facts per serving: 553 cal., 30 g total fat (17 g sat. fat), 298 mg chol., 640 mg sodium, 35 g carbo., 2 g fiber, 31 g pro.

CRANBERRY FRENCH STRATA

Prep: 25 minutes
Bake: 65 minutes

Oven: 350°F
Makes: 9 to 12 servings

12	ounces crusty French bread or sourdough bread, torn into 1-inch pieces (8 cups)
1	8-ounce package cream cheese
$1/2$	cup dried cranberries
6	eggs
$2^1/4$	cups milk
$1/3$	cup pure maple syrup or maple-flavored syrup
$1/2$	teaspoon ground cinnamon or ground nutmeg
1	recipe Orange Sauce

1 Grease a 2-quart rectangular baking dish. Arrange half of the bread in a single layer in prepared baking dish.

2 Cut the cream cheese into $1/2$-inch-thick slices. Arrange on top of bread in baking dish. Sprinkle with cranberries and top with remaining bread.

3 In a medium bowl beat together eggs, milk, and maple syrup. Pour over bread mixture in pan. Sprinkle with cinnamon. Press bread lightly with the back of a large spoon to coat with egg mixture. Cover and chill for at least 8 hours or up to 24 hours.

4 Preheat oven to 350°. Bake, covered, in preheated oven for 45 minutes. Uncover and bake for 20 minutes more.

5 Meanwhile, prepare Orange Sauce. Let strata stand for 10 minutes before serving. Serve strata warm with Orange Sauce.

Orange Sauce: In a small saucepan combine 4 teaspoons cornstarch and 1 tablespoon sugar. Stir in $1^1/4$ cups orange juice. Cook and stir over medium heat until thickened and bubbly. Add $1/2$ cup snipped dried cranberries and 1 tablespoon butter or margarine; cook and stir for 2 minutes more. Serve warm.

Nutrition Facts per serving: 381 cal., 16 g total fat (8 g sat. fat), 178 mg chol., 394 mg sodium, 48 g carbo., 2 g fiber, 12 g pro.

RICOTTA SOUFFLÉ PIE

Prep: 15 minutes
Bake: 30 minutes

Oven: 425°F
Makes: 6 servings

1	12-ounce package frozen spinach soufflé, thawed*
1	15-ounce carton ricotta cheese
½	cup finely shredded Parmesan cheese (2 ounces)
¼	teaspoon ground nutmeg
¼	teaspoon freshly ground black pepper
½	teaspoon bottled minced garlic (1 clove)
1	9-inch frozen unbaked deep-dish pastry shell

1 Preheat oven to 425°. In a large bowl combine spinach soufflé, ricotta cheese, Parmesan cheese, nutmeg, pepper, and garlic. Spoon into pastry shell, spreading top evenly. Place on a baking sheet.

2 Bake in preheated oven for 30 minutes. Let stand for 20 minutes before serving. Serve warm.

*Note: To thaw the spinach soufflé, follow microwave directions for thawing. (Or place the package of spinach soufflé in the refrigerator to thaw the night prior to making the pie.)

Nutrition Facts per serving: 414 cal., 27 g total fat (11 g sat. fat), 86 mg chol., 543 mg sodium, 26 g carbo., 1 g fiber, 17 g pro.

SPINACH BREAKFAST CASSEROLE

Prep: 30 minutes
Bake: 55 minutes

Oven: 325°F
Makes: 12 servings

4	cups seasoned croutons (about 7 ounces)
1	pound bulk pork sausage, cooked and drained
1	10-ounce package frozen chopped spinach, thawed and well drained
1/2	cup purchased shredded carrot
4	eggs
2	cups milk
1	10¾-ounce can condensed cream of mushroom soup
1	4-ounce can (drained weight) sliced mushrooms, drained
1	cup shredded cheddar cheese (4 ounces)
1	cup shredded Monterey Jack cheese (4 ounces)
1/4	teaspoon dry mustard
	Shredded cheddar and/or Monterey Jack cheese (optional)

1 Spread croutons in an even layer in a 3-quart rectangular baking dish. Spread sausage evenly over croutons. Sprinkle spinach and carrot evenly over sausage.

2 In a medium bowl beat eggs with a whisk; whisk in milk, mushroom soup, mushrooms, the 1 cup cheddar cheese, the 1 cup Monterey Jack cheese, and the dry mustard until well mixed. Pour over layers in dish. Cover and chill for at least 8 hours or up to 24 hours.

3 Preheat oven to 325°. Uncover casserole and bake in preheated oven for 45 minutes. If desired, sprinkle with additional cheese. Bake about 10 minutes more or until edges are bubbly and center is heated through. Let stand for 10 minutes before serving.

Nutrition Facts per serving: 346 cal., 24 g total fat (10 g sat. fat), 115 mg chol., 754 mg sodium, 15 g carbo., 2 g fiber, 15 g pro.

CORNBELT SPECIAL

Prep: 10 minutes
Bake: 1¼ hours

Oven: 350°F
Makes: 8 to 10 servings

2	eggs
1	15¼-ounce can cream-style corn
1	8-ounce carton dairy sour cream
¼	cup butter or margarine, melted
1	14¾-ounce can whole kernel corn, drained
1½	cups shredded cheddar cheese (6 ounces)
1	medium onion, chopped
1	4-ounce can chopped green chile peppers, drained
1	8½-ounce package corn muffin mix

1 Preheat oven to 350°. Grease a 2-quart casserole; set aside. In a large bowl beat eggs with a whisk. Stir in cream-style corn, sour cream, and melted butter. Stir in whole kernel corn, cheddar cheese, onion, and chile peppers. Add corn muffin mix, stirring just until moistened. Turn into prepared casserole.

2 Bake in preheated oven about 1¼ hours or until a knife inserted in center comes out clean and top is golden. Let stand for 5 minutes before serving.

Nutrition Facts per serving: 407 cal., 24 g total fat (12 g sat. fat), 104 mg chol., 730 mg sodium, 40 g carbo., 1 g fiber, 12 g pro.

EGG & POTATO CASSEROLE

Prep: 15 minutes
Bake: 40 minutes

Oven: 350°F
Makes: 6 servings

Nonstick cooking spray

2 cups loose-pack frozen diced hash brown potatoes with onion and peppers

1 cup loose-pack frozen cut broccoli or asparagus

⅓ cup finely chopped Canadian-style bacon or lean cooked ham (2 ounces)

⅓ cup evaporated fat-free milk

2 tablespoons all-purpose flour

2 8-ounce cartons refrigerated or frozen egg product, thawed

½ cup shredded reduced-fat cheddar cheese (2 ounces)

1 tablespoon snipped fresh basil or ½ teaspoon dried basil, crushed

¼ teaspoon black pepper

⅛ teaspoon salt

1 Preheat oven to 350°. Coat a 2-quart square baking dish with cooking spray. Arrange hash brown potatoes and broccoli in bottom of baking dish; top with Canadian bacon. Set aside.

2 In a medium bowl gradually stir evaporated milk into flour. Stir in egg product, half of the cheddar cheese, the basil, pepper, and salt. Pour egg product mixture over vegetables.

3 Bake in preheated oven for 40 to 45 minutes or until a knife inserted near center comes out clean. Sprinkle with remaining cheddar cheese. Let stand for 5 minutes before serving.

Make-Ahead Directions: Prepare as directed through step 2. Cover and chill for at least 4 hours or up to 24 hours. To serve, uncover and bake as directed in step 3.

Nutrition Facts per serving: 188 cal., 5 g total fat (2 g sat. fat), 11 mg chol., 373 mg sodium, 18 g carbo., 2 g fiber, 17 g pro.

WAFFLE BREAKFAST CASSEROLE

Prep: 15 minutes
Bake: 50 minutes

Chill: 4 to 24 hours
Oven: 350°F
Makes: 8 servings

1	pound bulk pork sausage
6	frozen waffles, toasted and cubed
1	cup shredded cheddar cheese (4 ounces)
6	eggs
2	cups milk
1	teaspoon dry mustard
⅛	teaspoon black pepper
	Frozen waffles, toasted (optional)
	Maple-flavored syrup or pure maple syrup (optional)

1 In a large skillet cook sausage until brown. Drain off fat.

2 Arrange 3 of the waffles in a 2-quart rectangular baking dish. Top with half of the sausage and about ⅓ cup of the cheese. Repeat layers.

3 In a large bowl beat eggs with a fork; stir in milk, mustard, and pepper. Pour over layers in dish. Cover and chill for at least 4 hours or up to 24 hours.

4 Preheat oven to 350°. Uncover and bake in preheated oven for 50 to 60 minutes or until a knife inserted near center comes out clean. Sprinkle with the remaining cheese. Let stand for 10 minutes before serving. If desired, serve on toasted waffles and drizzle with maple flavored syrup.

Nutrition Facts per serving: 413 cal., 28 g total fat (12 g sat. fat), 217 mg chol., 668 mg sodium, 15 g carbo., 1 g fiber, 19 g pro.

SALMON & BAGEL BAKE

Prep: 15 minutes
Bake: 35 minutes

Oven: 350°F
Makes: 6 servings

4	eggs
1	14-ounce can reduced-sodium chicken broth
¼	cup thinly sliced green onions
1	tablespoon snipped fresh dill or ¾ teaspoon dried dill, crushed
1	teaspoon bottled minced garlic (2 cloves)
4	onion bagels, split, or 10 mini bagels, split (8 to 10 ounces total)
1	7½-ounce can salmon, drained, flaked, and skin and bones removed
4	ounces Havarti cheese, shredded (1 cup)

1 Preheat oven to 350°. Grease a 2-quart square baking dish; set aside. In a medium bowl beat together eggs and chicken broth. Stir in green onions, dill, and garlic; set aside. Cut each split bagel into 2 or 3 pieces.

2 Place bagel bottom pieces, cut sides up, in prepared baking dish. Spoon salmon and cheese onto bagel bottoms. Stack bagel top pieces, cut sides down, on salmon and cheese. Gradually pour egg mixture over all.

3 Bake, uncovered, in preheated oven for 35 to 40 minutes or until a knife inserted near the center comes out clean. Let stand for 10 minutes before serving.

Make-Ahead Directions: Prepare as directed through step 2. Cover with plastic wrap. Chill for up to 24 hours. Uncover. Bake in a 350° oven for 40 to 45 minutes.

Nutrition Facts per serving: 325 cal., 15 g total fat (2 g sat. fat), 174 mg chol., 694 mg sodium, 27 g carbo., 1 g fiber, 20 g pro.

BREAKFAST BREAD PUDDINGS

Prep: 20 minutes
Bake: 35 minutes

Oven: 325°F
Makes: 6 servings

6	slices dry cinnamon-swirl bread or cinnamon-raisin bread*
	Nonstick cooking spray
1½	cups fat-free milk
¾	cup refrigerated or frozen egg product, thawed
3	tablespoons sugar
1	teaspoon vanilla
¼	teaspoon ground nutmeg
1	5 ½-ounce can apricot or peach nectar
2	teaspoons cornstarch

1 Preheat oven to 325°. Cut bread slices into ½-inch cubes (you should have 4 cups).

2 Coat six 6-ounce custard cups with cooking spray. Divide bread cubes among the custard cups. In a medium bowl whisk together milk, egg product, sugar, vanilla, and nutmeg. Pour the milk mixture evenly over the bread cubes. Lightly press bread cubes down with fork or back of a spoon.

3 Place the custard cups in a 13×9×2-inch baking pan. Place baking pan on oven rack. Carefully pour hot tap water into the baking pan around the custard cups to a depth of 1 inch.

4 Bake in the 325° oven for 35 to 40 minutes or until a knife inserted near centers comes out clean. Remove the custard cups from the baking pan. Let stand for 20 minutes on wire rack.

5 Meanwhile, for sauce, in a small saucepan gradually stir nectar into cornstarch. Cook and stir over medium heat until thickened and bubbly. Reduce heat. Cook and stir for 2 minutes more.

6 To serve, loosen edges of puddings with a knife. Invert into dessert dishes. Spoon warm sauce over puddings.

*Note: To dry the bread, arrange bread slices in a single layer on a wire rack; cover loosely and let stand overnight. (Or place bread slices in a single layer on a baking sheet. Bake, uncovered, in a 325° oven for 10 minutes, turning once. Cool on wire rack.)

Nutrition Facts per serving: 164 cal., 2 g total fat (1 g sat. fat), 1 mg chol., 189 mg sodium, 28 g carbo., 0 g fiber, 8 g pro.

CARAMEL BUBBLE RING

Prep: 25 minutes
Bake: 35 minutes

Oven: 350°F
Makes: 10 to 12 servings

⅓ cup chopped pecans

¾ cup sugar

4 teaspoons ground cinnamon

2 11-ounce packages (12 each) refrigerated breadsticks

⅓ cup butter or margarine, melted

½ cup caramel ice cream topping

2 tablespoons maple-flavored syrup

1 Preheat oven to 350°. Generously grease a 10-inch fluted tube pan. Sprinkle half of the pecans in the bottom of the prepared pan. Set aside. In a small bowl stir together sugar and cinnamon; set aside.

2 Separate each package of breadstick dough on the perforated lines into 6 spiral pieces, making 12 pieces total. Do not unroll. Cut the pieces in half crosswise. Dip each piece of dough into melted butter; roll in sugar cinnamon mixture to coat. Arrange dough pieces in the prepared pan.

3 Sprinkle with remaining pecans. In a measuring cup stir together caramel topping and maple-flavored syrup; drizzle over dough pieces in pan.

4 Bake in preheated oven about 35 minutes or until dough is light brown, covering with foil for the last 10 minutes of baking to prevent overbrowning.

5 Let stand for 1 minute only. (If it stands for more than 1 minute, the ring will be difficult to remove from pan.) Invert onto a serving platter. Spoon any topping and nuts remaining in the pan onto rolls. Serve warm.

Nutrition Facts per serving: 367 cal., 13 g total fat (5 g sat. fat), 18 mg chol., 587 mg sodium, 58 g carbo., 2 g fiber, 5 g pro.

PECAN STREUSEL COFFEE CAKE

Prep: 20 minutes
Bake: 35 minutes

. . . .

Oven: 350°F
Makes: 15 servings

1   cup chopped pecans
$^2/_3$ cup packed brown sugar
2   tablespoons butter, melted
$1^1/_2$ teaspoons ground cinnamon
1    $26^1/_2$-ounce package cinnamon streusel coffee cake mix
$^1/_2$ cup dairy sour cream

1 Preheat oven to 350°. Grease and flour a 13×9×2-inch baking pan; set aside. For topping, in a small bowl stir together pecans, brown sugar, butter, and cinnamon.

2 Prepare the coffee cake mix according to the package directions, except stir sour cream into prepared batter. Spread half (about 3 cups) of the batter into the prepared baking pan. Sprinkle batter with the streusel mix from the package of coffee cake mix. Carefully spread with the remaining batter. Sprinkle with the topping.

3 Bake in preheated oven for 35 to 40 minutes or until a toothpick inserted near center comes out clean. Cool slightly in pan.

4 Meanwhile, prepare glaze from the coffee cake mix according to package directions. Drizzle glaze over warm coffee cake.

Nutrition Facts per serving: 395 cal., 20 g total fat (5 g sat. fat), 50 mg chol., 248 mg sodium, 50 g carbo., 1 g fiber, 4 g pro.

APPLE-CHERRY-FILLED ROLLS

Prep: 30 minutes
Rise: 30 minutes
Bake: 13 minutes

Oven: 375°F
Makes: 16 rolls

Nonstick cooking spray
1   16-ounce package hot roll mix
1   cup chopped, peeled apple
¼   cup dried tart cherries
2   tablespoons brown sugar
½   teaspoon ground cinnamon
1   recipe Orange Icing

1 Lightly coat 2 baking sheets with cooking spray; set aside.

2 Prepare hot roll mix according to package directions through the resting step. Meanwhile, for filling, in a small bowl stir together apple, dried cherries, brown sugar, and cinnamon.

3 Divide dough into 16 portions. Flatten one portion of the dough to a 4-inch circle; spoon 1 rounded teaspoon of the filling onto dough circle. Shape the dough around the filling to enclose filling, pulling dough until smooth and rounded. Place, rounded side up, on prepared baking sheet. Repeat with remaining dough and filling. Cover; let rise in a warm place until double (about 30 minutes).

4 Preheat oven to 375°. Bake in preheated oven for 13 to 15 minutes or until golden. Cool slightly on a wire rack. Drizzle with Orange Icing. Serve warm.

Orange Icing: In a small bowl stir together 1 cup sifted powdered sugar and enough orange juice (1 to 2 tablespoons) to make an icing of drizzling consistency.

Nutrition Facts per roll: 165 cal., 2 g total fat (0 g sat. fat), 13 mg chol., 186 mg sodium, 33 g carbo., 0 g fiber, 4 g pro.

BERRY BREAKFAST ROLLS

Prep: 15 minutes
Bake: 12 minutes

Oven: 375°F
Makes: 16 rolls

1	11½-ounce package (8) refrigerated cinnamon rolls with icing
1	cup fresh blueberries
⅓	cup blueberry preserves
1	teaspoon finely shredded lemon peel
¼	cup chopped pecans
	Milk (optional)

1 Preheat oven to 375°. Lightly grease sixteen 2½-inch muffin cups. Cut each cinnamon roll in half crosswise; set icing aside. Press roll half in bottom and halfway up side of each muffin cup.

2 For filling, in a small bowl stir together blueberries, preserves, and lemon peel. Spoon filling into muffin cups. Sprinkle with pecans.

3 Bake in preheated oven about 12 minutes or until golden. Cool in cups on a wire rack for 10 minutes. Remove from cups and place on a wire rack.

4 For icing, if necessary, in a small bowl stir a little milk into the packaged icing to make drizzling consistency. Drizzle over rolls. Serve warm.

Nutrition Facts per roll: 110 cal., 4 g total fat (1 g sat. fat), 0 mg chol., 173 mg sodium, 18 g carbo., 0 g fiber, 1 g pro.

CARAMEL-PECAN ROLLS

Prep: 15 minutes
Bake: 20 minutes

· · · · · · · · · · · · · · · · · · · ·

Oven: 350°F
Makes: 12 rolls

½   cup sifted powdered sugar
2   tablespoons whipping cream
½   teaspoon ground cinnamon
¾   cup pecan pieces, toasted
1   16-ounce package frozen white roll dough (12 rolls)
1   tablespoon butter, melted

1 Grease a 9×1½-inch round baking pan; set aside. In a small bowl stir together powdered sugar, whipping cream, and cinnamon; spread into prepared pan. Sprinkle pecans evenly over powdered sugar mixture. Place rolls on mixture in pan. Brush rolls with melted butter. Cover and chill for at least 8 hours or up to 24 hours.

2 Before baking, let rolls stand at room temperature for 30 minutes. Preheat oven to 350°. Uncover and bake in preheated oven for 20 to 25 minutes or until browned. Cool in pan on a wire rack for 5 minutes. Carefully invert rolls onto a serving platter. Serve warm.

Nutrition Facts per roll: 181 cal., 9 g total fat (2 g sat. fat), 6 mg chol., 158 mg sodium, 23 g carbo., 1 g fiber, 4 g pro.

CINNAMON-ORANGE PULL-APARTS

Prep: 20 minutes
Rise: 1 hour
Bake: 35 minutes

Oven: 350°F
Makes: 16 servings

Nonstick cooking spray
24 frozen white roll dough (²/₃ of a 3-pound package)
1 cup sugar
2 teaspoons ground cinnamon
2 teaspoons finely shredded orange peel
¹/₃ cup butter or margarine, melted
¹/₃ cup light-colored corn syrup

1 Coat a baking sheet with cooking spray. Arrange frozen rolls in a single layer on baking sheet; cover with plastic wrap. Let stand for 15 minutes. Cut rolls in half horizontally and return to baking sheet; cover with plastic wrap. Let stand about 30 minutes more or until dough is completely thawed but not starting to rise.*

2 Grease a 10-inch fluted tube pan; set aside. In a shallow dish combine sugar, cinnamon, and orange peel. Dip half of the rolls in melted butter and coat with sugar mixture. Arrange coated rolls in prepared fluted tube pan. Drizzle half of the corn syrup over rolls in pan. Repeat with remaining rolls, adding them to the pan. Drizzle with remaining corn syrup and any remaining butter and sugar mixture.

3 Cover and let rise in a warm place until double in size (1 to 1¹/₄ hours). (Or preheat oven to 200°; turn oven off. Place pan in oven and let rolls rise until nearly double in size [about 35 minutes]. Remove rolls from oven and preheat oven to 350°.)

4 Bake rolls in preheated oven about 35 minutes or until golden. Cool in pan on a wire rack for 5 minutes. Invert onto a serving plate. Serve warm.

***Test Kitchen Tip:** To quickly thaw the roll dough, arrange 6 frozen rolls on a microwave-safe plate. Cover; microwave on 100% (high) power for 25 seconds. Give plate a half-turn. Turn rolls over; microwave for 20 to 25 seconds more or until thawed. Repeat with remaining rolls. Cut thawed rolls in half. Continue as directed in steps 2 through 4.

Nutrition Facts per serving: 252 cal., 7 g total fat (3 g sat. fat), 11 mg chol., 269 mg sodium, 44 g carbo., 1 g fiber, 5 g pro.

STICKY LEMON PINWHEELS

Prep: 10 minutes
Bake: 15 minutes

. . . .

Oven: 375°F
Makes: 6 servings

⅓   cup purchased lemon curd or orange curd
¼   cup sliced almonds, toasted
1   11-ounce package refrigerated breadsticks

1 Preheat oven to 375°. Grease an 8×1½-inch round baking pan; set aside. In a small bowl stir together lemon curd and almonds. Spread mixture evenly into the bottom of the prepared baking pan.

2 Separate, but do not uncoil, the breadsticks. Arrange coiled dough over the lemon mixture in the baking pan.

3 Bake in preheated oven for 15 to 18 minutes or until golden. Immediately invert onto a platter. Spread any remaining lemon mixture in the pan over the pinwheels. Serve warm.

Nutrition Facts per serving: 310 cal., 9 g total fat (2 g sat. fat), 13 mg chol., 593 mg sodium, 50 g carbo., 3 g fiber, 7 g pro.

STICKY RED RASPBERRY ROLLS

Prep: 10 minutes
Bake: 25 minutes

. . . .

Oven: 350°F
Makes: 8 servings

$\frac{1}{2}$ cup seedless red raspberry jam

1   11-ounce package refrigerated French bread dough

2   tablespoons sugar

$\frac{1}{4}$ of an 8-ounce tub cream cheese

1   tablespoon milk

1 Preheat oven to 350°. In a small saucepan heat and stir jam until melted. Set aside 2 tablespoons of the jam. Pour remaining jam into an 8×8×2-inch baking pan.

2 Cut bread dough into 16 slices. Lay bread dough slices on top of the jam in the baking pan; brush tops of dough with reserved jam. Sprinkle tops of dough slices with sugar.

3 Bake in preheated oven for 25 to 30 minutes or until brown. Invert onto a platter. Scrape any remaining jam from baking pan and spread over rolls.

4 In a small saucepan cook and stir cream cheese and milk over medium-low heat until mixture reaches drizzling consistency. Drizzle over rolls. Serve warm.

Nutrition Facts per serving: 186 cal., 4 g total fat (2 g sat. fat), 7 mg chol., 276 mg sodium, 34 g carbo., 1 g fiber, 4 g pro.

STRAWBERRY SWEET ROLLS

Prep: 25 minutes
Rise: 30 minutes
Bake: 25 minutes

. . . .

Oven: 375°F
Makes: 12 rolls

1   cup boiling water
½   cup dried strawberries
½   cup coarsely chopped pecans
⅓   cup strawberry preserves
⅓   cup packed brown sugar
2   tablespoons butter
1   tablespoon light-color corn syrup
12   frozen white roll dough (16-ounce package), thawed

1 In a small bowl pour the boiling water over the dried strawberries; let stand for 5 minutes. Drain. Coarsely snip the strawberries. In the small bowl combine snipped strawberries, ¼ cup of the pecans, and the strawberry preserves.

2 In a small saucepan combine brown sugar, butter, and corn syrup. Heat and stir over medium heat until combined. Spread in a 9×1½-inch round baking pan. Sprinkle with remaining ¼ cup pecans. Set aside.

3 On a lightly floured surface, roll each thawed roll to a 4-inch circle. Place about 1 rounded teaspoon of the strawberry mixture in center of each dough circle; pull edges to center and pinch to seal, shaping each into a round ball. Place balls, seam sides up, in prepared pan. Cover and let rise in a warm place until rolls are nearly double in size (30 to 45 minutes).

4 Preheat oven to 375°. Bake in preheated oven about 25 minutes or until golden. Carefully invert onto serving plate. Let stand for 15 minutes before serving.

Nutrition Facts per roll: 220 cal., 7 g total fat (2 g sat. fat), 5 mg chol., 177 mg sodium, 34 g carbo., 2 g fiber, 4 g pro.

FRENCH TOAST CASSEROLE

Prep: 20 minutes
Bake: 50 minutes

. . . .

Oven: 375°F
Makes: 8 servings

12	slices dry white bread,* cut into $\frac{1}{2}$-inch cubes (about 8 cups)
2	8-ounce packages cream cheese, cut into $\frac{3}{4}$-inch cubes
1	cup frozen blueberries
12	eggs
2	cups milk
$\frac{1}{2}$	cup pure maple syrup or maple-flavored syrup
	Blueberry-flavored, pure maple, or maple-flavored syrup

1 Generously butter a 3-quart rectangular baking dish. Spread half of the bread cubes evenly in bottom of prepared baking dish. Sprinkle cream cheese and blueberries over bread cubes. Arrange remaining bread cubes over blueberries.

2 In a large bowl beat eggs with a rotary beater; beat in milk and the $\frac{1}{2}$ cup maple syrup. Carefully pour egg mixture over the bread mixture. Cover and chill for at least 2 hours or up to 24 hours.

3 Preheat oven to 375°. Bake, covered, in preheated oven for 25 minutes. Uncover and bake about 25 minutes more or until a knife inserted near the center comes out clean and topping is puffed and golden. Let stand for 10 minutes before serving. Serve warm with desired syrup.

*Note: To dry the bread, arrange bread slices in a single layer on a wire rack; cover loosely and let stand overnight. (Or cut bread into $\frac{1}{2}$-inch cubes; spread in a large baking pan. Bake, uncovered, in a 300° oven for 10 to 15 minutes or until dry, stirring twice; cool.)

Nutrition Facts per serving: 608 cal., 30 g total fat (16 g sat. fat), 386 mg chol., 497 mg sodium, 66 g carbo., 1 g fiber, 19 g pro.

CREAM CHEESE-FILLED FRENCH TOAST

Prep: 20 minutes

Cook: 4 minutes per batch

....

Oven: 300°F

Makes: 9 servings

1	recipe Cream Cheese Filling
1	8-ounce French bread baguette
1	5-ounce can evaporated milk (²/₃ cup)
¹/₃	cup milk
¹/₄	cup butter or margarine
3	eggs
³/₄	cup sugar
1	teaspoon vanilla
2	tablespoons cooking oil
	Maple-flavored or fruit-flavored syrup

1 Prepare Cream Cheese Filling; set aside. Preheat oven to 300°. Cut bread into ³/₄-inch-thick slices; set aside. In small saucepan combine evaporated milk, milk, and butter; heat until butter melts. In a bowl beat eggs with a fork; stir in sugar, vanilla, and warm milk mixture. Pour egg-milk mixture into a shallow baking dish. Place bread slices in egg-milk mixture, turning to coat both sides. Let bread slices stand in egg-milk mixture about 5 minutes to thoroughly soak bread.

2 In a large skillet heat oil over medium heat. Add several bread slices; cook for 2 to 3 minutes on each side or until golden. Repeat with remaining bread.

3 Working with half of the slices, spread 1 heaping tablespoon of the Cream Cheese Filling on each slice; top with remaining slices. Serve with desired syrup.

Cream Cheese Filling: In a processor bowl or mixing bowl combine one 8-ounce package cream cheese, softened; ¹/₄ of an 8-ounce container frozen whipped dessert topping, thawed; 2 tablespoons sugar; and 2 tablespoons dairy sour cream. Cover and process or beat on low to medium speed until smooth.

Make-Ahead Directions: Prepare as directed through step 2. Place the cooked slices of toast on a baking sheet and freeze until firm. Place in freezer container. Seal, label, and freeze up to 3 months. To reheat, place frozen slices in a single layer on baking sheet., Bake in a 400° oven for 10 to 12 minutes or until heated through. Meanwhile, prepare Cream Cheese Filling. Fill and serve as directed in step 3.

Nutrition Facts per serving: 379 cal., 23 g total fat (13 g sat. fat), 120 mg chol., 330 mg sodium, 36 g carbo., 1 g fiber, 8 g pro.

LEMON POPPY SEED PANCAKES WITH RASPBERRY SYRUP

Start to Finish:

20 minutes

· · · · · · · · · · · · · · · · · · · ·

Makes: 4 servings
(8 pancakes)

2	eggs
²/₃	cup milk
1	7.6-ounce package lemon poppy seed muffin mix
1	10-ounce package frozen red raspberries in syrup, thawed
2	teaspoons cornstarch

1 In a medium bowl beat together eggs and milk. Add the muffin mix all at once. Stir just until moistened (batter should be nearly smooth).

2 For each pancake, pour or spread about ¼ cup of the batter into a 4-inch circle onto a hot, lightly greased griddle or heavy skillet. Cook over medium heat for 1½ to 2 minutes on each side or until pancakes are brown, turning to second sides when pancakes have bubbly surfaces and edges are slightly dry.

3 In a small saucepan combine raspberries and cornstarch. Cook and stir until thickened and bubbly. Serve over the pancakes.

Nutrition Facts per serving: 404 cal., 10 g total fat (3 g sat. fat), 114 mg chol., 387 mg sodium, 70 g carbo., 3 g fiber, 8 g pro.

MAPLE-BACON OVEN PANCAKE

Prep: 15 minutes
Bake: 13 minutes

....

Oven: 425°F
Makes: 12 servings

1½   cups packaged biscuit mix
1   cup shredded cheddar cheese (4 ounces)
2   eggs
¾   cup milk
¼   cup maple-flavored syrup
5   slices bacon, crisp-cooked, drained, and crumbled
      Maple-flavored syrup (optional)

1 Preheat oven to 425°. Grease and flour a 13×9×2-inch baking pan; set aside. In a medium bowl combine biscuit mix, half of the cheddar cheese, the eggs, milk, and the ¼ cup syrup; beat until nearly smooth. Spread in prepared baking pan.

2 Bake in preheated oven for 10 to 12 minutes or until toothpick inserted near center comes out clean. Sprinkle with remaining cheddar cheese and the bacon; bake for 3 minutes more. Cut into squares. If desired, serve with additional syrup.

Nutrition Facts per serving: 150 cal., 8 g total fat (3 g sat. fat), 49 mg chol., 294 mg sodium, 15 g carbo., 0 g fiber, 6 g pro.

BEEF

STEAKS WITH HORSERADISH-CREAM SAUCE

Start to Finish:
25 minutes

Oven: 400°F
Makes: 2 to 4 servings

1	tablespoon olive oil
2	1½-inch-thick beef tenderloin steaks (8 to 10 ounces each)
	Salt
	Freshly ground black pepper
½	cup whipping cream
3	tablespoons horseradish mustard
	Cracked black pepper

1 Preheat oven to 400°. In a large skillet heat oil over medium heat. Sprinkle both sides of steaks with salt and freshly ground pepper; add to hot skillet. Cook about 4 minutes or until brown, turning once. Transfer to a 2-quart square baking dish. Bake the steaks, uncovered, in preheated oven for 10 to 13 minutes or until medium-rare doneness (145°F).

2 Meanwhile, in a medium bowl beat the whipping cream with an electric mixer on medium speed until soft peaks form. Fold in horseradish mustard.

3 To serve, place steaks on warm dinner plates and spoon the cream sauce over steaks. Sprinkle with cracked pepper.

Nutrition Facts per serving: 641 cal., 47 g total fat (21 g sat. fat), 221 mg chol., 620 mg sodium, 4 g carbo., 0 g fiber, 50 g pro.

BORDELAISE PEPPERY STEAK

Start to Finish:

25 minutes

. . . .

Makes: 4 servings

1¼ cups water

1 cup sliced fresh mushrooms

½ cup finely chopped onion

1 0.87- to 1.2-ounce package dry brown gravy mix

¼ cup dry red wine

2 teaspoons garlic-pepper blend

4 6-ounce beef ribeye, top sirloin, or tenderloin steaks, cut ¾ inch thick

2 tablespoons olive oil

1 For sauce, in a medium saucepan bring the water to boiling. Add mushrooms and onion. Reduce heat. Cover and cook for 3 minutes. Stir in gravy mix and red wine. Cook, uncovered, about 3 minutes or until thickened, stirring occasionally. Cover; keep warm.

2 Meanwhile, rub garlic-pepper blend into both sides of each steak. In a large, heavy skillet heat oil over medium-high heat. Add steaks. Reduce heat to medium; cook to desired doneness, turning once halfway through cooking. Allow 5 to 7 minutes for medium-rare doneness (145°F) or 7 to 9 minutes for medium doneness (160°F).

3 Serve the steaks with the sauce on warmed plates.

Nutrition Facts per serving: 366 cal., 18 g total fat (5 g sat. fat), 81 mg chol., 954 mg sodium, 7 g carbo., 1 g fiber, 39 g pro.

STEAK WITH CREAMY ONION SAUCE

Prep: 10 minutes

Broil: 17 minutes

Makes: 4 servings

1   medium sweet onion (such as Vidalia, Maui, or Walla Walla), thinly sliced

4   6-ounce beef ribeye steaks, cut 1 inch thick

1   tablespoon Mediterranean seasoning blend or lemon-pepper seasoning

1   8-ounce carton dairy sour cream

2   tablespoons drained capers

1 Place onion slices on the rack of an unheated broiler pan. Broil 3 to 4 inches from heat for 5 minutes; turn onions. Meanwhile, sprinkle steaks with $1\frac{1}{2}$ teaspoons of the seasoning blend. Place steaks on the broiler pan rack with onion. Broil steaks and onions about 5 minutes or until onions are brown. Remove onions to a cutting board. Continue to broil steaks until desired doneness, turning once. Allow 7 to 9 minutes more for medium-rare doneness (145°F) or 10 to 13 minutes more for medium doneness (160°F), turning once.

2 Meanwhile, for sauce, coarsely chop broiled onion. In a small saucepan combine cooked onion, sour cream, capers, and remaining $1\frac{1}{2}$ teaspoons seasoning blend. Cook over medium-low heat until heated through (do not boil).

3 Transfer steaks to serving plates. Spoon sauce over steaks.

Nutrition Facts per serving: 398 cal., 22 g total fat (11 g sat. fat), 106 mg chol., 472 mg sodium, 4 g carbo., 0 g fiber, 39 g pro.

BEEF WITH CUCUMBER RAITA

Prep: 15 minutes
Broil: 15 minutes

Makes: 4 servings

1	8-ounce carton plain fat-free or low-fat yogurt
¼	cup coarsely shredded unpeeled cucumber
1	tablespoon finely chopped red or sweet onion
1	tablespoon snipped fresh mint
¼	teaspoon sugar
	Salt
	Black pepper
1	pound boneless beef top sirloin steak, cut 1 inch thick
½	teaspoon lemon-pepper seasoning
	Fresh mint leaves (optional)

1 Preheat broiler. For raita, in a small bowl combine yogurt, cucumber, onion, snipped mint, and sugar. Season to taste with salt and pepper; set aside.

2 Trim fat from meat. Sprinkle meat with lemon-pepper seasoning. Place meat on the unheated rack of a broiler pan. Broil 3 to 4 inches from heat until desired doneness, turning once halfway through broiling. Allow 15 to 17 minutes for medium-rare doneness (145°F) or 20 to 22 minutes for medium doneness (160°F).

3 Cut steak across the grain into thin slices. If desired, garnish with mint leaves. Serve with the raita.

Nutrition Facts per serving: 176 cal., 4 g total fat (1 g sat. fat), 55 mg chol., 312 mg sodium, 5 g carbo., 0 g fiber, 28 g pro.

GRILLED STEAK FAJITAS

Prep: 25 minutes
Grill: 20 minutes

Makes: 4 to 6 servings

3	green and/or red sweet peppers, sliced
1	medium onion, sliced
1	tablespoon olive oil
1½	teaspoons fajita seasoning
½	teaspoon bottled minced garlic (1 clove)
1	pound boneless beef top sirloin steak, cut 1 inch thick
4	to 6 burrito-size flour tortillas (10-inch)
	Bottled salsa (optional)
	Dairy sour cream (optional)

1 Fold a 36×18-inch piece of heavy foil in half crosswise. Place sweet peppers and onion in the center of foil. Drizzle with oil; sprinkle with ½ teaspoon of the fajita seasoning and the garlic. Bring up the opposite edges of foil and seal with a double fold. Fold in remaining edges, leaving space for steam to build. Set aside.

2 Rub remaining 1 teaspoon fajita seasoning on both sides of steak. Place steak and the vegetable packet on the rack of an uncovered grill directly over medium heat. Grill steak until desired doneness; remove steak and keep warm. Allow 14 to 18 minutes for medium-rare doneness (145°F) or 18 to 22 minutes for medium doneness (160°F). Grill vegetables about 20 minutes or until tender.

3 Meanwhile, wrap tortillas in foil. Place tortilla packet next to steak on grill rack; grill about 10 minutes or until tortillas are heated through. Slice meat into thin bite-size strips. Divide meat among tortillas; top with vegetables. Roll up. If desired, serve with salsa and sour cream.

Nutrition Facts per serving: 388 cal., 11 g total fat (3 g sat. fat), 53 mg chol., 327 mg sodium, 30 g carbo., 3 g fiber, 28 g pro.

GRILLED STEAK, MANGO & PEAR SALAD

Prep: 15 minutes
Grill: 14 minutes

Makes: 4 servings

12	ounces boneless beef top loin steak, cut 1 inch thick
1	tablespoon olive oil or cooking oil
1/2	teaspoon salt
1/4	teaspoon black pepper
1	10-ounce package torn mixed salad greens (about 8 cups)
1	24-ounce jar refrigerated sliced mango, drained
1	medium pear, peeled, cored, and chopped
3/4	cup refrigerated blue cheese salad dressing
	Cracked black pepper

1 Brush steak with oil; sprinkle both sides with salt and the 1/4 teaspoon pepper.

2 Place steak on the rack of an uncovered grill directly over medium heat. Grill until desired doneness, turning once halfway through grilling. Allow 14 to 18 minutes for medium-rare doneness (145°F) or 18 to 22 minutes for medium doneness (160°F).

3 To serve, thinly slice steak across the grain. Arrange greens on a serving platter; top with meat and fruit. Pour salad dressing over the fruit. Sprinkle with cracked black pepper.

Nutrition Facts per serving: 492 cal., 31 g total fat (6 g sat. fat), 48 mg chol., 869 mg sodium, 36 g carbo., 2 g fiber, 22 g pro.

BLACKENED BEEF STIR-FRY

Start to Finish:
25 minutes

Makes: 4 servings

12	ounces boneless beef top sirloin steak or top round steak
2¼	teaspoons blackened seasoning for beef
⅔	cup water
2	tablespoons tomato paste
2	teaspoons cornstarch
½	teaspoon instant beef bouillon granules
1	tablespoon cooking oil
1	16-ounce package frozen stir-fry vegetables (any combination)
	Hot cooked rice

1 If desired, partially freeze beef (about 30 minutes) for easier slicing. Trim fat from beef. Thinly slice beef across the grain into thin bite-size strips.

2 Sprinkle steak strips with 2 teaspoons of the blackened seasoning; toss to coat well.

3 For sauce, in a small bowl stir together the water, tomato paste, cornstarch, beef bouillon granules, and remaining ¼ teaspoon blackened seasoning. Set aside.

4 In a wok or large skillet heat oil over medium-high heat. Add stir-fry vegetables. Cook and stir for 2 to 3 minutes or until crisp-tender. Remove vegetables from wok. Add beef strips to hot wok. (Add more oil during cooking as necessary.) Cook and stir for 2 to 3 minutes or until desired doneness.

5 Push meat from center of wok. Stir sauce. Add to center of wok. Cook and stir until thickened and bubbly. Return vegetables to wok. Stir together to coat all ingredients with sauce. Heat through. Serve over rice.

Nutrition Facts per serving: 342 cal., 7 g total fat (2 g sat. fat), 40 mg chol., 367 mg sodium, 43 g carbo., 3 g fiber, 25 g pro.

GREEK BEEF & PASTA SKILLET

Makes: 4 servings

8   ounces dried rotini pasta

12   ounces boneless beef top sirloin steak or top round steak

1   tablespoon cooking oil

1   26-ounce jar ripe olive and mushroom pasta sauce, ripe olive and green olive pasta sauce, or marinara pasta sauce

¼   teaspoon salt

¼   teaspoon ground cinnamon

½   of a 10-ounce package frozen chopped spinach, thawed and well drained

⅓   cup crumbled feta cheese

1 Cook pasta according to package directions; drain. Meanwhile, trim fat from meat. Thinly slice beef across the grain into bite-size strips.

2 In a large skillet cook and stir beef in hot oil for 2 to 3 minutes or until desired doneness. Add pasta sauce, salt, and cinnamon. Cook and stir until sauce is bubbly. Add cooked pasta and spinach. Cook and stir until heated through. Sprinkle each serving with feta cheese.

Nutrition Facts per serving: 483 cal., 12 g total fat (3 g sat. fat), 63 mg chol., 1,063 mg sodium, 60 g carbo., 6 g fiber, 32 g pro.

FLANK STEAK SANDWICHES

Prep: 20 minutes
Grill: 17 minutes

....

Makes: 4 to 6 servings

1	1- to 1¼-pound beef flank steak
½	cup balsamic vinaigrette salad dressing
1½	cups sliced fresh portobello mushrooms
2	tablespoons butter
½	cup bottled roasted red sweet peppers, cut into strips
1	teaspoon soy sauce
4	to 6 hard rolls, halved lengthwise and toasted (if desired)
	Balsamic vinaigrette salad dressing (optional)

1 Score both sides of steak in a diamond pattern by making shallow diagonal cuts at 1-inch intervals. Place steak in a resealable plastic bag set in a shallow baking dish. Add the ½ cup balsamic dressing. Seal bag; turn to coat steak. Marinate in the refrigerator for at least 2 hours or up to 24 hours, turning bag occasionally.

2 Drain steak, discarding marinade. Place steak on the rack of an uncovered grill directly over medium heat. Grill for 17 to 21 minutes or until medium doneness (160°F), turning once halfway through grilling.

3 Meanwhile, in a large skillet cook mushrooms in hot butter just until tender. Stir in roasted red peppers and soy sauce; remove from heat. Slice steak thinly across the grain.

4 Serve steak slices in rolls. Top with mushroom mixture. If desired, drizzle with additional balsamic dressing.

Nutrition Facts per serving: 503 cal., 26 g total fat (9 g sat. fat), 62 mg chol., 861 mg sodium, 35 g carbo., 2 g fiber, 32 g pro.

ASIAN BEEF & NOODLE BOWL

Start to Finish:

30 minutes

Makes: 4 servings

4	cups water
2	3-ounce packages ramen noodles (any flavor)
2	teaspoons chile oil, or 2 teaspoons cooking oil plus ⅛ teaspoon cayenne pepper
12	ounces beef flank steak or top round steak, cut into thin bite-size strips
1	teaspoon grated fresh ginger
1	teaspoon bottled minced garlic (2 cloves)
1	cup beef broth
2	tablespoons soy sauce
2	cups torn fresh spinach
1	cup purchased shredded carrots
¼	cup snipped fresh cilantro

1 In a large saucepan bring the water to boiling. If desired, break up noodles; drop noodles into the boiling water. (Reserve the flavor packets for another use.) Return to boiling; boil for 2 to 3 minutes or just until noodles are tender but firm, stirring occasionally. Drain noodles; set aside.

2 Meanwhile, in an extra large skillet heat oil over medium-high heat. Add beef, ginger, and garlic; cook and stir for 2 to 3 minutes or until beef is desired doneness. Carefully stir beef broth and soy sauce into skillet. Bring to boiling; reduce heat.

3 Add spinach, carrots, cilantro, and cooked noodles to skillet; stir to combine. Heat through.

Nutrition Facts per serving: 381 cal., 17 g total fat (3 g sat. fat), 34 mg chol., 1,503 mg sodium, 30 g carbo., 2 g fiber, 26 g pro.

BEEF POT ROAST SANDWICHES AU JUS

Prep: 25 minutes
Cook: 1³/₄ hours

Makes: 8 to 10 servings

1   2¹/₂- to 3-pound boneless beef chuck pot roast
1   tablespoon cooking oil
1   10¹/₂-ounce can condensed beef consommé
³/₄   cup water
1   0.6- to 0.75-ounce package dry au jus mix
1   teaspoon dried Italian seasoning, crushed
8   to 10 crusty French rolls, split and toasted

1 Trim fat from meat. In a 4- to 6-quart Dutch oven brown roast on all sides in hot oil. Drain off fat.

2 In a medium bowl combine beef consommé, the water, dry au jus mix, and Italian seasoning. Pour over roast. Bring to boiling; reduce heat. Simmer, covered, about 1³/₄ hours or until meat is tender.

3 Slice or shred meat. If necessary, skim fat from cooking juices. Place meat on rolls. Serve sandwiches with cooking juices.

Slow-Cooker Directions: Trim fat from meat. Brown meat as directed in step 1. Transfer meat to a 3¹/₂- to 4¹/₂-quart slow cooker. In a small bowl combine beef consommé, dry au jus mix, and Italian seasoning (omit water); pour over roast. Cover and cook on low-heat setting for 10 to 12 hours or on high-heat setting for 5 to 6 hours. Serve as directed in step 3.

Nutrition Facts per serving: 307 cal., 9 g total fat (2 g sat. fat), 84 mg chol., 785 mg sodium, 21 g carbo., 1 g fiber, 35 g pro.

BEEF ROAST WITH VEGETABLES

Prep: 15 minutes

Cook: 20 minutes

Makes: 4 servings

1	17-ounce package refrigerated cooked beef roast au jus
1½	cups packaged peeled baby carrots
8	ounces tiny new potatoes, quartered
2	stalks celery, cut into 1-inch pieces
¼	cup water
½	teaspoon dried thyme, crushed
½	teaspoon garlic-pepper blend

1 Transfer liquid from beef roast package to a large skillet. Halve any large carrots lengthwise. Add carrots, new potatoes, celery, and the water to skillet. Place beef roast on top of vegetables. Sprinkle thyme and garlic-pepper blend over all. Bring to boiling; reduce heat. Simmer, covered, about 20 minutes or until vegetables are tender and meat is heated through.

2 Serve meat with vegetables and juices.

Nutrition Facts per serving: 239 cal., 9 g total fat (4 g sat. fat), 64 mg chol., 591 mg sodium, 18 g carbo., 3 g fiber, 25 g pro.

FRUITED POT ROAST

Makes: 4 servings

1   17-ounce package refrigerated cooked beef pot roast with juices

1   tablespoon butter or margarine

2   tablespoons minced shallots

2   tablespoons tarragon vinegar

2   cups fresh fruit wedges (such as peaches, green plums, and/or red plums)

     Hot cooked spaetzle (optional)

1   teaspoon snipped fresh tarragon

1 Remove meat from package, reserving juices. In a large skillet melt butter over medium heat. Add shallots; cook for 1 minute. Add pot roast; reduce heat. Cover and cook about 10 minutes or until pot roast is heated through.

2 In a small bowl stir together reserved meat juices and tarragon vinegar. Pour over meat. Spoon fruit over top. Cover and heat for 2 minutes more. If desired, serve with cooked spaetzle. Sprinkle with snipped tarragon.

Nutrition Facts per serving: 259 cal., 12 g total fat (5 g sat. fat), 64 mg chol., 459 mg sodium, 19 g carbo., 2 g fiber, 24 g pro.

STROGANOFF-SAUCED BEEF ROAST

Start to Finish:

30 minutes

....

Makes: 3 or 4 servings

1 16- or 17-ounce package refrigerated cooked beef pot roast with gravy

2 cups fresh shiitake, crimini, or button mushrooms

1/2 cup dairy sour cream French onion dip

2 cups hot cooked noodles

1 Transfer beef with gravy to a large skillet (leave meat whole). Remove stems from shiitake mushrooms; halve or quarter mushrooms. Add mushrooms to skillet. Cover and cook over medium-low heat about 15 minutes or until heated through, stirring mushrooms once and turning roast over halfway through cooking time.

2 Use a wooden spoon to break meat into bite-size pieces. Stir onion dip into meat mixture; heat through (do not boil). Stir in hot cooked noodles.

Nutrition Facts per serving: 542 cal., 7 g total fat (11 g sat. fat), 99 mg chol., 787 mg sodium, 46 g carbo., 4 g fiber, 8 g pro.

CALIENTE POT ROAST

Start to Finish:

25 minutes

. . . .

Makes: 4 to 6 servings

1	16- or 17-ounce package refrigerated cooked beef pot roast with juices
1½	cups sliced fresh mushrooms
1	8-ounce bottle picante sauce
1	14-ounce can reduced-sodium chicken broth
1	cup quick-cooking couscous
2	tablespoons snipped fresh cilantro
	Dairy sour cream (optional)
	Chopped fresh tomato (optional)
	Sliced avocado (optional)
	Fresh cilantro sprigs (optional)

1 Transfer liquid from pot roast package to a large skillet; add mushrooms and picante sauce. Cut pot roast into 1- to 1½-inch cubes; add to mushrooms in skillet. Bring to boiling; reduce heat. Simmer, covered, for 10 minutes.

2 Meanwhile, in a medium saucepan bring chicken broth to boiling; stir in couscous. Remove from heat. Cover and let stand for 5 minutes. Fluff with a fork; stir in snipped cilantro.

3 Spoon pot roast mixture over hot cooked couscous mixture. If desired, serve with sour cream, tomato, and/or avocado; top with cilantro sprigs.

Nutrition Facts per serving 479 cal., 13 g total fat (4 g sat. fat), 120 mg chol., 1,000 mg sodium, 43 g carbo., 3 g fiber, 46 g pro.

BEEF RAGOUT

Start to Finish:

25 minutes

. . . .

Makes: 6 servings

10   ounces dried wide egg noodles

1   17-ounce package refrigerated cooked beef tips with gravy

1   10³/₄-ounce can condensed cheddar cheese soup

1   9-ounce package frozen Italian-style green beans

1   4¹/₂-ounce jar (drained weight) whole mushrooms, drained

¹/₂   cup water

3   tablespoons tomato paste

2   tablespoons dried minced onion

¹/₂   cup dairy sour cream

1 Prepare noodles according to package directions. Drain and keep warm.

2 Meanwhile, in a 4-quart Dutch oven combine beef tips with gravy, cheddar cheese soup, green beans, drained mushrooms, the water, tomato paste, and dried minced onion. Bring to boiling; reduce heat. Simmer, covered, for 10 to 15 minutes or until green beans are crisp-tender, stirring occasionally. Stir in sour cream; cook for 2 to 3 minutes more or until heated through. Serve over hot cooked noodles.

Nutrition Facts per serving: 378 cal., 13 g total fat (5 g sat. fat), 90 mg chol., 954 mg sodium, 49 g carbo., 4 g fiber, 22 g pro.

ROAST BEEF & MASHED POTATO STACKS

Start to Finish:

15 minutes

. . . .

Makes: 4 servings

1   17-ounce package refrigerated cooked beef tips with gravy

½   cup onion-seasoned beef broth

1   20-ounce package refrigerated mashed potatoes

2   tablespoons butter or margarine

⅛   teaspoon black pepper

4   slices thick-sliced white bread

1 In a large skillet combine beef tips with gravy and beef broth. Cook and stir over medium heat until heated through.

2 Meanwhile, prepare mashed potatoes according to package directions, adding the butter and pepper.

3 To serve, place bread slices on 4 dinner plates. Divide mashed potatoes among bread slices. Ladle beef mixture over potatoes and bread. Serve immediately.

Nutrition Facts per serving: 372 cal., 15 g total fat (6 g sat. fat), 64 mg chol., 1,174 mg sodium, 36 g carbo., 2 g fiber, 23 g pro.

BEEF BURGUNDY

Prep: 20 minutes
Cook: 20 minutes

Makes: 5 or 6 servings

1	17-ounce package refrigerated cooked beef tips with gravy
½	teaspoon dried basil, crushed
¼	teaspoon black pepper
1	10¾-ounce can condensed golden mushroom soup
½	cup Burgundy wine
1½	cups sliced fresh mushrooms
1	cup packaged peeled baby carrots, halved lengthwise
1	cup loose-pack frozen small whole onions
12	ounces dried wide egg noodles (6 cups)

1 In a large saucepan combine beef tips with gravy, basil, and pepper. Stir in golden mushroom soup and Burgundy. Bring to boiling. Add mushrooms, carrots, and onions. Return to boiling; reduce heat to low. Simmer, covered, for 20 to 25 minutes or until vegetables are tender, stirring frequently.

2 Meanwhile, cook noodles according to package directions; drain. Serve meat mixture over noodles.

Nutrition Facts per serving: 458 cal., 10 g total fat (3 g sat. fat), 106 mg chol., 1,017 mg sodium, 63 g carbo., 5 g fiber, 26 g pro.

BEEF TIPS WITH CORNICHONS

Start to Finish:

35 minutes

. . . .

Makes: 4 servings

1	tablespoon cooking oil
½	cup chopped onion
1	teaspoon bottled minced garlic (2 cloves)
¼	cup dry white wine
1	17-ounce package refrigerated cooked beef tips with gravy
⅓	cup cornichons,* sliced lengthwise
½	teaspoon dried tarragon, crushed
½	cup dairy sour cream
	Hot cooked noodles or rice

1 In a large skillet heat oil over medium heat. Add onion and garlic; cook and stir until onion is tender. Add white wine. Bring to boiling; reduce heat. Simmer, uncovered, until reduced by half.

2 Add beef tips with gravy, cornichons, and tarragon to skillet; cook until heated through. Stir in sour cream. Serve immediately over hot cooked noodles.

*Note: Look for the small sour pickles called cornichons with other pickles at your supermarket or specialty food store.

Nutrition Facts per serving: 347 cal., 16 g total fat (6 g sat. fat), 84 mg chol., 828 mg sodium, 28 g carbo., 2 g fiber, 22 g pro.

EASY SHEPHERD'S PIE

Prep: 20 minutes
Bake: 20 minutes

Oven: 375°F
Makes: 4 servings

1	17-ounce package refrigerated cooked beef tips with gravy
2	cups loose-pack frozen mixed vegetables
1	10^3/$_4$-ounce can condensed tomato bisque soup
1	tablespoon Worcestershire sauce
1	teaspoon dried minced onion
^{1}/$_2$	teaspoon dried thyme, crushed
^{1}/$_8$	teaspoon black pepper
1	20-ounce package refrigerated mashed potatoes
^{1}/$_2$	cup shredded cheddar cheese (2 ounces)

1 Preheat oven to 375°. Lightly grease a 2-quart rectangular baking dish. In a large saucepan combine beef tips with gravy, mixed vegetables, tomato bisque soup, Worcestershire sauce, dried minced onion, thyme, and pepper. Bring to boiling over medium heat, stirring occasionally. Transfer to prepared baking dish.

2 Place potatoes in a large bowl; stir until nearly smooth. Spoon potatoes into 6 mounds on top of meat mixture.

3 Bake, uncovered, in preheated oven for 20 to 25 minutes or until heated through and bubbly on edges. Sprinkle with cheese. Let stand for 10 minutes before serving.

Nutrition Facts per serving: 442 cal., 15 g total fat (6 g sat. fat), 64 mg chol., 1,609 mg sodium, 50 g carbo., 6 g fiber, 27 g pro.

CHIPOTLE BRISKET SANDWICH

Start to Finish:

15 minutes

Makes: 6 servings

1   17-ounce package refrigerated cooked, seasoned, and sliced beef brisket with barbecue sauce

1   to 2 canned chipotle peppers in adobo sauce, chopped

½   of a 16-ounce package shredded cabbage with carrot (coleslaw mix) (about 4 cups)

⅓   cup bottled coleslaw dressing

6   kaiser rolls, split and toasted

1 In a large saucepan combine the beef brisket with barbecue sauce and chipotle peppers. Cook and stir about 5 minutes or until heated through.

2 Meanwhile, in a large bowl combine the shredded cabbage mixture and coleslaw dressing.

3 To serve, spoon beef mixture onto roll bottoms. Top with coleslaw mixture and roll tops.

Nutrition Facts per serving: 414 cal., 18 g total fat (5 g sat. fat), 39 mg chol., 1,085 mg sodium, 47 g carbo., 2 g fiber, 16 g pro.

THAI BEEF STIR-FRY

Start to Finish:

15 minutes

. . . .

Makes: 4 servings

4   ounces dried rice noodles

2   tablespoons cooking oil

1   16-ounce package frozen pepper stir-fry vegetables (yellow, green, and red peppers and onion)

12   ounces packaged beef stir-fry strips

½   cup bottled Thai peanut stir-fry sauce

1 Prepare the noodles according to package directions. Drain and set aside.

2 In a large skillet heat 1 tablespoon of the oil over medium-high heat. Add the stir-fry vegetables; cook and stir for 2 to 3 minutes or until tender. Drain; place stir-fry vegetables in a bowl.

3 In the same skillet stir-fry beef strips in remaining 1 tablespoon hot oil for 2 to 3 minutes or until desired doneness. Return stir-fry vegetables to skillet; add stir-fry sauce. Stir to combine; heat through. Serve over rice noodles.

Nutrition Facts per serving: 404 cal., 16 g total fat (4 g sat. fat), 50 mg chol., 597 mg sodium, 39 g carbo., 3 g fiber, 23 g pro.

BARBECUE BEEF CALZONES

Prep: 20 minutes
Bake: 30 minutes

. . . .

Oven: 400°F
Makes: 4 calzones

1	10-ounce package refrigerated pizza dough (for 1 crust)
1/2	of an 18- to 20-ounce package refrigerated cooked shredded beef with barbecue sauce
1/2	of a 16-ounce package frozen pepper stir-fry vegetables (yellow, green, and red peppers and onion), thawed
4	ounces Monterey Jack cheese with jalapeño peppers or cheddar cheese, shredded (1 cup)
2	tablespoons cornmeal
1	tablespoon milk
1/4	teaspoon garlic salt

1 Preheat oven to 400°. Grease a 15×10×1-inch baking pan; set aside. Unroll pizza dough onto a lightly floured surface. Roll to a 12-inch square. Cut into four 6-inch squares.

2 Divide shredded beef, thawed vegetables, and cheese among dough squares, placing ingredients on half of each square. Fold remaining half of each dough square over filling to form a rectangle. Press edges with the tines of a fork to seal.

3 Sprinkle 1 tablespoon of the cornmeal on prepared baking pan. Place calzones on pan; brush tops lightly with milk. In a small bowl combine the remaining cornmeal and the garlic salt; sprinkle over calzones.

4 Bake in preheated oven about 30 minutes or until golden. Serve warm.

Nutrition Facts per calzone: 434 cal., 17 g total fat (8 g sat. fat), 69 mg chol., 832 mg sodium, 42 g carbo., 2 g fiber, 28 g pro.

CHILI CORN PIE

Prep: 20 minutes
Bake: 20 minutes

. . . .

Oven: 375°F
Makes: 4 servings

2 11-ounce packages frozen chunky beef and bean chili

1 11.5-ounce package refrigerated corn bread twists

⅓ cup shredded cheddar cheese

1 tablespoon snipped fresh cilantro

¼ cup dairy sour cream

1 Preheat oven to 375°. Heat the frozen chili according to the package directions for microwave.

2 Meanwhile, on a lightly floured surface, unroll sheet of corn bread twist dough (do not separate into strips). Press at perforations to seal. Roll the dough to an 11×7-inch rectangle.

3 Spoon hot chili into a 2-quart rectangular baking dish. Immediately place sheet of corn bread twist dough on chili in baking dish. Use a sharp knife to cut slits in corn bread dough to allow steam to escape.

4 Bake in preheated oven about 20 minutes or until corn bread is lightly browned. Sprinkle with cheese and cilantro. Let stand for 5 minutes before serving. Top each serving with sour cream.

Nutrition Facts per serving: 512 cal., 24 g total fat (9 g sat. fat), 44 mg chol., 1,429 mg sodium, 50 g carbo., 3 g fiber, 22 g pro.

DELI ROAST BEEF SANDWICHES

Start to Finish:

15 minutes

. . . .

Makes: 2 sandwiches

8	ounces thinly sliced deli roast beef
4	slices pumpernickel, rye, or whole wheat bread
½	cup purchased coleslaw
	Herb-pepper seasoning

1 Arrange roast beef on 2 of the bread slices. Spread coleslaw over beef; sprinkle with herb-pepper seasoning. Top with the remaining bread slices.

Nutrition Facts per sandwich: 369 cal., 8 g total fat (2 g sat. fat), 80 mg chol., 507 mg sodium, 34 g carbo., 5 g fiber, 39 g pro.

MIDDLE EASTERN-STYLE PITAS

Start to Finish:

10 minutes

. . . .

Makes: 4 servings

1   7- or 8-ounce container roasted-garlic-flavored hummus

4   pita rounds, halved crosswise

12   ounces thinly sliced deli roast beef

½   cup plain yogurt

½   cup chopped cucumber

1 Spread hummus in the pita halves. Add beef to pita halves. In a small bowl stir together yogurt and cucumber; spoon over beef in pita halves.

Nutrition Facts per serving: 463 cal., 18 g total fat (5 g sat. fat), 70 mg chol., 735 mg sodium, 44 g carbo., 3 g fiber, 34 g pro.

REUBEN LOAF

Prep: 30 minutes
Rise: 30 minutes
Bake: 25 minutes

Oven: 375°F
Makes: 10 servings

1   16-ounce package hot roll mix

1   cup bottled Thousand Island salad dressing

1   pound sliced cooked corned beef

8   ounces Swiss cheese, thinly sliced or shredded

1   14- to 16-ounce jar or can sauerkraut, rinsed and drained

1 Prepare the hot roll mix according to package directions. Let rest for 5 minutes. Meanwhile, line an extra-large baking sheet with foil; grease foil. Set aside.

2 Divide dough in half; roll each half into a 12×8-inch rectangle. On each dough rectangle, layer $1/4$ cup of the Thousand Island salad dressing, half of the corned beef, half of the cheese, and half of the sauerkraut, spreading to within 1 inch of the edges. Starting from a long side, roll up each rectangle to form a loaf. Brush edges with water and press to seal.

3 Place loaves, seam sides down, on the prepared baking sheet. Lightly cover; let rise in a warm place for 30 minutes.

4 Meanwhile, preheat oven to 375°. Make 4 diagonal slits, $1/4$ inch deep, in the top of each loaf. Bake in preheated oven for 25 to 30 minutes or until golden. Serve with remaining salad dressing.

Nutrition Facts per serving: 492 cal., 27 g total fat (8 g sat. fat), 91 mg chol., 1,305 mg sodium, 41 g carbo., 1 g fiber, 22 g pro.

ROASTED VEGETABLE & PASTRAMI PANINI

Start to Finish:

30 minutes

Makes: 4 servings

4   thin slices provolone cheese (2 ounces)

8   ½-inch slices sourdough or Vienna bread

1   cup roasted or grilled vegetables from a deli or deli-marinated vegetables, coarsely chopped

4   thin slices pastrami (3 ounces)

1   tablespoon olive oil or basil-flavored olive oil

1 Place a cheese slice on each of 4 of the bread slices. Spread vegetables evenly over cheese. Top with pastrami and remaining 4 bread slices. Brush the outsides of the sandwiches with oil.

2 If desired, wrap a brick completely in foil. Heat a nonstick griddle pan or large skillet over medium heat. Place a sandwich on heated pan; place brick on top to flatten slightly.* Cook for 4 to 6 minutes or until sandwich is golden and cheese is melted, turning once. Repeat for remaining sandwiches.

*Note: Or place sandwich on a covered indoor grill or panini grill. Close lid; grill for 4 to 5 minutes or until golden and cheese is melted.

Nutrition Facts per serving: 314 cal., 16 g total fat (6 g sat. fat), 29 mg chol., 689 mg sodium, 30 g carbo., 2 g fiber, 12 g pro.

SAUCY ASIAN-STYLE MEATBALLS

Prep: 25 minutes
Cook: 12 minutes

Makes: 4 servings

1   egg
³/₄   cup purchased shredded carrot
¹/₂   cup soft bread crumbs
1   teaspoon ground ginger
¹/₄   teaspoon salt
¹/₄   teaspoon garlic powder
12   ounces lean ground beef
¹/₂   of a 14-ounce jar sweet ginger sesame grill sauce (about ³/₄ cup) or ³/₄ cup bottled stir-fry sauce
¹/₂   cup water
1   small onion, cut into thin wedges
1   8-ounce can sliced water chestnuts, drained
1   medium red or green sweet pepper, cut into 1-inch pieces
    Hot cooked rice

1 In a medium bowl beat egg with a fork. Stir in ¹/₄ cup of the shredded carrot, the bread crumbs, ginger, salt, and garlic powder; add meat and mix well. Shape meat mixture into 8 meatballs. In a large skillet cook meatballs over medium heat until brown, turning to brown evenly (meatballs will not be done). Remove meatballs from skillet. Wipe skillet with paper towels.

2 Add ginger sesame grill sauce and the water to skillet. Add onion, water chestnuts, sweet pepper, and remaining ¹/₂ cup shredded carrot to skillet; bring to boiling. Return meatballs to skillet. Reduce heat. Simmer, covered, for 12 to 15 minutes or until done (160°F).* Serve meatballs and sauce with hot cooked rice.

*Note: The internal color of a meatball is not a reliable doneness indicator. A beef, veal, lamb, or pork meatball cooked to 160°F is safe, regardless of color. To measure the doneness of a meatball, insert an instant-read thermometer into the center of meatball.

Nutrition Facts per serving: 537 cal., 10 g total fat (4 g sat. fat), 107 mg chol., 1,367 mg sodium, 83 g carbo., 3 g fiber, 23 g pro.

CATSUP-GLAZED MEAT LOAF

Prep: 20 minutes
Bake: 45 minutes

Oven: 350°F
Makes: 4 servings

1	egg
¼	cup hot and spicy catsup
1	cup soft bread crumbs
¼	cup chopped onion
½	teaspoon salt
⅛	teaspoon black pepper
2	teaspoons bottled minced garlic (4 cloves)
1	pound lean ground beef
2	tablespoons hot and spicy catsup

1 Preheat oven to 350°. In a large bowl beat egg with a whisk; whisk in the ¼ cup catsup. Stir in bread crumbs, onion, salt, pepper, and garlic. Add meat; mix well. Lightly pat meat mixture into an 8×4×2-inch loaf pan.

2 Bake in preheated oven for 45 to 50 minutes or until done (160°F).* Spoon off fat. Let stand for 10 minutes before serving. Spoon the 2 tablespoons catsup over meat loaf before serving.

*Note: The internal color of a meat loaf is not a reliable doneness indicator. A meat loaf made with beef, veal, lamb, or pork cooked to 160°F is safe, regardless of color. To measure the doneness of a meat loaf, insert an instant-read thermometer into the center of the meat loaf.

Nutrition Facts per serving: 264 cal., 12 g total fat (5 g sat. fat), 125 mg chol., 675 mg sodium, 14 g carbo., 1 g fiber, 23 g pro.

MEXICAN MEAT LOAF

Prep: 20 minutes
Bake: 55 minutes

. . . .

Oven: 350°F
Makes: 6 servings

2	eggs
½	cup purchased black bean salsa or bottled salsa
1	cup corn chips, finely crushed
1¼	pounds lean ground beef
¼	cup purchased black bean salsa, bottled salsa, or tomato sauce
⅓	cup corn chips, coarsely crushed
	Dairy sour cream (optional)
	Sliced green onions (optional)
	Shredded cheddar cheese (optional)

1 Preheat oven to 350°. In a large bowl beat eggs with a fork; stir in the ½ cup salsa and the finely crushed corn chips. Add ground beef; mix well. Pat mixture into an 8×4×2-inch loaf pan.

2 Bake in preheated oven for 55 to 60 minutes or until done (160°F).* If desired, carefully drain off fat. Cool in pan for 10 minutes.

3 Transfer to a serving platter. Spread the ¼ cup black bean salsa over meat loaf. Sprinkle with the coarsely crushed corn chips. If desired, serve with sour cream, green onions, and/or cheddar cheese.

*Note: The internal color of a meat loaf is not a reliable doneness indicator. A meat loaf made with beef, veal, lamb, or pork cooked to 160°F is safe, regardless of color. To measure the doneness of a meat loaf, insert an instant-read thermometer into the center of the meat loaf.

Nutrition Facts per serving: 330 cal., 23 g total fat (8 g sat. fat), 139 mg chol., 238 mg sodium, 9 g carbo., 1 g fiber, 20 g pro.

HAMBURGER STROGANOFF

Start to Finish:
25 minutes

Makes: 3 or 4 servings

12   ounces ground beef

½   teaspoon bottled minced garlic (1 clove) or ⅛ teaspoon garlic powder

1½   cups water

1½   cups half-and-half, light cream, or milk

1   4-ounce can (drained weight) sliced mushrooms, drained

1   1½-ounce envelope dry stroganoff sauce mix

4   ounces dried medium egg noodles (2 cups)

1 In a large saucepan cook ground beef and garlic until meat is brown. Drain off fat. Stir the water, half-and-half, mushrooms, and dry stroganoff sauce mix into meat mixture in skillet. Bring to boiling. Stir in noodles. Reduce heat. Simmer, covered, for 6 to 8 minutes or until noodles are tender, stirring occasionally.

Nutrition Facts per serving: 528 cal., 34 g total fat (16 g sat. fat), 132 mg chol., 949 mg sodium, 31 g carbo., 1 g fiber, 23 g pro.

SPAGHETTI WITH CINCINNATI-STYLE MARINARA

Start to Finish:
30 minutes

. . . .

Makes: 6 servings

12	ounces dried spaghetti
1	pound ground beef
1	cup chopped onion
1	to 2 tablespoons chili powder
¼	teaspoon ground cinnamon
1	15-ounce can red kidney beans, rinsed and drained
1	14-ounce jar marinara sauce
½	cup water
1	cup shredded cheddar cheese (4 ounces)

1 Cook spaghetti according to package directions. Meanwhile, in a large skillet cook beef and onion until meat is brown and onion is tender. Drain off fat. Stir chili powder and cinnamon into meat mixture; cook and stir for 2 minutes.

2 Add kidney beans, marinara sauce, and the water. Cook over medium heat until boiling, stirring occasionally.

3 Place hot cooked spaghetti in a large serving bowl. Spoon sauce over spaghetti; sprinkle with cheddar cheese.

Nutrition Facts per serving: 522 cal., 17 g total fat (7 g sat. fat), 67 mg chol., 527 mg sodium, 62 g carbo., 7 g fiber, 32 g pro.

BEEF & NOODLE CASSEROLE

Prep: 15 minutes
Bake: 30 minutes

. . . .

Oven: 350°F
Makes: 4 servings

1	pound ground beef
½	cup milk
½	of an 8-ounce tub cream cheese with chives and onion (½ cup)
1	medium carrot, shredded
1	4.6-ounce package vermicelli with garlic and olive oil or one 4.8-ounce package angel hair pasta with herbs
1½	cups boiling water

1 Preheat oven to 350°. Grease a 1½-quart casserole; set aside. In a large skillet cook ground beef until brown. Drain off fat.

2 Meanwhile, in prepared casserole gradually whisk milk into cream cheese until smooth. Stir in carrot and seasoning packet from pasta mix. Stir in meat. Break pasta from pasta mix into 1-inch-long pieces; stir into meat mixture.

3 Slowly pour boiling water over meat mixture. Bake, covered, in preheated oven for 30 to 35 minutes or until noodles are tender, stirring twice. Let stand, covered, for 5 minutes. Stir before serving.

Nutrition Facts per serving: 463 cal., 25 g total fat (13 g sat. fat), 101 mg chol., 619 mg sodium, 28 g carbo., 2 g fiber, 28 g pro.

SHORTCUT LASAGNA

Prep: 20 minutes
Bake: 40 minutes

Oven: 350°F
Makes: 8 servings

8	ounces ground beef
8	ounces bulk Italian sausage
1	26-ounce jar tomato-basil pasta sauce
1	egg
1	15-ounce carton ricotta cheese or cream-style cottage cheese
1	2¼-ounce can sliced pitted ripe olives
9	no-boil lasagna noodles
1	8-ounce package sliced mozzarella cheese
¼	cup grated Parmesan cheese (1 ounce)
	Snipped fresh basil (optional)

1 Preheat oven to 350°. In a large saucepan cook beef and sausage until brown. Drain off fat. Stir pasta sauce into meat mixture in saucepan; bring to boiling.

2 Meanwhile, in a medium bowl beat egg slightly with a fork. Stir in ricotta and olives.

3 To assemble lasagna, spread about 1 cup of the hot meat mixture in the bottom of a 3-quart rectangular baking dish. Cover with 3 of the lasagna noodles, making sure that noodles do not touch the edge of the dish. Cover with one-third of the ricotta mixture, one-third of the remaining meat mixture, and one-third of the mozzarella cheese. Repeat with 2 more layers of noodles, meat mixture, ricotta cheese mixture, and mozzarella. (Make sure noodles are covered with sauce.) Sprinkle with Parmesan cheese.

4 Cover with foil. Bake in preheated oven for 30 minutes. Uncover and bake for 10 to 15 minutes more or until cheese is golden and noodles are tender. Let stand for 5 minutes before serving. If desired, garnish with fresh basil.

Nutrition Facts per serving: 449 cal., 25 g total fat (12 g sat. fat), 115 mg chol., 766 mg sodium, 23 g carbo., 2 g fiber, 30 g pro.

SKILLET TOSTADAS

Start to Finish:

25 minutes

. . . .

Makes: 4 servings

8	ounces ground beef
$\frac{1}{2}$	cup chopped onion
1	15-ounce can light red kidney beans, rinsed and drained
1	11-ounce can condensed nacho cheese soup
$\frac{1}{3}$	cup bottled salsa
8	tostada shells
1	cup shredded taco cheese (4 ounces)
	Shredded lettuce
	Chopped tomatoes
	Dairy sour cream or guacamole (optional)

1 In a 10-inch skillet cook ground beef and onion until meat is brown and onion is tender. Drain off fat. Stir kidney beans, nacho cheese soup, and salsa into beef mixture. Heat through.

2 Divide beef-salsa mixture among tostada shells. Top with cheese. Top with lettuce and tomatoes. If desired, serve with sour cream.

Nutrition Facts per serving: 576 cal., 33 g total fat (15 g sat. fat), 81 mg chol., 1,277 mg sodium, 42 g carbo., 11 g fiber, 26 g pro.

CHILI & DUMPLINGS

Prep: 25 minutes
Cook: 17 minutes

. . . .

Makes: 6 servings

1	pound ground beef
1	15-ounce can red kidney beans, rinsed and drained
1	14½-ounce can diced tomatoes, undrained
1	11½-ounce can tomato juice
½	cup water
4	teaspoons chili powder
½	teaspoon salt
1	7.75-ounce package cheese-garlic complete biscuit mix
	Snipped fresh cilantro or parsley (optional)

1 In a large saucepan cook beef until brown. Drain off fat. Stir kidney beans, undrained tomatoes, tomato juice, the water, chili powder, and salt into beef in saucepan. Bring to boiling; reduce heat. Simmer, uncovered, for 5 minutes.

2 Meanwhile, prepare biscuit mix according to package directions. Drop biscuit dough by spoonfuls into mounds onto the simmering chili mixture. Simmer, covered, for 12 to 15 minutes or until a toothpick inserted into dumplings comes out clean. If desired, garnish with cilantro.

Nutrition Facts per serving: 482 cal., 28 g total fat (10 g sat. fat), 64 mg chol., 1,155 mg sodium, 38 g carbo., 6 g fiber, 19 g pro.

QUICK CHILI

Start to Finish:

15 minutes

· ·

Makes: 4 servings

1   pound ground beef

2   15-ounce cans chili beans with chili gravy

1¹/₂   cups tomato juice

4   teaspoons chili powder

     Dairy sour cream dip with toasted onion or dairy sour cream

1 In a medium saucepan cook ground beef over medium-high heat until brown, stirring frequently. Drain off fat.

2 Stir chili beans, tomato juice, and chili powder into beef in saucepan. Bring to boiling; reduce heat. Simmer, uncovered, for 5 minutes. Top servings with sour cream dip.

Nutrition Facts per serving: 526 cal., 21 g total fat (8 g sat. fat), 101 mg chol., 1,097 mg sodium, 41 g carbo., 13 g fiber, 43 g pro.

CHEESY ITALIAN PIE

Prep: 20 minutes
Bake: 25 minutes

Oven: 425°F
Makes: 6 servings

1	15-ounce package folded refrigerated unbaked piecrusts (2 crusts)
1	pound ground beef or Italian sausage
2	8-ounce cans pizza sauce
1	10-ounce package frozen chopped spinach, thawed and well drained
2	eggs
1	cup ricotta cheese or cottage cheese
½	cup grated Parmesan cheese (2 ounces)
½	teaspoon dried Italian seasoning, crushed

1 Preheat oven to 425°. Let piecrusts stand at room temperature for 15 minutes as directed on package.

2 Meanwhile, for filling, in a large skillet cook the ground beef until brown. Drain off fat. Stir pizza sauce and spinach into ground beef in skillet. Set aside.

3 In a medium bowl stir together eggs, ricotta, Parmesan cheese, and Italian seasoning. Line a 9-inch pie plate with 1 of the piecrusts. Spoon ricotta mixture into crust. Top with beef mixture. Place remaining piecrust over filling. Seal and flute edge. Cut slits in top crust to allow steam to escape.

4 Bake in preheated oven about 25 minutes or until crust is golden.

Nutrition Facts per serving: 715 cal., 48 g total fat (20 g sat. fat), 173 mg chol., 844 mg sodium, 43 g carbo., 1 g fiber, 26 g pro.

ITALIAN BEEF & SPINACH PIE

Prep: 20 minutes
Bake: 30 minutes

Oven: 350°F
Makes: 8 servings

12	ounces lean ground beef
3/4	cup chopped red and/or yellow sweet pepper
1/2	teaspoon bottled minced garlic (1 clove)
1	cup water
1	6-ounce can Italian-style tomato paste
1	4-ounce can (drained weight) sliced mushrooms, drained
1/2	teaspoon dried Italian seasoning, crushed
1	10-ounce package frozen chopped spinach, thawed and well drained
3/4	cup shredded mozzarella cheese (3 ounces)
2/3	cup light or regular ricotta cheese
1/2	teaspoon salt
1	baked 9-inch pastry shell*

1 Preheat oven to 350°. In a large skillet cook beef, sweet pepper, and garlic until meat is brown and sweet pepper is tender. Stir in the water, tomato paste, drained mushrooms, and Italian seasoning. Bring to boiling; reduce heat. Simmer, covered, for 10 minutes.

2 Meanwhile, in a medium bowl stir together spinach, 1/4 cup of the mozzarella cheese, the ricotta cheese, and salt. Spoon spinach mixture into baked pastry shell. Top with the meat mixture. Cover edge of pastry with foil to prevent overbrowning.

3 Bake in preheated oven for 30 to 35 minutes or until heated through. Remove foil. Top with remaining mozzarella cheese. Let pie stand for 10 minutes before serving.

***Note:** For a baked pastry shell, bake one 9-inch frozen unbaked deep-dish pastry shell according to package directions. Or prepare and bake 1 folded refrigerated unbaked piecrust (1/2 of a 15-ounce package) according to package directions.

Nutrition Facts per serving: 237 cal., 12 g total fat (4 g sat. fat), 38 mg chol., 635 mg sodium, 16 g carbo., 2 g fiber, 15 g pro.

TAMALE PIE

Prep: 20 minutes
Bake: 22 minutes

. . . .

Oven: 375°F
Makes: 6 servings

1   8½-ounce package corn muffin mix
1   4-ounce package shredded cheddar cheese (1 cup)
1   4-ounce can diced green chile peppers, drained
1   pound ground beef or bulk pork sausage
1   15-ounce can red kidney beans, rinsed and drained
1   10-ounce can enchilada sauce
    Dairy sour cream (optional)

1 Preheat oven to 375°. Grease a 2-quart rectangular baking dish; set aside.

2 Prepare muffin mix according to package directions. Stir in ½ cup of the cheese and the chile peppers. Spread the corn muffin batter into prepared baking dish.

3 Bake in preheated oven for 12 to 15 minutes or until a toothpick inserted near the center comes out clean.

4 Meanwhile, in a large skillet cook ground beef until brown. Drain off fat. Stir kidney beans and enchilada sauce into meat. Spread meat mixture over baked corn muffin mixture.

5 Bake for 7 minutes more. Sprinkle with remaining cheese. Bake about 3 minutes more or until cheese melts and mixture is heated through. To serve, cut into squares. If desired, serve with sour cream.

Nutrition Facts per serving: 464 cal., 21 g total fat (8 g sat. fat), 67 mg chol., 778 mg sodium, 44 g carbo., 4 g fiber, 27 g pro.

TACO PIZZA

Prep: 15 minutes
Bake: 20 minutes

. . . .

Oven: 400°F
Makes: 6 wedges

8	ounces lean ground beef and/or bulk pork sausage
1	medium sweet pepper, chopped
1	11½-ounce package refrigerated corn bread twists
½	cup bottled salsa
3	cups shredded taco cheese (12 ounces)

1 Preheat oven to 400°. Grease a 12-inch pizza pan; set aside. In a medium skillet cook and stir beef and/or sausage and sweet pepper over medium heat until meat is done. Drain off fat. Set aside.

2 Unroll corn bread dough (do not separate into strips). Press dough into the bottom and up the edge of prepared pan. Spread salsa on top of dough. Sprinkle with meat mixture and cheese.

3 Bake in preheated oven about 20 minutes or until bottom of crust is golden when lifted slightly with a spatula. Cut into wedges.

Nutrition Facts per wedge: 465 cal., 30 g total fat (15 g sat. fat), 73 mg chol., 870 mg sodium, 27 g carbo., 1 g fiber, 22 g pro.

BACON-CHEESE BURGERS

Prep: 15 minutes
Broil: 11 minutes

. . . .

Makes: 4 servings

1¼   pounds lean ground beef

8   thin slices Colby and Monterey Jack cheese or cheddar cheese (4 ounces)

4   slices bacon, crisp-cooked and crumbled

4   hamburger buns, split and toasted

¼   cup dairy sour cream onion dip

1 Shape the ground beef into eight ¼-inch-thick patties. Place 1 cheese slice on top of each of 4 of the patties; sprinkle with crumbled bacon. Place remaining 4 patties on top of the bacon-and-cheese-topped patties. Seal edges well.

2 Place patties on the unheated rack of a broiler pan. Broil 3 to 4 inches from the heat for 10 to 12 minutes or until cooked through, turning once halfway through cooking time. Place remaining 4 cheese slices on top of patties. Broil the patties for 1 minute more.

3 Meanwhile, spread cut sides of toasted buns with the onion dip. Serve burgers on prepared buns.

Nutrition Facts per serving: 635 cal., 41 g total fat (19 g sat. fat), 133 mg chol., 691 mg sodium, 25 g carbo., 1 g fiber, 37 g pro.

DRIED TOMATO BURGERS

Prep: 15 minutes
Grill: 10 minutes

. . . .

Makes: 4 servings

1	pound lean ground beef
2	tablespoons dried tomato-flavored light mayonnaise dressing
2	tablespoons oil-packed dried tomatoes, drained and chopped
1	teaspoon finely shredded lemon peel
4	onion hamburger buns
¼	cup dried tomato-flavored light mayonnaise dressing
2	tablespoons snipped fresh basil
1	small red onion, thinly sliced
1	cup fresh spinach leaves

1 In a medium bowl combine beef, the 2 tablespoons mayonnaise dressing, the dried tomatoes, and lemon peel. Mix lightly but thoroughly. Shape into four ½-inch-thick patties.

2 Place patties on the rack of an uncovered grill directly over medium heat. Grill for 10 to 13 minutes or until done (160°F),* turning patties once halfway through grilling. For the last 1 to 2 minutes of grilling, place buns, cut sides down, on grill rack to toast.

3 Meanwhile, in a small bowl combine the ¼ cup mayonnaise dressing and the basil. Top bun bottoms with patties. Top with mayonnaise dressing mixture, onion slices, and spinach. Add bun tops.

*Note: The internal color of a burger is not a reliable doneness indicator. A beef, veal, lamb, or pork patty cooked to 160°F is safe, regardless of color. To measure the doneness of a patty, insert an instant-read thermometer through the side of the patty to a depth of 2 to 3 inches.

Nutrition Facts per serving: 509 cal., 34 g total fat (12 g sat. fat), 100 mg chol., 496 mg sodium, 25 g carbo., 2 g fiber, 24 g pro.

BLUE CHEESE BURGERS

Prep: **25** minutes

Grill: **14** minutes

Makes: 4 servings

1	egg
1/3	cup fine dry seasoned bread crumbs
2	to 3 teaspoons bottled hot pepper sauce
1/4	teaspoon salt
1 1/4	pounds lean ground beef
1/3	cup crumbled blue cheese
4	kaiser rolls, split and toasted
	Sliced tomatoes (optional)
	Sliced red onion (optional)
	Lettuce leaves (optional)
1/4	cup bottled blue cheese salad dressing

1 In a medium bowl beat egg with a fork. Stir in bread crumbs, hot pepper sauce, and salt. Add ground beef; mix well. Shape meat mixture into eight 1/4-inch-thick patties. Divide crumbled blue cheese among 4 of the patties, placing cheese in center of each patty. Top with remaining 4 patties. Seal edges well.

2 Place patties on the rack of an uncovered grill directly over medium heat. Grill for 14 to 18 minutes or until cooked through (160°),* turning once halfway through grilling.

3 If desired, line roll bottoms with tomatoes, red onion, and lettuce. Place burgers on roll bottoms; top with blue cheese dressing and add roll tops.

Broiler Directions: Prepare burgers as directed in step 1. Place burgers on the unheated rack of a broiler pan. Broil 3 to 4 inches from heat for 12 to 14 minutes or until cooked through, turning once halfway through grilling. Serve as directed in step 3.

*Note: The internal color of the burger or any ground meat mixture is not a reliable doneness indicator. A beef mixture cooked to 160°F is safe, regardless of color.

Nutrition Facts per serving: 567 cal., 29 g total fat (10 g sat. fat), 153 mg chol., 1,106 mg sodium, 38 g carbo., 1 g fiber, 37 g pro.

FIESTA BURGERS

Prep: 15 minutes
Broil: 11 minutes

Makes: 4 servings

1   pound ground beef
½   cup bottled salsa
⅓   cup chopped avocado
⅓   cup mayonnaise or dairy sour cream
½   teaspoon chili powder
¼   teaspoon garlic salt
4   kaiser rolls or hamburger buns, split and toasted
1   cup shredded lettuce

1 Shape ground beef into four ½-inch-thick patties. Place patties on the unheated rack of a broiler pan. Broil 3 to 4 inches from heat for 11 to 13 minutes or until done (160°F).*

2 Meanwhile, in a small bowl combine salsa and avocado. In another small bowl stir together mayonnaise, chili powder, and garlic salt. Spread chili powder mixture on roll bottoms. Top with shredded lettuce, cooked patties, salsa mixture, and roll tops.

*Note: The internal color of a burger is not a reliable doneness indicator. A beef, veal, lamb, or pork patty cooked to 160°F is safe, regardless of color. To measure the doneness of a patty, insert an instant-read thermometer through the side of the patty to a depth of 2 to 3 inches.

Nutrition Facts per serving: 542 cal., 33 g total fat (8 g sat. fat), 78 mg chol., 601 mg sodium, 32 g carbo., 2 g fiber, 28 g pro.

ITALIAN PIZZA BURGERS

Prep: **15** minutes

Broil: **11** minutes

Makes: 4 servings

4   3³/₄-ounce purchased refrigerated uncooked hamburger patties*

4   ³/₄-inch slices sourdough bread

1   cup purchased mushroom pasta sauce

1   cup shredded provolone or mozzarella cheese (4 ounces)

2   tablespoons thinly sliced fresh basil

1 Place hamburger patties on the unheated rack of a broiler pan. Broil 3 to 4 inches from heat for 10 to 12 minutes or until done (160°F),** turning once halfway through broiling. Add bread slices to broiler pan for the last 2 to 3 minutes of broiling; turn once to toast evenly.

2 Meanwhile, in a medium saucepan heat the pasta sauce over medium heat until bubbly, stirring occasionally. Place patties on bread slices. Spoon pasta sauce over patties; sprinkle with cheese. Place on the rack of the broiler pan. Return to broiler; broil for 1 to 2 minutes more or until cheese melts. Top with basil.

***Note:** If refrigerated uncooked hamburger patties are not available, shape 1 pound ground beef into four ¹/₂-inch-thick patties.

****Note:** The internal color of a burger is not a reliable doneness indicator. A beef, veal, lamb, or pork patty cooked to 160°F is safe, regardless of color. To measure the doneness of a patty, insert an instant-read thermometer through the side of the patty to a depth of 2 to 3 inches.

Nutrition Facts per serving: 504 cal., 30 g total fat (13 g sat. fat), 96 mg chol., 815 mg sodium, 27 g carbo., 2 g fiber, 30 g pro.

GERMAN MEATBALLS WITH SPAETZLE

Prep: 20 minutes
Cook: 16 minutes

. . . .

Makes: 4 to 6 servings

1   10½-ounce package dried spaetzle

1   16-ounce package frozen cooked meatballs (32)

1   14-ounce can beef broth

1   4-ounce can (drained weight) mushroom stems and pieces, drained

½   cup chopped onion

1   8-ounce carton dairy sour cream

2   tablespoons all-purpose flour

½   to 1 teaspoon caraway seeds

    Snipped fresh parsley (optional)

1 Cook spaetzle according to package directions. Drain.

2 Meanwhile, in a large saucepan combine meatballs, beef broth, mushrooms, and onion. Bring to boiling; reduce heat. Simmer, covered, for 15 to 20 minutes or until meatballs are heated through.

3 In a small bowl combine sour cream, flour, and caraway seeds; stir into meatball mixture. Cook and stir until mixture is thickened and bubbly. Cook and stir for 1 minute more.

4 To serve, spoon the meatball mixture over the spaetzle. If desired, sprinkle with parsley.

Nutrition Facts per serving: 796 cal., 44 g total fat (20 g sat. fat), 122 mg chol., 2,128 mg sodium, 70 g carbo., 7 g fiber, 30 g pro.

POULTRY

SAUCY CRANBERRY CHICKEN

Prep: 15 minutes
Bake: 1½ hours

. . . .

Oven: 325°F
Makes: 4 to 6 servings

1	16-ounce can whole cranberry sauce
1	cup bottled Russian salad dressing or French salad dressing
1	envelope (½ of a 2-ounce package) dry onion soup mix
2½	to 3 pounds meaty chicken pieces (breast halves, thighs, and drumsticks)
	Hot cooked rice (optional)

1 Preheat oven to 325°. In a bowl stir together cranberry sauce, salad dressing, and soup mix. Skin chicken, if desired. Arrange chicken pieces, meaty sides down, in a 3-quart rectangular baking dish. Pour the cranberry mixture over chicken pieces.

2 Bake, uncovered, in the preheated oven about 1½ hours or until chicken is no longer pink (170°F for breast pieces; 180°F for thighs and drumsticks), stirring glaze and spooning it over the chicken once or twice. If desired, serve over hot cooked rice.

Nutrition Facts per serving: 810 cal., 47 g total fat (7 g sat. fat), 141 mg chol., 901 mg sodium, 54 g carbo., 2 g fiber, 43 g pro.

CHICKEN WITH BUTTERMILK GRAVY

Prep: 15 minutes
Broil: 12 minutes

Makes: 6 servings

⅓	cup fine dry seasoned bread crumbs
2	tablespoons grated Parmesan cheese
½	teaspoon paprika
6	skinless, boneless chicken breast halves (about 2 pounds total)
3	tablespoons butter or margarine, melted
	Salt (optional)
	Black pepper (optional)
1	1-ounce envelope chicken gravy mix
1	cup buttermilk
¼	teaspoon dried sage, crushed

1 Preheat broiler. In a shallow dish combine bread crumbs, Parmesan cheese, and paprika; set aside. Brush chicken with some of the melted butter. If desired, sprinkle chicken with salt and pepper. Dip chicken into crumb mixture, turning to coat evenly.

2 Arrange chicken on the unheated rack of a broiler pan. Drizzle with any remaining melted butter. Broil 4 to 5 inches from the heat for 12 to 15 minutes or until chicken is no longer pink (170°F), turning once halfway through broiling.

3 Meanwhile, for gravy, in a small saucepan prepare chicken gravy mix according to package directions, except use the 1 cup buttermilk in place of the water called for in the package directions. Stir sage into gravy. Serve with chicken.

Nutrition Facts per serving: 288 cal., 9 g total fat (5 g sat. fat), 107 mg chol., 644 mg sodium, 10 g carbo., 0 g fiber, 38 g pro.

ASIAN CHICKEN & VEGETABLES

Prep: 10 minutes
Bake: 40 minutes

· · · · · · · · · · · · · · · · · · ·

Oven: 400°F
Makes: 4 servings

8	chicken drumsticks and/or thighs, skinned (about 2 pounds total)
1	tablespoon cooking oil
1½	teaspoons five-spice powder
⅓	cup bottled plum sauce or sweet-and-sour sauce
1	14-ounce package frozen baby whole potatoes, broccoli, carrots, baby corn, and red pepper mix or one 16-ounce package frozen stir-fry vegetables (any combination)

1 Preheat oven to 400°. Arrange the chicken pieces in a 13×9×2-inch baking pan, making sure pieces do not touch. Brush chicken pieces with oil; sprinkle with 1 teaspoon of the five-spice powder. Bake, uncovered, in preheated oven for 25 minutes.

2 Meanwhile, in a large bowl combine remaining ½ teaspoon five-spice powder and the plum sauce. Add frozen vegetables; toss to coat.

3 Move chicken pieces to one side of the baking pan. Add vegetable mixture to the other side of the baking pan. Bake for 15 to 20 minutes more or until chicken is no longer pink (180°F), stirring vegetables once during baking. Using a slotted spoon, transfer chicken and vegetables to a serving platter.

Nutrition Facts per serving: 277 cal., 9 g total fat (2 g sat. fat), 98 mg chol., 124 mg sodium, 21 g carbo., 2 g fiber, 30 g pro.

PASTRY-WRAPPED CHICKEN

Prep: 30 minutes
Bake: 12 minutes

Oven: 400°F
Makes: 4 servings

2	tablespoons butter or margarine
½	teaspoon dried tarragon, crushed
4	skinless, boneless chicken breast halves (about 1¼ pounds total)
1	8-ounce package (8) refrigerated crescent rolls
1	cup shredded Swiss cheese (4 ounces)
1	recipe Honey Mustard Sauce

1 Preheat oven to 400°. In a large skillet melt butter over medium heat; stir in tarragon. Add chicken; cook for 8 to 10 minutes or until no longer pink (170°F), turning once. Remove from skillet.

2 Meanwhile, separate crescent rolls into 4 rectangles. Pinch perforations to seal. On a floured surface, roll each dough rectangle into a 6½×4½-inch rectangle. Divide cheese among rectangles, sprinkling in center of each rectangle. Place chicken breast halves on cheese. Fold dough over chicken and cheese. Crimp edges to seal.

3 Place bundles, seam sides down, on an ungreased baking sheet. Bake in preheated oven about 12 minutes or until pastry is golden. Serve with Honey Mustard Sauce.

Honey Mustard Sauce: In a small bowl stir together ¼ cup mayonnaise or salad dressing and 2 tablespoons honey mustard. Makes about ⅓ cup.

Nutrition Facts per serving: 621 cal., 38 g total fat (13 g sat. fat), 132 mg chol., 808 mg sodium, 25 g carbo., 0 g fiber, 45 g pro.

TANGY LEMON CHICKEN

Prep: 10 minutes

Grill: 12 minutes

Makes: 4 servings

4   skinless, boneless chicken breast halves (about 1¼ pounds total)

1   cup bottled creamy Italian salad dressing

1½   teaspoons finely shredded lemon peel

2   tablespoons lemon juice

     Dash black pepper

8   cups torn mixed salad greens

1 Place the chicken in a resealable plastic bag set in a shallow dish. For marinade, in a small bowl stir together ½ cup of the salad dressing, the lemon peel, lemon juice, and pepper. Pour marinade over chicken. Seal bag; turn to coat chicken. Marinate in the refrigerator for at least 8 hours or up to 24 hours, turning bag occasionally.

2 Drain chicken, reserving marinade. Place chicken on the rack of an uncovered grill directly over medium heat. Grill for 12 to 15 minutes or until no longer pink (170°F), turning once and brushing once with reserved marinade halfway through grilling. Discard any remaining marinade.

3 Serve chicken with greens and remaining salad dressing.

Nutrition Facts per serving: 451 cal., 31 g total fat (5 g sat. fat), 82 mg chol., 550 mg sodium, 9 g carbo., 2 g fiber, 34 g pro.

ORIENTAL-STYLE CHICKEN

Start to Finish:

25 minutes

Makes: 4 servings

2	cups loose-pack frozen stir-fry vegetables (any combination)
1	8-ounce can pineapple tidbits (juice pack)
½	cup bottled teriyaki sauce
2	teaspoons cornstarch
½	teaspoon ground ginger
1	tablespoon cooking oil
12	ounces packaged skinless, boneless chicken breast strips (stir-fry strips)
	Coarsely chopped honey-roasted peanuts
	Hot cooked rice

1 In a colander run hot water over frozen vegetables just until thawed. Drain well. Meanwhile, drain pineapple, reserving ¼ cup of the juice. Set pineapple aside. In a small bowl stir together reserved pineapple juice, teriyaki sauce, cornstarch, and ginger. Set aside.

2 In a large skillet heat oil over medium-high heat. Add chicken; cook for 2 to 3 minutes or until no longer pink, (165°F),* turning occasionally. Add vegetables and pineapple; cook for 1 minute more.

3 Push chicken and vegetables to the edge of the skillet. Add teriyaki mixture to the skillet. Cook and stir until thickened and bubbly. Cook and stir for 2 minutes more. Sprinkle with peanuts. Serve with hot cooked rice.

*Note: The internal color is not a reliable doneness indicator. Chicken mixtures must be cooked to 165°F.

Nutrition Facts per serving: 374 cal., 9 g total fat (1 g sat. fat), 49 mg chol., 2,184 mg sodium, 42 g carbo., 3 g fiber, 28 g pro.

BLACKENED CHICKEN ALFREDO

Prep: 15 minutes
Grill: 12 minutes

Makes: 4 servings

3　skinless, boneless chicken breast halves (12 to 16 ounces total)

2　tablespoons olive oil

2　teaspoons blackened redfish seasoning

8　ounces dried mostaccioli ($2^2/_3$ cups)

2　cups broccoli florets

1　cup halved, packaged peeled baby carrots

1　10-ounce container refrigerated Alfredo pasta sauce

$^1/_2$　teaspoon blackened redfish seasoning

1 Preheat grill. In a resealable plastic bag place the chicken, oil, and the 2 teaspoons blackened seasoning. Turn bag to coat chicken.

2 Place chicken on the rack of an uncovered grill directly over medium heat. Grill for 12 to 15 minutes or until no longer pink (170°F), turning once halfway through grilling. (Or in a large skillet cook chicken in 1 tablespoon hot olive oil or cooking oil for 8 to 10 minutes or until no longer pink [170°F], turning once.) Cut chicken into $^1/_2$-inch cubes; set aside.

3 Meanwhile, cook pasta according to the package directions except add the broccoli and carrots the last 8 minutes of cooking. Drain; return to pan. Stir in grilled chicken, Alfredo sauce, and the $^1/_2$ teaspoon blackened seasoning. Heat through.

Nutrition Facts per serving: 615 cal., 31 g total fat (1 g sat. fat), 85 mg chol., 567 mg sodium, 52 g carbo., 4 g fiber, 32 g pro.

SWEET GINGER STIR-FRY

Start to Finish:

20 minutes

. . . .

Makes: 4 servings

12   ounces skinless, boneless chicken breast halves or skinless, boneless chicken thighs

2   tablespoons cooking oil

2   cups loose-pack frozen mixed vegetables (any combination)

½   cup bottled sweet ginger stir-fry sauce

    Hot cooked rice

1 Cut chicken into 1-inch pieces; set aside. In a wok or large skillet heat oil over medium-high heat. Add vegetables; stir-fry about 3 minutes or until vegetables are crisp-tender. Remove vegetables from wok.

2 Add chicken to hot wok. (Add more oil if necessary.) Stir-fry for 3 to 4 minutes or until chicken is no longer pink. Push chicken from center of the wok. Add sauce to center of the wok. Cook and stir until bubbly. Return cooked vegetables to wok. Stir to coat. Cook and stir about 1 minute more or until heated through.

3 Serve over hot cooked rice.

Nutrition Facts per serving: 382 cal., 9 g total fat (1 g sat. fat), 49 mg chol., 879 mg sodium, 50 g carbo., 3 g fiber, 24 g pro.

ORANGE CHICKEN & FRIED RICE

Start to Finish:
25 minutes

Makes: 4 servings

1	6-ounce package Oriental-flavored fried rice mix
2	tablespoons butter or margarine
1	pound packaged skinless, boneless chicken breast strips (stir-fry strips)
8	green onions, bias-sliced into 1-inch pieces
1	teaspoon bottled minced garlic (2 cloves) or ¼ teaspoon garlic powder
1	teaspoon ground ginger
1	tablespoon frozen orange juice concentrate, thawed
¼	cup chopped cashews

1 Cook rice according to package directions.

2 Meanwhile, in a large skillet melt butter over medium-high heat. Add chicken strips, green onions, garlic, and ginger; cook and stir for 3 to 5 minutes or until chicken is no longer pink.

3 Stir the orange juice concentrate into cooked rice. Stir rice mixture into chicken mixture in skillet. Cook and stir until heated through. To serve, sprinkle with cashews.

Nutrition Facts per serving: 396 cal., 13 g total fat (5 g sat. fat), 82 mg chol., 985 mg sodium, 38 g carbo., 2 g fiber, 32 g pro.

RANCH-STYLE CHICKEN STRIPS

Prep: 15 minutes
Bake: 12 minutes

Oven: 425°F
Makes: 4 servings

Nonstick cooking spray

2 cups crushed cornflakes

2 tablespoons snipped fresh basil or 1 teaspoon dried basil, crushed

1 8-ounce bottle buttermilk ranch salad dressing

12 ounces packaged skinless, boneless chicken breast strips

1 Preheat oven to 425°. Lightly coat a 15×10×1-inch baking pan with cooking spray; set aside. In a shallow dish combine cornflakes and basil. In another shallow dish place $1/2$ cup of the salad dressing. Dip chicken strips into the dressing, allowing excess to drip off; dip into crumb mixture, turning to coat. Arrange strips in prepared baking pan. Discard any remaining dressing used to dip chicken.

2 Bake in preheated oven for 12 to 15 minutes or until chicken is no longer pink. Serve with remaining salad dressing.

Nutrition Facts per serving: 543 cal., 32 g total fat (5 g sat. fat), 54 mg chol., 928 mg sodium, 38 g carbo., 0 g fiber, 24 g pro.

CHILE-LIME CHICKEN SKEWERS

Prep: 20 minutes
Grill: 10 minutes

Makes: 4 servings

1	pound skinless, boneless chicken breasts
2	limes
1½	teaspoons ground ancho chile pepper
1	teaspoon garlic-herb seasoning

1 Preheat grill. Cut the chicken into 1-inch-wide strips. Place chicken strips in a shallow dish; set aside. Finely shred enough peel from 1 of the limes to measure 1 teaspoon (chill this lime and use for juice another time). Cut remaining lime into wedges and set aside.

2 For rub, in a small bowl combine lime peel, ground ancho chile pepper, and garlic-herb seasoning. Sprinkle rub evenly over chicken; rub in with your fingers.

3 On 4 long metal skewers, thread chicken accordion-style, leaving a ¼-inch space between pieces. Place skewers on the rack of an uncovered grill directly over medium heat. Grill for 10 to 12 minutes or until chicken is no longer pink, turning once. (Or place skewers on the unheated rack of a broiler pan. Broil 4 to 5 inches from the heat for 10 to 12 minutes or until chicken is no longer pink, turning once.) Serve with lime wedges.

Nutrition Facts per serving: 132 cal., 2 g total fat (0 g sat. fat), 66 mg chol., 62 mg sodium, 1 g carbo., 0 g fiber, 26 g pro.

CHICKEN & ARTICHOKE PIZZA

Prep: 20 minutes
Bake: 22 minutes

Oven: 375°F
Makes: 6 main-dish or 10 appetizer servings

1	10-ounce package refrigerated pizza dough (for 1 crust)
8	ounces skinless, boneless chicken breasts or thighs, chopped
1/2	teaspoon garlic salt
1	tablespoon cooking oil
1/2	cup thinly sliced celery
1/3	cup pizza sauce
1/2	cup chopped green sweet pepper
1	6-ounce jar marinated artichoke hearts, drained and quartered
1/4	cup sliced green onions
1	cup shredded mozzarella cheese (4 ounces)
1/2	cup crumbled blue cheese (2 ounces) (optional)

1 Preheat oven to 375°. Grease a 12-inch pizza pan. Unroll pizza dough; press into prepared pan, building up edge slightly. Bake in preheated oven about 12 minutes or until lightly browned. Set aside.

2 Meanwhile, toss together chicken and 1/4 teaspoon of the garlic salt. In a large skillet heat oil over medium-high heat. Add chicken and celery; stir-fry about 3 minutes or until chicken is no longer pink.

3 Combine pizza sauce and the remaining garlic salt; spread over prebaked crust. Top with chicken mixture, sweet pepper, artichoke hearts, and green onions. Sprinkle mozzarella and, if desired, blue cheese over pizza.

4 Bake in the 375° oven for 10 to 15 minutes more or until cheese is melted and bubbly. Cut into wedges to serve.

Nutrition Facts per main-dish serving: 242 cal., 9 g total fat (3 g sat. fat), 33 mg chol., 442 mg sodium, 23 g carbo., 2 g fiber, 17 g pro.

FETTUCCINE VERONA

Start to Finish:

20 minutes

· · · · · · · · · · · · · · · · · ·

Makes: 4 servings

1	9-ounce package refrigerated red sweet pepper fettuccine
¼	of a 7-ounce jar oil-packed dried tomato strips or pieces (¼ cup)
1	large zucchini or yellow summer squash, halved lengthwise and sliced (about 2 cups)
8	ounces packaged skinless, boneless chicken breast strips (stir-fry strips)
2	tablespoons olive oil
½	cup finely shredded Parmesan, Romano, or Asiago cheese (2 ounces)
	Freshly ground black pepper

1 Using kitchen scissors, cut fettuccine strands in half. Cook fettuccine in lightly salted boiling water according to package directions; drain. Return fettuccine to hot pan.

2 Meanwhile, drain tomatoes, reserving 2 tablespoons of the oil from the jar. Set drained tomatoes aside. In a large skillet heat 1 tablespoon of the reserved oil over medium-high heat. Add zucchini; cook and stir for 2 to 3 minutes or until crisp-tender. Remove from skillet. Add remaining 1 tablespoon reserved oil to skillet. Add chicken; cook and stir for 2 to 3 minutes or until no longer pink.

3 Add chicken, zucchini, drained tomatoes, and olive oil to cooked fettuccine; toss gently to combine. Sprinkle servings with cheese. Season to taste with pepper.

Nutrition Facts per serving: 384 cal., 14 g total fat (4 g sat. fat), 93 mg chol., 356 mg sodium, 37 g carbo., 4 g fiber, 28 g pro.

QUICK-FRIED CHICKEN SALAD WITH STRAWBERRIES

Makes: 6 servings

3/4   cup all-purpose flour

4   tablespoons snipped fresh basil

1   tablespoon finely shredded lemon peel

2   beaten eggs

1   pound packaged skinless, boneless chicken breast strips

2   tablespoons cooking oil

8   cups packaged torn mixed salad greens

2   cups sliced fresh strawberries

1/2   cup bottled balsamic vinaigrette salad dressing

1 In a shallow dish combine flour, 2 tablespoons of the basil, and the lemon peel. Place eggs in another shallow dish. Dip chicken into flour mixture, then into eggs, and again into flour mixture to coat.

2 In a heavy, 12-inch skillet heat oil over medium-high heat. Add chicken breast strips; cook for 6 to 8 minutes or until chicken is no longer pink, turning once. (If necessary, reduce heat to medium to prevent overbrowning and add more oil as needed during cooking.) Cool slightly.

3 Meanwhile, in a large bowl toss together salad greens, strawberries, and remaining basil. Drizzle vinaigrette over salad mixture; toss gently to coat. Top with chicken.

Nutrition Facts per serving: 291 cal., 14 g total fat (2 g sat. fat), 115 mg chol., 305 mg sodium, 20 g carbo., 2 g fiber, 23 g pro.

CHICKEN & POLENTA

Start to Finish:

35 minutes

Makes: 4 servings

1½	pounds skinless, boneless chicken thighs
⅛	teaspoon salt
	Nonstick cooking spray
2	medium green sweet peppers, coarsely chopped
1	medium onion, coarsely chopped
2	teaspoons ground cumin
1	14½-ounce can diced tomatoes, undrained
1	tablespoon olive oil
1	16-ounce tube refrigerated cooked polenta, cut into 8 slices
2	tablespoons snipped fresh cilantro

1 Sprinkle chicken with salt. Lightly coat an unheated 12-inch nonstick skillet with cooking spray. Preheat skillet over medium-high heat. Add chicken; cook for 10 to 12 minutes or until no longer pink (180°F), turning once. Remove from skillet.

2 Add sweet peppers and onion to skillet. Cook and stir for 3 to 4 minutes or until sweet peppers are crisp-tender. Stir the cumin into undrained tomatoes; stir into sweet pepper mixture. Bring to boiling. Return chicken to skillet; heat through.

3 Meanwhile, in a 10-inch nonstick skillet heat oil over medium-high heat. Add polenta slices; cook for 10 to 12 minutes or until golden, turning once.

4 To serve, arrange chicken and polenta slices on dinner plates. Top with chicken and sweet pepper mixture. Sprinkle with cilantro.

Nutrition Facts per serving: 392 cal., 10 g total fat (2 g sat. fat), 136 mg chol., 802 mg sodium, 32 g carbo., 5 g fiber, 39 g pro.

CHUTNEY CHICKEN

Prep: 20 minutes
Cook: 35 minutes

. . . .

Makes: 4 to 6 servings

2 to 2½ pounds chicken thighs (4 to 6), skinned
Salt
Black pepper
1   tablespoon butter or margarine
1   9-ounce jar mango chutney (about ⅔ cup)
2   tablespoons lemon juice

1 Season chicken with salt and pepper. In a large skillet melt butter over medium heat. Add chicken; cook about 8 minutes or until brown, turning once. Drain off fat.

2 In a small bowl stir together the mango chutney and lemon juice. Pour over chicken in skillet. Bring to boiling; reduce heat. and simmer, covered, for 15 minutes. Turn chicken. Cook, uncovered, about 20 minutes more or until chicken is no longer pink (180°F). Remove chicken to a serving platter. Spoon chutney mixture over chicken.

Nutrition Facts per serving: 280 cal., 8 g total fat (3 g sat. fat), 115 mg chol., 187 mg sodium, 27 g carbo., 1 g fiber, 26 g pro.

CHUNKY CHICKEN CHILI

Start to Finish:

20 minutes

. . . .

Makes: 4 servings

Nonstick cooking spray

12 ounces skinless, boneless chicken thighs, cut into 1-inch pieces

2 15-ounce cans chili beans with chili gravy, undrained

1½ cups frozen pepper stir-fry vegetables (yellow, green, and red peppers and onion)

¾ cup bottled salsa

Dairy sour cream (optional)

1 Lightly coat an unheated large saucepan with cooking spray. Preheat over medium-high heat. Add chicken; cook and stir until chicken is brown. Stir in undrained chili beans, frozen vegetables, and salsa.

2 Bring to boiling; reduce heat. Simmer, uncovered, about 7 minutes or until chicken is no longer pink. If desired, top each serving with sour cream.

Nutrition Facts per serving: 320 cal., 5 g total fat (1 g sat. fat), 70 mg chol., 930 mg sodium, 39 g carbo., 12 g fiber, 29 g pro.

ASIAN CHICKEN WRAPS

Makes: 8 servings

1	2- to 2¼-pound deli-roasted chicken
8	8- to 10-inch flour tortillas
½	cup bottled hoisin sauce
¼	cup finely chopped peanuts
¼	cup finely chopped green onions
½	cup shredded daikon, well drained
3	tablespoons soy sauce
3	tablespoons Chinese black vinegar or rice vinegar
1	tablespoon water
1	teaspoon chile oil or toasted sesame oil

1 Remove skin from chicken and discard. Remove chicken from bones and shred chicken (you should have about 4 cups shredded chicken); set aside.

2 Spread one side of each tortilla with some of the hoisin sauce; sprinkle with peanuts and green onions. Top with shredded chicken and shredded daikon. Roll up tortillas; halve each tortilla crosswise.

3 For dipping sauce, in a small bowl combine soy sauce, vinegar, the water, and chile oil. Serve with chicken wraps.

Nutrition Facts per serving: 283 cal., 9 g total fat (2 g sat. fat), 50 mg chol., 869 mg sodium, 26 g carbo., 1 g fiber, 20 g pro.

HAWAIIAN-STYLE BARBECUE PIZZA

Prep: 20 minutes
Bake: 10 minutes

Oven: 425°F
Makes: 4 servings

1	16-ounce Italian bread shell (Boboli)
1/2	cup bottled barbecue sauce
1	cup shredded pizza cheese (4 ounces)
1	to 1½ cups deli-roasted chicken cut into strips or chunks (about ½ of a chicken)
1	8-ounce can pineapple chunks (juice pack), drained
1	papaya, peeled, seeded, and sliced
1	medium green sweet pepper, cut into thin strips
1/4	of a small red or yellow onion, thinly sliced and separated into rings

1 Preheat oven to 425°. Place the bread shell on a baking sheet. Spread barbecue sauce on the bread shell. Sprinkle with ½ cup of the cheese. Arrange chicken, pineapple, papaya, sweet pepper, and onion. Sprinkle with the remaining ½ cup cheese.

2 Bake in preheated oven about 10 minutes or until heated through.

Nutrition Facts per serving: 573 cal., 16 g total fat (5 g sat. fat), 56 mg chol., 1,104 mg sodium, 77 g carbo., 5 g fiber, 32 g pro.

CHICKEN FOCACCIA SANDWICHES

Start to Finish:

15 minutes

· · · · · · · · · · · · · · · · · ·

Makes: 4 servings

1   8- to 10-inch tomato or onion Italian flatbread (focaccia) or 1 loaf sourdough bread

⅓   cup light mayonnaise dressing or salad dressing

1   cup lightly packed fresh basil

1½   cups sliced or shredded deli-roasted chicken

½   of a 7-ounce jar roasted red sweet peppers, drained and cut into strips (about ½ cup)

1 Using a long serrated knife, cut bread in half horizontally. Spread cut sides of bread halves with mayonnaise dressing.

2 Layer basil leaves, chicken, and roasted sweet peppers between bread halves. Cut into quarters.

Nutrition Facts per serving: 314 cal., 10 g total fat (1 g sat. fat), 40 mg chol., 597 mg sodium, 40 g carbo., 1 g fiber, 19 g pro.

SOUTHWESTERN CHICKEN WRAPS

Start to Finish:

15 minutes

Makes: 4 servings

½ cup dairy sour cream

2 tablespoons purchased guacamole

4 10-inch dried tomato, spinach, and/or plain flour tortillas

2 5½-ounce packages Southwestern-flavored refrigerated cooked chicken breast strips

2 Roma tomatoes, sliced

2 cups shredded lettuce

1 In a small bowl stir together sour cream and guacamole. Divide sour cream mixture among tortillas, spreading over one side of each tortilla. Divide chicken, tomatoes, and lettuce among tortillas. Roll up.

Nutrition Facts per serving: 395 cal., 13 g total fat (4 g sat. fat), 49 mg chol., 1,015 mg sodium, 45 g carbo., 2 g fiber, 25 g pro.

TEQUILA-LIME CHICKEN

Start to Finish:

15 minutes

· · · · · · · · · · · · · · · ·

Makes: 4 servings

1	9-ounce package refrigerated fettuccine
2	limes
1	10-ounce container refrigerated regular or light Alfredo pasta sauce
¼	cup tequila or milk
2	5½-ounce packages refrigerated cooked grilled chicken breast strips

1 Cook the fettuccine according to package directions; drain. Meanwhile, finely shred enough peel from 1 of the limes to measure 1 teaspoon (chill this lime and use for juice another time). Cut remaining lime into wedges and set aside.

2 In a medium saucepan combine shredded lime peel, Alfredo sauce, and tequila; cook and stir just until boiling. Stir in chicken strips; heat through. Toss chicken mixture with hot fettuccine. Serve with lime wedges.

Nutrition Facts per serving: 547 cal., 24 g total fat (1 g sat. fat), 133 mg chol., 981 mg sodium, 39 g carbo., 2 g fiber, 11 g pro.

CHICKEN & ORZO CASSEROLE

Prep: **15** minutes
Bake: **20** minutes

Oven: 350°F
Makes: 4 to 6 servings

2	teaspoons cumin seeds
1	14-ounce can chicken broth
1	14½-ounce can Mexican-style stewed tomatoes or one 10-ounce can diced tomatoes and green chile peppers, undrained
¼	cup oil-packed dried tomatoes, drained and cut up
1	cup dried orzo pasta
2	9-ounce packages Southwestern-flavored frozen cooked chicken breast strips, thawed, or two 5½-ounce packages Southwestern-flavor refrigerated cooked chicken breast strips
	Paprika (optional)
	Fresh jalapeño or serrano chile peppers, seeded and chopped (optional)*

1 Preheat oven to 350°. Place cumin seeds in a large saucepan. Heat over medium heat for 3 to 4 minutes or until seeds are toasted and aromatic, shaking pan occasionally. Carefully stir in the chicken broth, undrained tomatoes, dried tomatoes, and uncooked orzo. Bring to boiling. Transfer to a 2-quart baking dish. Top with chicken breast strips.

2 Bake, covered, in preheated oven about 20 minutes or until orzo is tender. Let stand, covered, for 10 minutes before serving. To serve, if desired, sprinkle with paprika and top with chopped jalapeño chile peppers.

***Note:** Because chile peppers contain volatile oils that can burn your skin and eyes, avoid direct contact with them as much as possible. When working with chile peppers, wear plastic or rubber gloves. If your bare hands do touch the chile peppers, wash your hands well with soap and warm water.

Nutrition Facts per serving: 388 cal., 7 g total fat (2 g sat. fat), 60 mg chol., 1,227 mg sodium, 44 g carbo., 3 g fiber, 35 g pro.

THREE-CORNER CHICKEN SALAD

Prep: 10 minutes
Bake: 15 minutes

Oven: 400°F
Makes: 4 servings

- 1 10-ounce package refrigerated pizza dough (for 1 crust)
- 1 9- or 10-ounce package frozen cooked chicken strips
- 6 cups torn mixed salad greens
- ⅓ cup bottled salad dressing (any flavor)

1 Preheat oven to 400°. Invert four 10-ounce custard cups in a shallow baking pan; generously grease the outside of each custard cup. Set aside.

2 Unroll refrigerated pizza dough on a cutting board. Shape into a 10-inch square. Cut the square diagonally into 4 triangles. Drape each triangle over one of the prepared custard cups.

3 Bake in preheated oven about 15 minutes or until deep golden. Remove from cups; cool.

4 Meanwhile, prepare frozen cooked chicken strips as directed on the package. To serve, divide the mixed salad greens and the chicken among bread "bowls." Drizzle with salad dressing.

Nutrition Facts per serving: 419 cal., 21 g total fat (4 g sat. fat), 43 mg chol., 1,333 mg sodium, 37 g carbo., 2 g fiber, 21 g pro.

ORANGE-BARLEY CHICKEN SALAD

Prep: 25 minutes

Chill: 1 hour

. . . .

Makes: 4 servings

½   cup quick-cooking barley
     Leaf lettuce
1   9-ounce package frozen cooked chicken breast strips, thawed
1½   cups cubed fresh pineapple or one 15¼-ounce can pineapple chunks (juice pack), drained
1   cup halved seedless grapes
1   recipe Orange-Basil Vinaigrette or ½ cup bottled vinaigrette salad dressing
2   tablespoons chopped pecans, toasted

1 Cook barley according to package directions. Drain. Rinse under cold water; drain again. Cover; chill for at least 1 hour.

2 Line 4 dinner plates with lettuce. Top lettuce with chicken, pineapple, and grapes. Shake Orange-Basil Vinaigrette; pour over salads. Top with pecans.

Orange-Basil Vinaigrette: In a screw-top jar combine 1 teaspoon finely shredded orange peel; ¼ cup orange juice; ¼ cup salad oil; 2 tablespoons white balsamic vinegar or white wine vinegar; 2 tablespoons snipped fresh basil or 1 teaspoon dried basil, crushed; and 1 tablespoon honey. Cover and shake to mix. Makes ¼ cup.

Nutrition Facts per serving: 381 cal., 20 g total fat (3 g sat. fat), 45 mg chol., 379 mg sodium, 36 g carbo., 4 g fiber, 19 g pro.

THAI CHICKEN PASTA

Start to Finish:

20 minutes

· · · · · · · · · · · · · · · ·

Makes: 4 servings

8   ounces dried angel hair pasta

3   cups cooked chicken, cut into strips

1   14-ounce can unsweetened coconut milk

1   teaspoon Thai seasoning

¼   cup roasted peanuts

1 Cook the pasta according to package directions; drain well. Return pasta to pan; keep warm.

2 Meanwhile, in a large skillet combine chicken, coconut milk, and Thai seasoning. Cook and gently stir over medium heat until heated through. Pour hot chicken mixture over cooked pasta in pan. Toss gently to coat.

3 Transfer to a serving platter or bowl. Sprinkle with peanuts.

Nutrition Facts per serving: 644 cal., 31 g total fat (19 g sat. fat), 93 mg chol., 236 mg sodium, 47 g carbo., 2 g fiber, 42 g pro.

UPSIDE-DOWN PIZZA PIE

Prep: 20 minutes
Bake: 25 minutes

Oven: 375°F
Makes: 4 servings

1	14½-ounce can diced tomatoes with basil, garlic, and oregano, undrained
2	cups cubed cooked chicken (about 10 ounces)
1½	cups sliced fresh mushrooms
1	8-ounce can pizza sauce
1	cup shredded pizza cheese (4 ounces)
¼	cup grated Parmesan cheese (1 ounce)
1	11-ounce package (12) refrigerated breadsticks
	Milk
1	tablespoon grated Parmesan cheese
	Additional toppings (such as sliced pitted black or green olives, chopped green or yellow sweet pepper, and/or chopped tomato) (optional)

1 Preheat oven to 375°. Grease four 12- to 16-ounce baking dishes; set aside. In a medium bowl stir together undrained tomatoes, chicken, mushrooms, and pizza sauce. Spoon mixture into prepared baking dishes. Sprinkle pizza cheese evenly over tomato mixture. Sprinkle with the ¼ cup Parmesan cheese.

2 Unroll the breadstick dough. Separate along perforations to form 12 strips. Weave 3 strips over filling in each baking dish to form a lattice crust on chicken mixture. (Depending on the width of your bowls, you may need to cut strips to length or piece strips together.) Brush dough with a little milk. Sprinkle with the 1 tablespoon Parmesan cheese.

3 Bake in preheated oven about 25 minutes or until breadsticks are golden and filling is bubbly. Let stand for 5 minutes before serving. To serve, loosen edges and invert onto plates; remove baking dishes. If desired, sprinkle pizza pie with additional toppings.

Nutrition Facts per serving: 562 cal., 20 g total fat (8 g sat. fat), 88 mg chol., 1,865 mg sodium, 52 g carbo., 3 g fiber, 40 g pro.

CHIPOTLE CHICKEN ENCHILADAS

Prep: 25 minutes
Bake: 40 minutes

Oven: 350°F
Makes: 4 servings

2½	cups chopped cooked chicken (about 12 ounces)
1	to 2 teaspoons ground chipotle chile pepper
1	10¾-ounce can condensed cream of chicken soup
1	8-ounce carton dairy sour cream
1	4-ounce can diced green chile peppers
8	7- to 8-inch flour tortillas
2	cups shredded cheddar cheese (8 ounces)
¼	cup sliced green onions

1 Preheat oven to 350°. Grease a 3-quart rectangular baking dish; set aside. In a medium bowl combine chicken and chipotle chile pepper; set aside.

2 For sauce, in a large bowl combine cream of chicken soup, sour cream, and undrained green chile peppers. Stir ½ cup of the sauce into the chicken mixture.

3 Divide chicken mixture among tortillas. Sprinkle 1½ cups of the cheese and the green onions over chicken mixture on tortillas. Roll up tortillas; place, seam sides down, in prepared baking dish. Pour remaining sauce over all. Cover baking dish with foil.

4 Bake in preheated oven about 35 minutes or until edges are bubbly. Uncover; sprinkle with the remaining ½ cup cheese. Bake, uncovered, about 5 minutes more or until cheese is melted.

Nutrition Facts per serving: 786 cal., 47 g total fat (24 g sat. fat), 169 mg chol., 1,376 mg sodium, 42 g carbo., 2 g fiber, 47 g pro.

CHICKEN POTPIE

Prep: 15 minutes
Bake: 15 minutes

Oven: 450°F
Makes: 4 servings

½ of a 15-ounce package folded refrigerated unbaked piecrusts (1 crust)

1 10¾-ounce can condensed cream of onion soup

1 cup milk

1 3-ounce package cream cheese, cut up

½ teaspoon dried sage, crushed

¼ teaspoon black pepper

1 10-ounce can chunk-style chicken, drained and flaked

1 10-ounce package frozen mixed vegetables

½ cup uncooked instant rice

1 Preheat oven to 450°. Let piecrust stand at room temperature for 15 minutes as directed on package.

2 Meanwhile, for filling, in a large saucepan combine cream of onion soup, milk, cream cheese, sage, and pepper. Cook and stir over medium-high heat until cream cheese melts. Stir in chicken, vegetables, and uncooked rice. Bring to boiling.

3 Pour chicken mixture into a 1½-quart casserole. Top with piecrust. Trim crust to ½ inch beyond edge of the casserole. Fold under extra crust; crimp edge. Cut slits in crust to allow steam to escape.

4 Bake in preheated oven about 15 minutes or until crust is golden.

Nutrition Facts per serving: 629 cal., 33 g total fat (19 g sat. fat), 47 mg chol., 1,221 mg sodium, 57 g carbo., 3 g fiber, 25 g pro.

EASY CHICKEN TURNOVERS

Prep: 25 minutes
Bake: 25 minutes

Oven: 400°F
Makes: 4 servings

1   15-ounce package folded refrigerated unbaked piecrusts (2 crusts)

1   10-ounce can chunk-style chicken, drained and broken up, or 1½ cups chopped cooked chicken (about 8 ounces)

1   cup loose-pack frozen mixed vegetables or peas and carrots

1   cup shredded cheddar cheese (4 ounces)

⅓   cup purchased pasta sauce or bottled barbecue sauce
     Milk

1 Preheat oven to 400°. Let piecrusts stand at room temperature according to package directions. Meanwhile, for filling, in a large bowl stir together chicken, frozen vegetables, shredded cheese, and pasta sauce.

2 Unfold piecrusts; cut each crust in half. Spoon one-fourth of the filling (about ¾ cup) onto one half of each piecrust piece. Moisten edges of piecrust pieces with water. Fold each piecrust piece in half over filling to make a turnover. Seal edges of turnovers with the tines of a fork; prick tops. Place on an ungreased baking sheet.

3 Brush turnovers with milk. Bake in preheated oven about 25 minutes or until lightly browned. Let stand for 10 minutes before serving.

Make-Ahead Directions: Prepare as directed through step 2. Cover and chill for up to 24 hours. Continue as directed in step 3.

Nutrition Facts per serving: 714 cal., 41 g total fat (19 g sat. fat), 85 mg chol., 859 mg sodium, 60 g carbo., 2 g fiber, 27 g pro.

SAUCY CHICKEN CASSEROLE

Prep: 20 minutes

Bake: 1 hour

. . . .

Oven: 375°F

Makes: 6 servings

1	10³/₄-ounce can condensed cream of chicken soup
¹/₂	cup milk
1	tablespoon dried minced onion
¹/₄	teaspoon dried basil or dried sage, crushed
¹/₈	teaspoon black pepper
4	1-ounce slices American cheese
1	10-ounce can chunk-style chicken
1	cup dried elbow macaroni
1	2-ounce jar sliced pimiento, drained, or ¹/₄ cup chopped red sweet pepper

1 In a 1¹/₂-quart casserole combine cream of chicken soup, milk, dried minced onion, basil, and black pepper.

2 Tear American cheese into small pieces. Add cheese, undrained chicken, uncooked macaroni, and drained pimiento to soup mixture in casserole; mix well. Cover and chill for at least 3 hours or up to 24 hours.

3 Preheat oven to 375°. Bake chicken-macaroni mixture, covered, in preheated oven about 1 hour or until macaroni is tender, stirring once.

Nutrition Facts per serving: 265 cal., 12 g total fat (5 g sat. fat), 46 mg chol., 815 mg sodium, 22 g carbo., 1 g fiber, 19 g pro.

CHICKEN & PASTA SALAD WITH TOMATOES

Prep: 15 minutes
Freeze: 10 minutes

· ·

Makes: 4 servings

1   16-ounce package frozen pasta and vegetables in a seasoned sauce (such as pasta, broccoli, peas, and carrots in onion and herb seasoned sauce)

1   5-ounce can chunk-style chicken, drained and flaked, or 1 cup chopped cooked chicken or turkey (about 5 ounces)

½   cup diary sour cream dip with chives

2   medium tomatoes, coarsely chopped

½   cup shredded cheddar cheese (2 ounces)

1 In a 2-quart saucepan cook the pasta and vegetables according to package directions.

2 Meanwhile, in a large bowl stir together chicken and sour cream dip with chives. Gently fold the undrained cooked pasta mixture and the tomatoes into the chicken mixture. Cover and chill in freezer for 10 minutes.

3 To serve, sprinkle with cheddar cheese.

Nutrition Facts per serving: 329 cal., 18 g total fat (10 g sat. fat), 58 mg chol., 935 mg sodium, 24 g carbo., 5 g fiber, 18 g pro.

MEAT-&-CHEESE SANDWICH LOAF

Prep: 10 minutes
Bake: 15 minutes

Oven: 375°F
Makes: 6 servings

¼   cup creamy Dijon-style mustard blend

1   tablespoon prepared horseradish (optional)

1   unsliced loaf Italian bread (about 12 inches long)

1   6-ounce package Swiss cheese slices

2   2½-ounce packages very thinly sliced smoked chicken or very thinly sliced smoked turkey

1   2½-ounce package very thinly sliced pastrami

1 Preheat oven to 375°. In a small bowl stir together the mustard blend and, if desired, horseradish. Set aside.

2 Cut bread loaf into 1-inch slices by cutting from the top to, but not through, the bottom crust. (You should have 11 pockets.)

3 To assemble loaf, spread a scant tablespoon of the mustard blend on both sides of every other pocket in the bread loaf, starting with the first pocket on one end.

4 Divide cheese slices, chicken slices, and pastrami slices among the mustard-spread pockets.

5 Place the bread loaf on a baking sheet. Bake in preheated oven about 15 minutes or until heated through.

6 To serve, cut bread loaf into sandwiches by cutting through the bottom crusts of the unfilled pockets.

Nutrition Facts per serving: 389 cal., 14 g total fat (7 g sat. fat), 48 mg chol., 1,004 mg sodium, 42 g carbo., 2 g fiber, 21 g pro.

APRICOT TURKEY STEAKS

Start to Finish:

25 minutes

. . . .

Makes: 4 servings

1	6-ounce package chicken-flavored rice and vermicelli mix
2	turkey breast tenderloins (about 1¼ pounds total)
1	5½-ounce can apricot nectar
½	teaspoon salt
⅛	teaspoon ground cinnamon
	Dash black pepper
3	tablespoons apricot preserves
1½	teaspoons cornstarch

1 Prepare rice mix according to package directions. Set aside.

2 Meanwhile, split each turkey breast tenderloin in half horizontally to make 4 turkey steaks. In a large skillet combine apricot nectar, salt, cinnamon, and pepper. Add turkey steaks. Bring to boiling; reduce heat. Simmer, covered, about 10 minutes or until turkey is no longer pink (170°F).

3 Transfer turkey steaks to a serving platter, reserving cooking liquid in the skillet. Keep turkey warm.

4 For sauce, in a small bowl combine apricot preserves and cornstarch; stir into cooking liquid in the skillet. Cook and stir until thickened and bubbly. Cook and stir for 2 minutes more. Spoon rice mixture onto the serving platter. Pour some of the sauce over turkey; pass remaining sauce.

Nutrition Facts per serving: 374 cal., 2 g total fat (1 g sat. fat), 88 mg chol., 1,054 mg sodium, 48 g carbo., 1 g fiber, 39 g pro.

TURKEY STEAKS WITH CRANBERRY-ORANGE SAUCE

Start to Finish:

30 minutes

Makes: 4 servings

1	6-ounce package long grain and wild rice mix
1	pound turkey breast tenderloin
	Salt
	Black pepper
2	tablespoons butter or margarine
1	10-ounce package frozen cranberry-orange relish, thawed
2	tablespoons orange liqueur or orange juice

1 Cook rice mix according to package directions.

2 Meanwhile, split turkey breast tenderloin in half horizontally. Cut each piece in half, making 4 portions. Sprinkle turkey with salt and pepper. In a large skillet melt butter over medium heat. Add turkey; cook for 10 to 12 minutes or until no longer pink (170°F), turning once.

3 Transfer turkey to a serving platter. Keep warm. Remove skillet from heat; let cool for 2 minutes. Carefully add cranberry-orange relish to drippings in skillet; add liqueur. Return to heat; cook and stir over low heat until heated through. Spoon sauce over turkey. Serve with rice.

Nutrition Facts per serving: 481 cal., 8 g total fat (4 g sat. fat), 84 mg chol., 941 mg sodium, 68 g carbo., 0 g fiber, 31 g pro.

NUTTY TURKEY TENDERLOINS

Prep: 15 minutes
Bake: 18 minutes

. . . .

Oven: 375°F
Makes: 4 servings

2	turkey breast tenderloins (about 1 pound total)
¼	cup creamy Dijon-style mustard blend
1	cup purchased corn bread stuffing mix
½	cup finely chopped pecans
2	tablespoons butter, melted

1 Preheat oven to 375°. Split each turkey breast tenderloin in half horizontally to make 4 turkey steaks. Brush turkey generously with the mustard blend. In a shallow dish combine the dry stuffing mix and pecans; dip turkey in stuffing mixture, turning to coat both sides. Place in a shallow baking pan. Drizzle with melted butter.

2 Bake, uncovered, in preheated oven for 18 to 20 minutes or until turkey is no longer pink (170°F).

Nutrition Facts per serving: 395 cal., 21 g total fat (5 g sat. fat), 84 mg chol., 566 mg sodium, 21 g carbo., 1 g fiber, 30 g pro.

TURKEY TENDERLOIN WITH BEAN & CORN SALSA

Start to Finish:

25 minutes

Makes: 4 servings

1	pound turkey breast tenderloin
	Salt
	Black pepper
¼	cup red jalapeño chile pepper jelly
1¼	cups bottled black bean and corn salsa
2	tablespoons snipped fresh cilantro

1 Preheat broiler. Split turkey breast tenderloin in half horizontally. Place turkey on the unheated rack of a broiler pan. Season with salt and pepper. Broil 4 to 5 inches from the heat for 5 minutes.

2 Meanwhile, in a small saucepan melt jelly. Remove 2 tablespoons of the jelly. Turn turkey and brush with the 2 tablespoons jelly. Broil for 4 to 6 minutes more or until no longer pink (170°F). Transfer turkey to a serving platter. Spoon remaining jelly over turkey; cover and keep warm.

3 In a small saucepan heat the salsa. Spoon salsa over the turkey. Sprinkle with cilantro.

Nutrition Facts per serving: 196 cal., 2 g total fat (1 g sat. fat), 66 mg chol., 377 mg sodium, 16 g carbo., 1 g fiber, 27 g pro.

FIVE-SPICE TURKEY STIR-FRY

Start to Finish:

25 minutes

Makes: 4 servings

1	4.4-ounce package beef lo-mein noodle mix
12	ounces turkey breast tenderloin, cut into bite-size strips
¼	teaspoon five-spice powder
¼	teaspoon salt
¼	teaspoon black pepper
2	tablespoons cooking oil
½	of a 16-ounce package frozen pepper stir-fry vegetables (yellow, green, and red peppers and onion)
2	tablespoons chopped honey-roasted peanuts or peanuts

1 Prepare noodle mix according to package directions. Set aside. In a small bowl toss together turkey strips, five-spice powder, salt, and black pepper; set aside.

2 Pour 1 tablespoon of the oil into a wok. Heat over medium-high heat. Carefully add frozen vegetables to wok; cook and stir for 3 minutes. Remove vegetables from wok. Add remaining 1 tablespoon oil to hot wok. Add turkey mixture to wok; cook and stir for 2 to 3 minutes or until turkey is done. Return cooked vegetables to wok. Cook and stir about 1 minute more or until heated through.

3 To serve, divide noodle mixture among 4 dinner plates. Top with turkey mixture. Sprinkle with peanuts.

Nutrition Facts per serving: 314 cal., 11 g total fat (2 g sat. fat), 76 mg chol., 670 mg sodium, 26 g carbo., 3 g fiber, 27 g pro.

DIJON-TURKEY POTPIE

Prep: 25 minutes
Bake: 15 minutes

Oven: 375°F
Makes: 4 servings

1½ cups loose-pack frozen broccoli, cauliflower, and carrots

1 11½-ounce package (8) refrigerated corn bread twists

1 1.8-ounce envelope white sauce mix

10 ounces cooked turkey breast portion, chopped (about 2 cups)

2 tablespoons Dijon-style mustard

1 teaspoon instant chicken bouillon granules

1 Preheat oven to 375°. Place frozen vegetables in a colander. Run hot water over vegetables just until thawed. Drain well. Cut up any large pieces.

2 Meanwhile, unroll corn bread twists. Separate into 16 pieces. Set aside.

3 In a medium saucepan prepare white sauce mix according to package directions, except after mixture starts to boil, stir in vegetables, chopped turkey, mustard, and chicken bouillon granules. Return to boiling; reduce heat. Cook and stir for 1 minute more.

4 Transfer turkey mixture to a 2-quart rectangular baking dish. Arrange corn bread dough pieces in a single layer on top of the turkey mixture.

5 Bake, uncovered, in preheated oven for 15 to 20 minutes or until corn bread sticks are golden.

Nutrition Facts per serving: 496 cal., 18 g total fat (6 g sat. fat), 50 mg chol., 1,875 mg sodium, 51 g carbo., 1 g fiber, 29 g pro.

TURKEY-BISCUIT PIE

Prep: 15 minutes
Bake: 12 minutes

· · · · · · · · · · · · · · · · · · · ·

Oven: 450°F
Makes: 4 servings

1	10³/₄-ounce can condensed cream of chicken soup
¹/₂	cup milk
¹/₄	cup dairy sour cream
6	ounces cooked turkey breast, cubed (about 1 cup)
1¹/₂	cups loose-pack frozen mixed vegetables (any combination)
¹/₂	teaspoon dried basil, crushed
¹/₈	teaspoon black pepper
1	5-ounce package (5) refrigerated biscuits, quartered

1 Preheat oven to 450°. Lightly grease a 1¹/₂-quart casserole; set aside.

2 In a medium saucepan stir together cream of chicken soup, milk, and sour cream. Stir in turkey, frozen vegetables, basil, and pepper. Cook and stir over medium heat until boiling. Transfer to prepared casserole. Top with biscuit quarters.

3 Bake, uncovered, in preheated oven for 12 to 15 minutes or until biscuits are brown.

Nutrition Facts per serving: 335 cal., 14 g total fat (5 g sat. fat), 49 mg chol., 1,049 mg sodium, 33 g carbo., 3 g fiber, 20 g pro.

TURKEY-POTATO BAKE

Prep: 15 minutes
Bake: 30 minutes

· · · · · · · · · · · · · · ·

Oven: 400°F
Makes: 4 servings

2¼	cups water
1	4.6- to 5-ounce package dry julienne potato mix
10	ounces boneless cooked turkey breast, cubed (about 2 cups)
1	4-ounce package shredded cheddar cheese (1 cup)
1	teaspoon dried parsley, crushed
⅔	cup milk

1 Preheat oven to 400°. Bring the water to boiling. Meanwhile, in a 2-quart square baking dish combine dry potatoes and sauce mix from potato mix. Stir in turkey, ½ cup of the cheddar cheese, and the parsley flakes. Stir in the boiling water and milk.

2 Bake, uncovered, in preheated oven for 30 to 35 minutes or until potatoes are tender. Sprinkle with remaining cheese. Let stand for 10 minutes before serving (mixture will thicken on standing).

Nutrition Facts per serving: 373 cal., 15 g total fat (8 g sat. fat), 87 mg chol., 994 mg sodium, 27 g carbo., 1 g fiber, 32 g pro.

MEXICAN TURKEY PIE

Prep: 25 minutes
Bake: 24 minutes

Oven: 400°F
Makes: 6 servings

1 8½-ounce package corn muffin mix

1 cup all-purpose flour

1 9-ounce can plain bean dip

½ cup bottled thick-and-chunky salsa

10 ounces cooked turkey breast, chopped (about 2 cups)

1 4-ounce can diced green chile peppers, drained

1 2¼-ounce can sliced pitted ripe olives, drained

4 ounces sharp American cheese, shredded (1 cup)

Bottled thick-and-chunky salsa (optional)

1 Preheat oven to 400°. Grease a 12-inch pizza pan; set aside. For crust, prepare corn muffin mix according to package directions, except stir in ¾ cup of the flour with the dry corn muffin mix. Using a wooden spoon, stir in as much of the remaining flour as you can. Turn out dough onto a lightly floured surface. Knead in remaining flour to make a moderately soft dough. Shape dough into a ball. Roll into a 13-inch circle. Carefully transfer the dough to prepared pizza pan, building up edge slightly.

2 Bake in preheated oven about 12 minutes or until golden.

3 Meanwhile, in a small bowl combine bean dip and the ½ cup salsa. Spread over hot crust. Top with turkey breast, chile peppers, and olives. Sprinkle with cheese. Bake in the 400° oven for 12 to 15 minutes more or until hot. If desired, serve with additional salsa.

Nutrition Facts per serving: 435 cal., 14 g total fat (4 g sat. fat), 71 mg chol., 1,505 mg sodium, 54 g carbo., 3 g fiber, 22 g pro.

TURKEY STRUDEL

Prep: 20 minutes
Bake: 20 minutes

Oven: 350°F
Makes: 6 servings

2	8-ounce packages (16) refrigerated crescent rolls
6	ounces Havarti cheese with dill, thinly sliced*
10	ounces cooked turkey, chopped (about 2 cups)
1	4-ounce can (drained weight) sliced mushrooms, drained

1 Preheat oven to 350°. Unroll crescent roll dough. On a large baking sheet, press dough from 1 of the packages into a 12×8-inch rectangle; set aside. On a sheet of waxed paper, press dough from remaining package into a 12×8-inch rectangle; set aside.

2 Arrange cheese slices on dough rectangle on baking sheet, leaving a ½-inch space around the edges. Top with turkey and mushrooms. Invert remaining dough rectangle over filling; peel off waxed paper. Pinch edges to seal. Cut 3 slits in top. Bake in preheated oven for 20 to 25 minutes or until golden.

*Note: If you can't find Havarti cheese with dill, substitute 6 ounces regular Havarti cheese and sprinkle with 1 teaspoon dried dill after placing cheese on dough.

Nutrition Facts per serving: 472 cal., 29 g total fat (3 g sat. fat), 71 mg chol., 868 mg sodium, 30 g carbo., 1 g fiber, 26 g pro.

EASY TURKEY-PESTO POTPIE

Prep: 15 minutes
Bake: 15 minutes

....

Oven: 375°F
Makes: 6 servings

1	18-ounce jar turkey gravy
¼	cup purchased basil or dried tomato pesto
3	cups cubed, cooked turkey (about 1 pound)
1	16-ounce package loose-pack frozen peas and carrots
1	7-ounce package (6) refrigerated breadsticks

1 Preheat oven to 375°. In a large saucepan combine turkey gravy and pesto; stir in the turkey and vegetables. Bring to boiling, stirring frequently. Divide turkey mixture evenly among six 8-ounce au gratin dishes. Unroll and separate breadsticks. Arrange a breadstick on top of each au gratin dish.

2 Bake in preheated oven about 15 minutes or until breadsticks are golden.

Nutrition Facts per serving: 372 cal., 14 g total fat (2 g sat. fat), 59 mg chol., 988 mg sodium, 30 g carbo., 3 g fiber, 30 g pro.

MOCK MONTE CRISTO SANDWICHES

Prep: 10 minutes
Bake: 15 minutes

. . . .

Oven: 400°F
Makes: 6 half sandwiches

6	slices frozen French toast
2	tablespoons honey mustard
3	ounces sliced cooked turkey breast
3	ounces sliced cooked ham
3	ounces thinly sliced Swiss cheese

1 Preheat oven to 400°. Lightly grease a baking sheet; set aside. To assemble sandwiches, spread one side of each of the frozen French toast slices with honey mustard. Layer 3 of the toast slices, mustard sides up, with the turkey, ham, and cheese. Cover with remaining toast slices, mustard sides down.

2 Place sandwiches on prepared baking sheet. Bake in preheated oven for 15 to 20 minutes or until sandwiches are heated through, turning sandwiches over once. Cut each sandwich in half diagonally.

Nutrition Facts per half sandwich: 221 cal., 9 g total fat (4 g sat. fat), 75 mg chol., 704 mg sodium, 21 g carbo., 1 g fiber, 14 g pro.

ITALIAN-STYLE TURKEY BURGERS

Prep: 20 minutes

Broil: 10 minutes

Makes: 4 servings

1   egg

¼   cup seasoned fine dry bread crumbs

¼   teaspoon salt

1   pound uncooked ground turkey

4   slices provolone or mozzarella cheese (4 ounces)

4   kaiser rolls or hamburger buns, split and toasted

      Fresh basil leaves or shredded lettuce

¼   cup dried tomato-flavored light mayonnaise dressing

1 Preheat broiler. In a large bowl beat egg with a fork; stir in bread crumbs and salt. Add ground turkey; mix well. Shape into 4 patties, each 4 inches in diameter.

2 Grease the unheated rack of a broiler pan. Place patties on prepared rack. Broil 3 to 4 inches from the heat for 10 to 12 minutes or until no longer pink (165°F),* turning once halfway through broiling time. Top each patty with a slice of cheese; broil about 30 seconds more or until cheese melts.

3 Serve patties on rolls topped with basil leaves and mayonnaise dressing.

*Note: The internal color of a burger is not a reliable doneness indicator. A turkey patty cooked to 165°F is safe, regardless of color. To measure the doneness of a patty, insert an instant-read thermometer through the side of the patty to a depth of 2 to 3 inches.

Nutrition Facts per serving: 531 cal., 26 g total fat (9 g sat. fat), 172 mg chol., 1,087 mg sodium, 37 g carbo., 1 g fiber, 35 g pro.

MEXICAN STROMBOLI

Prep: **30** minutes
Bake: **25** minutes

Oven: 375°F
Makes: 8 servings

12	ounces uncooked ground turkey or chicken breast
1	15-ounce can black beans or pinto beans, rinsed and drained
1	cup bottled salsa
	Nonstick cooking spray
2	10-ounce packages refrigerated pizza dough (each for 1 crust)
3	ounces Monterey Jack cheese with jalapeño peppers or Monterey Jack cheese, shredded (³⁄₄ cup)
	Water
1	tablespoon cornmeal
	Bottled salsa

1 Preheat oven to 375°. For filling, in a large skillet cook turkey until no longer pink; drain off fat. Stir in half of the drained beans (about ³⁄₄ cup) and the 1 cup salsa. Place the remaining beans in a small bowl and mash with a potato masher or fork; add mashed beans to the turkey mixture. Heat through. Set aside.

2 Lightly coat a 15×10×1-inch baking pan with cooking spray; set aside. On a lightly floured surface, unroll a sheet of the pizza dough. Roll dough into a 10-inch square.

3 Spoon half of the shredded cheese down the center of the dough square to within 1 inch of edges. Spoon half of the turkey mixture (about 1³⁄₄ cups) over the cheese, spreading to a 4-inch-wide strip. Moisten the dough edges with water. Bring the side edges of dough together over the filling, stretching as necessary; pinch to seal well. Fold up the ends of the dough; pinch to seal well. Place, seam side down, on prepared baking pan. Repeat with the remaining dough, cheese, and turkey mixture.

4 Prick the tops of each stromboli with a fork. Brush the stromboli tops with water and sprinkle with cornmeal. Bake, uncovered, in preheated oven for 25 to 30 minutes or until golden. Cool for 10 minutes before serving. Serve with additional salsa.

Nutrition Facts per serving: 331 cal., 10 g total fat (4 g sat. fat), 45 mg chol., 762 mg sodium, 43 g carbo., 4 g fiber, 20 g pro.

POLENTA WITH TURKEY SAUSAGE FLORENTINE

Start to Finish:

25 minutes

. . . .

Makes: 2 servings

1	9- or 10-ounce package frozen creamed spinach
8	ounces bulk turkey sausage
½	of a 16-ounce tube refrigerated cooked polenta with wild mushrooms, cut into ¾-inch slices
1	tablespoon olive oil
2	tablespoons sliced almonds or pine nuts, toasted

1 Cook the spinach according to package directions. Meanwhile, in a medium skillet cook sausage until brown. Drain in colander. In the same skillet cook polenta slices in hot oil about 6 minutes or until golden, turning once. Transfer polenta to serving plate.

2 Stir cooked sausage into hot creamed spinach; heat through. Spoon mixture onto the polenta. Sprinkle with toasted nuts.

Nutrition Facts per serving: 607 cal., 41 g total fat (8 g sat. fat), 119 mg chol., 1,586 mg sodium, 33 g carbo., 6 g fiber, 28 g pro.

PORK & LAMB

PORK CHOPS DIJON

Start to Finish:

30 minutes

Makes: 4 servings

3 tablespoons Dijon-style mustard

2 tablespoons bottled reduced-calorie Italian salad dressing

¼ teaspoon black pepper

4 pork loin chops, cut ½ inch thick (about 1½ pounds total)
   Nonstick cooking spray

1 medium onion, halved and sliced

1 In a small bowl combine mustard, Italian dressing, and pepper; set aside. Trim fat from the chops. Coat an unheated 10-inch skillet with cooking spray. Preheat the skillet over medium-high heat. Add the chops; cook until brown on both sides, turning once. Remove chops from skillet.

2 Add onion to skillet. Cook and stir over medium heat for 3 minutes. Push onion aside; return chops to skillet. Spread mustard mixture over chops. Cover and cook over medium-low heat about 15 minutes or until done (160°F). Spoon onion mixture over chops.

Nutrition Facts per serving: 163 cal., 5 g total fat (2 g sat. fat), 53 mg chol., 403 mg sodium, 2 g carbo., 0 g fiber, 22 g pro.

BALSAMIC & GARLIC PORK

Start to Finish:

15 minutes

. . . .

Makes: 4 servings

4	boneless pork loin chops, cut ½ inch thick (12 to 16 ounces total)
½	teaspoon dried rosemary, crushed
¼	teaspoon salt
1	tablespoon olive oil
2	teaspoons bottled minced roasted garlic
½	cup bottled balsamic salad dressing
1	tablespoon honey mustard

1 Sprinkle chops with rosemary and salt, pressing into surface of meat.

2 In a large nonstick skillet heat oil over medium heat. Add chops; cook for 8 to 12 minutes or until done (160°F) and juices run clear, turning meat halfway through cooking time. Remove chops, reserving drippings in skillet; keep chops warm while preparing sauce.

3 For sauce, in same skillet cook garlic in hot drippings for 30 seconds. Stir in balsamic salad dressing and honey mustard. Bring to boiling. To serve, spoon sauce over chops.

Nutrition Facts per serving: 276 cal., 18 g total fat (4 g sat. fat), 54 mg chol., 562 mg sodium, 5 g carbo., 0 g fiber, 22 g pro.

CHEESY CHOPS & CORN BREAD DRESSING

Prep: 20 minutes
Bake: 40 minutes

. . . .

Oven: 400°F
Makes: 4 servings

3	cups packaged corn bread stuffing mix
1	4-ounce can diced green chile peppers, undrained
1/2	cup orange juice or water
1/4	cup butter or margarine, melted
4	pork loin chops, cut 1 inch thick (about 2 1/2 pounds total)
	Salt
	Black pepper
1	9-ounce can nacho cheese sauce or dip (3/4 cup)

1 Preheat oven to 400°. In a medium bowl stir together dry stuffing mix, undrained chile peppers, orange juice, and melted butter. Spoon stuffing mixture evenly into the bottom of a 3-quart rectangular baking dish. Arrange chops over stuffing mixture in baking dish. Season chops with salt and pepper.

2 Bake, uncovered, in preheated oven about 30 minutes or until an instant-read thermometer inserted in center of chops registers 140°F (thermometer should not touch bone). Carefully spoon cheese sauce over chops and stuffing mixture. Bake about 10 minutes more or until thermometer registers 160°F.

Nutrition Facts per serving: 624 cal., 30 g total fat (13 g sat. fat), 131 mg chol., 1,346 mg sodium, 42 g carbo., 2 g fiber, 44 g pro.

CREAMY PORK CHOPS & RICE

Prep: 20 minutes
Bake: 30 minutes

. . . .

Oven: 375°F
Makes: 4 servings

1½	cups uncooked instant rice
1⅓	cups water
1	11-ounce can whole kernel corn with sweet peppers, undrained
½	cup purchased shredded carrot
1	tablespoon dried minced onion
½	teaspoon dried thyme, crushed
1	10¾-ounce can condensed cream of mushroom soup
4	pork loin or rib chops, cut ½ inch thick (about 1½ pounds total)
	Salt
	Black pepper
¼	cup seasoned fine dry bread crumbs
¼	teaspoon paprika
1	tablespoon butter or margarine, melted

1 Preheat oven to 375°. In a medium saucepan combine uncooked rice, the water, undrained corn, carrot, dried minced onion, and thyme; bring to boiling. Stir in cream of mushroom soup. Spoon mixture into a 2-quart rectangular baking dish, spreading evenly.

2 Trim fat from chops. Season chops with salt and pepper. Arrange chops on rice mixture. Cover with foil. Bake in preheated oven for 15 minutes.

3 Meanwhile, in a small bowl stir together bread crumbs and paprika. Add melted butter; toss gently to mix.

4 Uncover baking dish; sprinkle bread crumb mixture evenly over chops. Bake, uncovered, about 15 minutes more or until rice is tender and pork is done (160°F).

Nutrition Facts per serving: 480 cal., 15 g total fat (6 g sat. fat), 62 mg chol., 1,218 mg sodium, 57 g carbo., 3 g fiber, 29 g pro.

OVEN-FRIED PORK CHOPS

Prep: 10 minutes
Bake: 20 minutes

....

Oven: 425°F
Makes: 4 servings

3 tablespoons butter or margarine

1 egg

2 tablespoons milk

1 cup packaged corn bread stuffing mix

4 pork loin chops, cut ½ inch thick (about 1½ pounds total)
   Applesauce (optional)

1 Preheat oven to 425°. Place butter in a 13×9×2-inch baking pan; place in the preheated oven about 3 minutes or until butter melts.

2 Meanwhile, in a shallow dish beat egg with a fork; stir in milk. Place dry stuffing mix in another shallow dish. Dip pork chops into egg mixture. Coat both sides with stuffing mix. Place chops in the baking pan with the butter.

3 Bake in the 425° oven for 20 to 25 minutes or until done (160°F), turning once. If desired, serve with applesauce.

Nutrition Facts per serving: 326 cal., 16 g total fat (8 g sat. fat), 131 mg chol., 392 mg sodium, 17 g carbo., 0 g fiber, 26 g pro.

PORK TENDERLOIN WITH SWEET POTATOES

Start to Finish:

25 minutes

Makes: 4 servings

1   12-ounce pork tenderloin

1   large onion, cut into wedges

1   tablespoon cooking oil

2   10-ounce packages or one 16-ounce package frozen candied sweet potatoes with sauce, thawed

1   tablespoon snipped fresh thyme or $\frac{1}{2}$ teaspoon dried thyme, crushed

1 Cut tenderloin into $\frac{1}{2}$-inch-thick slices. In a large skillet cook pork slices and onion in hot oil about 6 minutes or until pork is tender and juices run clear, turning slices once. Remove pork slices from the skillet; set aside.

2 Stir sweet potatoes with sauce and dried thyme (if using) into onions in skillet. Bring to boiling; reduce heat. Cover and cook over medium heat about 10 minutes or until sweet potatoes are tender. Return pork slices to skillet. Heat through. Stir in fresh thyme, if using.

Nutrition Facts per serving: 386 cal., 13 g total fat (2 g sat. fat), 55 mg chol., 484 mg sodium, 44 g carbo., 4 g fiber, 20 g pro.

PEPPERED PORK & APRICOT SALAD

Prep: 25 minutes

Broil: 9 minutes

Makes: 4 servings

½	cup snipped dried apricots
1	6.1-ounce package quick-cooking long grain and wild rice mix
½	cup loose-pack frozen peas
½	of a 1½-pound refrigerated peppercorn marinated pork tenderloin, cut into ¾-inch slices
¼	cup bottled Italian salad dressing
2	green onions, thinly sliced
2	tablespoons frozen orange juice concentrate, thawed

1 Preheat broiler. Stir the apricots into the rice mix. Prepare the rice mix according to package directions. Gently stir the frozen peas into the cooked rice mixture. Spread mixture into shallow baking pan; cool for 20 minutes.

2 Meanwhile, place pork tenderloin slices on unheated rack of a broiler pan. Broil 3 to 4 inches from the heat for 9 to 11 minutes or until done (160°F). Transfer pork slices to a plate; cover loosely with foil. Let stand for 10 minutes.

3 For dressing, in a small bowl combine salad dressing, green onions, and orange juice concentrate. Transfer the cooled rice mixture to a large bowl; drizzle with dressing. Toss lightly to coat.

4 Spoon rice mixture onto a large serving platter. Cut pork tenderloin crosswise into thin strips; arrange slices over rice mixture.

Make-Ahead Directions: Prepare as directed through step 3. Cover and chill rice mixture and meat slices separately for up to 24 hours. Continue as directed in step 4. Let stand at room temperature for 15 minutes before serving.

Nutrition Facts per serving: 377 cal., 11 g total fat (2 g sat. fat), 38 mg chol., 1,382 mg sodium, 52 g carbo., 2 g fiber, 20 g pro.

PEPPERY PORK SANDWICHES

Prep: 25 minutes

Bake: 2½ hours

Oven: 325°F

Makes: 8 or
9 sandwiches

1   large onion, thinly sliced

1   2- to 2½-pound boneless pork shoulder roast

1   tablespoon hot paprika

2   14½-ounce cans diced tomatoes, undrained

1   4-ounce can diced green chile peppers, undrained

2   teaspoons dried oregano, crushed

1   teaspoon black pepper

¼   teaspoon salt

8   or 9 (6-inch) French-style rolls, split and toasted

1 Preheat oven to 325°. Arrange onion slices in bottom of a 4-quart Dutch oven. Sprinkle pork roast evenly with paprika. Place roast on top of onion. In a medium bowl combine undrained tomatoes, undrained chile peppers, oregano, black pepper, and salt. Pour over roast in Dutch oven. Bake, covered, in preheated oven for 2½ to 3 hours or until roast is very tender.

2 Remove pork to cutting board, reserving tomato mixture in Dutch oven. Using 2 forks, pull pork into shreds. Skim fat from tomato mixture. Add shredded meat to tomato mixture; stir until combined. Heat through. Spoon pork mixture onto rolls.

Nutrition Facts per sandwich: 383 cal., 18 g total fat (6 g sat. fat), 79 mg chol., 964 mg sodium, 29 g carbo., 3 g fiber, 25 g pro.

CRISPY PORK BURRITOS

Prep: 25 minutes

Bake: 20 minutes

....

Oven: 350°F

Makes: 10 servings

1	17-ounce package refrigerated cooked pork roast au jus
1	16-ounce jar salsa
1	16-ounce can refried beans with green chiles
1	1½-ounce envelope dry burrito seasoning mix
10	10-inch flour tortillas
8	ounces shredded Colby and Monterey Jack cheese or cheddar cheese
	Bottled salsa (optional)
	Dairy sour cream (optional)

1 Preheat oven to 350°. Discard au jus from pork roast or reserve for another use. Cut pork into bite-size pieces (should have about 2 cups pork pieces).

2 In a large skillet combine pork pieces, the 16-ounce jar salsa, the beans, and dry burrito seasoning mix. Cook and stir over medium heat until heated through.

3 Meanwhile, wrap tortillas tightly in foil. Heat in preheated oven for 10 minutes to soften.

4 To assemble, place ½ cup of the meat mixture onto each tortilla, just below the center. Sprinkle with cheese. Fold bottom edge of each tortilla up and over filling. Fold opposite sides in and over filling. Roll up from the bottom. Secure rolled tortillas with wooden toothpicks, if necessary. Place burritos on a baking sheet, seam sides down.

5 Bake in the 350° oven about 20 minutes or until heated through. Remove and discard toothpicks. If desired, serve with additional salsa and sour cream.

Nutrition Facts per serving: 347 cal., 13 g total fat (7 g sat. fat), 50 mg chol., 1,232 mg sodium, 34 g carbo., 4 g fiber, 21 g pro.

MU SHU-STYLE PORK ROLL-UPS

Start to Finish:

20 minutes

....

Oven: 350°F
Makes: 4 servings

4	10-inch flour tortillas
1	teaspoon toasted sesame oil
12	ounces lean boneless pork, cut into strips
2	cups loose-pack frozen stir-fry vegetables (any combination)
¼	cup bottled plum or hoisin sauce

1 Preheat oven to 350°. Wrap tortillas tightly in foil. Heat in preheated oven for 10 minutes to soften. (Or wrap tortillas in microwave-safe paper towels; microwave on 100% power for 15 to 30 seconds or until tortillas are softened.)

2 Meanwhile, in a large skillet heat sesame oil over medium-high heat. Add pork strips; stir-fry for 2 to 3 minutes or until done Add stir-fry vegetables. Cook and stir for 3 to 4 minutes or until vegetables are crisp-tender.

3 Spread each tortilla with 1 tablespoon of the plum sauce; place a quarter of the meat mixture just below the center of each tortilla. Fold the bottom edge of each tortilla up and over the filling. Fold in the sides until they meet; roll up over the filling.

Nutrition Facts per serving: 302 cal., 8 g total fat (2 g sat. fat), 53 mg chol., 311 mg sodium, 34 g carbo., 2 g fiber, 22 g pro.

PORK & GREEN CHILE CASSEROLE

Prep: 25 minutes
Bake: 25 minutes

Oven: 375°F
Makes: 6 servings

1¼	pounds lean boneless pork
1	tablespoon cooking oil
1	15-ounce can black beans or pinto beans, rinsed and drained
1	14½-ounce can diced tomatoes, undrained
1	10¾-ounce can condensed cream of chicken soup
2	4-ounce cans diced green chile peppers, drained
1	cup uncooked instant brown rice
¼	cup water
2	tablespoons bottled salsa
1	teaspoon ground cumin
½	cup shredded cheddar cheese (2 ounces)

1 Preheat oven to 375°. Cut pork into thin bite-size strips. In a large skillet stir-fry pork, half at a time, in hot oil until done. Drain. Return all meat to skillet. Stir in beans, undrained tomatoes, cream of chicken soup, chile peppers, uncooked brown rice, the water, salsa, and cumin. Heat and stir just until bubbly; pour into a 2-quart casserole.

2 Bake, uncovered, in preheated oven for 25 minutes. Remove from oven. Sprinkle with cheese; let stand for 3 to 4 minutes or until cheese melts.

Nutrition Facts per serving: 350 cal., 14 g total fat (5 g sat. fat), 69 mg chol., 1,242 mg sodium, 28 g carbo., 5 g fiber, 30 g pro.

BARBECUED RIBS & KRAUT

Prep: 15 minutes
Cook: 25 minutes

Makes: 3 servings

1   14½-ounce can sauerkraut, rinsed and drained
2   cups loose-pack frozen diced hash brown potatoes with onion and peppers
1   30.4-ounce package refrigerated cooked pork ribs in barbecue sauce
¼   cup chicken broth

1 In a large nonstick skillet combine sauerkraut and potatoes. Cut ribs into 2-rib portions; arrange on sauerkraut mixture. In a small bowl combine any barbecue sauce from package and the chicken broth; drizzle over the mixture in the skillet. Cover and cook over medium heat about 25 minutes or until heated through.

Nutrition Facts per serving: 751 cal., 43 g total fat (16 g sat. fat), 111 mg chol., 2,700 mg sodium, 54 g carbo., 7 g fiber, 39 g pro.

TEX-MEX SKILLET

Start to Finish:

30 minutes

Makes: 4 servings

8	ounces ground pork
4	ounces bulk chorizo sausage
1	10-ounce can diced tomatoes and green chile peppers, undrained
1	cup loose-pack frozen whole kernel corn
¾	cup water
½	cup chopped red sweet pepper
1	cup uncooked instant rice
½	cup shredded cheddar cheese or Monterey Jack cheese (2 ounces)
	Flour tortillas, warmed (optional)
	Dairy sour cream (optional)

1 In a large skillet cook the pork and sausage until brown. Drain off fat. Stir in undrained tomatoes, corn, the water, and sweet pepper. Bring to boiling.

2 Stir uncooked rice into tomato mixture in skillet. Remove from heat. Top with cheese. Cover and let stand about 5 minutes or until rice is tender. If desired, serve in flour tortillas and top with sour cream.

Nutrition Facts per serving: 395 cal., 20 g total fat (9 g sat. fat), 66 mg chol., 748 mg sodium, 33 g carbo., 1 g fiber, 21 g pro.

WHITE & GREEN CHILI

Prep: 15 minutes
Cook: 15 minutes

Makes: 4 servings

1   pound unseasoned meat loaf mix (⅓ pound each ground beef, pork, and veal), lean ground beef, or ground pork

1   small onion, chopped

2   15-ounce cans Great Northern beans or white beans, rinsed and drained

1   16-ounce jar green salsa

1   14-ounce can reduced-sodium chicken broth

1½ teaspoons ground cumin

2   tablespoons snipped fresh cilantro

¼   cup dairy sour cream (optional)

1 In a 4-quart Dutch oven cook meat loaf mix and onion over medium heat about 5 minutes or until brown, breaking up pieces of meat with a spoon. Drain off fat. Add beans, salsa, chicken broth, and cumin. Bring to boiling; reduce heat. Simmer, covered, for 15 minutes.

2 To serve, stir in 1 tablespoon of the cilantro. Divide chile among 4 serving bowls. Sprinkle with remaining 1 tablespoon cilantro. If desired, top each serving with sour cream.

Nutrition Facts per serving: 440 cal., 15 g total fat (5 g sat. fat), 81 mg chol., 1,256 mg sodium, 41 g carbo., 13 g fiber, 32 g pro.

PORK & APPLE CASSEROLE

Prep: 25 minutes
Bake: 30 minutes

Oven: 400°F
Makes: 6 servings

1	pound bulk pork sausage
2	medium apples, cored and chopped
1⅓	cups packaged corn bread stuffing mix
1	tablespoon dried minced onion
2	eggs
1¼	cups apple juice or apple cider
½	cup shredded cheddar cheese (2 ounces)

1 Preheat oven to 400°. Grease a 2-quart square baking dish; set aside. In a large skillet cook sausage until brown. Drain off fat. Stir in chopped apples, dry stuffing mix, and dried minced onion. In a small bowl whisk together eggs and apple juice; add to sausage mixture. Toss to coat. Transfer mixture to prepared baking dish.

2 Bake, covered, in preheated oven for 20 minutes. Uncover; stir sausage and stuffing mixture and sprinkle with cheese. Bake, uncovered, about 10 minutes more or until hot in center (160°F).

Nutrition Facts per serving: 429 cal., 29 g total fat (11 g sat. fat), 138 mg chol., 776 mg sodium, 24 g carbo., 2 g fiber, 17 g pro.

COUNTRY-STYLE STUFFED PEPPERS

Prep: 30 minutes
Bake: 25 minutes

. . . .

Oven: 375°F
Makes: 8 servings

4	medium green sweet peppers
1	pound bulk pork sausage
1	cup purchased shredded carrot
1	stalk celery, finely chopped
1½	cups shredded smoked Gouda, smoked cheddar, or regular cheddar cheese (6 ounces)
½	cup packaged corn bread stuffing mix

1 Preheat oven to 375°. Cut sweet peppers in half lengthwise. Remove seeds and membrane. In a covered large saucepan cook sweet pepper halves in enough boiling water to cover for 4 to 5 minutes or just until tender; drain well. Pat dry with paper towels.

2 Meanwhile, in a large skillet cook sausage, carrot, and celery until sausage is brown. Drain off fat. Stir 1 cup of the cheese and the dry corn bread stuffing mix into sausage mixture.

3 Spoon about ½ cup of the sausage and stuffing mixture into each sweet pepper half. Place pepper halves, filling sides up, in a 15×10×1-inch baking pan.

4 Bake, uncovered, in preheated oven for 20 minutes. Sprinkle tops with remaining ½ cup cheese. Bake, uncovered, about 5 minutes more or until cheese is melted and stuffing is heated through.

Nutrition Facts per serving: 304 cal., 23 g total fat (10 g sat. fat), 60 mg chol., 815 mg sodium, 11 g carbo., 2 g fiber, 13 g pro.

ITALIAN-SAUSAGE PIZZA

Prep: 25 minutes
Bake: 10 minutes

Oven: 425°F
Makes: 6 servings

1   10-ounce package refrigerated pizza dough (for 1 crust)
8   ounces bulk Italian sausage
½   of a medium green sweet pepper, cut into thin strips
1   8-ounce can pizza sauce
1   4-ounce can (drained weight) sliced mushrooms, drained
1   8-ounce package shredded pizza cheese (2 cups)

1 Preheat oven to 425°. Grease a 12-inch pizza pan; press pizza dough into prepared pan, building up side. Bake in preheated oven for 5 minutes.

2 Meanwhile, in a medium skillet cook sausage and sweet pepper until sausage is brown. Drain off fat. Stir in pizza sauce and mushrooms.

3 Sprinkle half of the cheese on the crust. Spoon meat mixture over cheese. Top with remaining cheese. Bake in the 425° oven for 10 to 15 minutes or until cheese is bubbly. Let stand for 5 minutes before serving.

Nutrition Facts per serving: 403 cal., 21 g total fat (11 g sat. fat), 53 mg chol., 1,049 mg sodium, 28 g carbo., 1 g fiber, 23 g pro.

SAUSAGE-CAVATELLI SKILLET

Start to Finish:

30 minutes

Makes: 4 servings

8   ounces dried cavatelli (1¾ cups)

1   pound bulk Italian sausage or ground beef

1   medium green sweet pepper, chopped (optional)

1   20-ounce jar spaghetti sauce with mushrooms

1   cup shredded mozzarella cheese (4 ounces)

1 Cook cavatelli according to package directions. Drain well.

2 Meanwhile, in a large skillet cook Italian sausage and sweet pepper (if using) until sausage is brown. Drain off fat. Stir in spaghetti sauce; cook about 2 minutes or until heated through. Stir in the drained cavatelli. Sprinkle with cheese. Cover and cook about 2 minutes more or until cheese melts.

Nutrition Facts per serving: 677 cal., 32 g total fat (13 g sat. fat), 93 mg chol., 1,469 mg sodium, 60 g carbo., 4 g fiber, 32 g pro.

CANADIAN BACON & PINEAPPLE CALZONE

Prep: 25 minutes
Bake: 20 minutes

Oven: 425°F
Makes: 4 servings

1   8-ounce can crushed pineapple (juice pack)

4   ounces sliced Canadian-style bacon or turkey ham, cut into bite-size pieces (about 1 cup)

½   cup purchased chunky meatless spaghetti sauce

1   10-ounce package refrigerated pizza dough (for 1 crust)

1   8-ounce package shredded mozzarella cheese (2 cups)

1   tablespoon milk

2   tablespoons grated Parmesan cheese

1 Preheat oven to 425°. Drain pineapple, pressing out as much liquid as possible. In a medium bowl stir together drained pineapple, Canadian-style bacon, and spaghetti sauce.

2 Grease a 12-inch pizza pan; press pizza dough into pan. Sprinkle half of the mozzarella cheese over one half of the dough to within ½ inch of the edge. Spoon meat mixture over cheese. Sprinkle with remaining mozzarella cheese.

3 Fold the pizza dough over the filling, making a half circle. Seal the edges with the tines of a fork. Make slits in the top to allow steam to escape. Brush top with milk and sprinkle with Parmesan cheese. Bake in preheated oven about 20 minutes or until golden.

Nutrition Facts per serving: 431 cal., 16 g total fat (9 g sat. fat), 61 mg chol., 1,128 mg sodium, 46 g carbo., 1 g fiber, 24 g pro.

CANADIAN BACON PIZZA

Prep: 20 minutes
Grill: 5 minutes

Makes: 4 servings

1	6-ounce jar marinated artichoke hearts, quartered
2	6-inch Italian bread shells (Boboli)
1	cup shredded fontina or mozzarella cheese (4 ounces)
6	slices Canadian-style bacon, cut into strips (about 5 ounces)
3	Roma tomatoes, sliced
¼	cup crumbled feta cheese (1 ounce)
2	green onions, thinly sliced (¼ cup)
1	tablespoon snipped fresh oregano or basil

1 Preheat grill. Drain artichoke hearts, reserving marinade. Brush the bread shells with some of the reserved marinade (discard any remaining marinade). Sprinkle half of the fontina cheese over bread shells. In a large bowl toss together the artichoke hearts, Canadian-style bacon, tomatoes, feta cheese, green onions, and oregano; divide among bread shells. Sprinkle with remaining fontina cheese.

2 Transfer the bread shells to a pizza grill pan or a large piece of double-thickness heavy foil. On a grill that has a cover, place the pan or foil on the rack directly over medium heat. Cover and grill for 5 to 8 minutes or until cheese is melted and pizza is heated through.

Nutrition Facts per serving: 385 cal., 19 g total fat (7 g sat. fat), 59 mg chol., 1,253 mg sodium, 33 g carbo., 2 g fiber, 23 g pro.

PEPPY PEPPERONI PIZZA

Prep: 20 minutes
Bake: 18 minutes

Oven: 425°F
Makes: 6 servings

1   10-ounce package refrigerated pizza dough (for 1 crust)
1   8-ounce package shredded Monterey Jack cheese (2 cups)
1   cup bottled salsa
1   4-ounce can (drained weight) sliced mushrooms, drained
1/2   of a 3 1/2-ounce package sliced pepperoni

1 Preheat oven to 425°. Grease a baking sheet; roll pizza dough into a 15×10-inch rectangle on prepared baking sheet. Build up edges of dough slightly. Sprinkle 1 1/2 cups of the cheese on the dough. Spoon salsa evenly over cheese. Top with mushrooms and pepperoni. Sprinkle with remaining 1/2 cup cheese.

2 Bake in the preheated oven for 18 to 20 minutes or until crust is golden and cheese is melted.

Nutrition Facts per serving: 309 cal., 17 g total fat (9 g sat. fat), 40 mg chol., 774 mg sodium, 24 g carbo., 1 g fiber, 16 g pro.

RASPBERRY-PEPPER GLAZED HAM

Prep: 15 minutes
Bake: 1½ hours **+ 15** minutes

....

Oven: 325°F
Makes: 16 to 20 servings

1   9- to 10-pound cooked bone-in ham (rump half or shank portion)
1   recipe Raspberry Sauce
1   tablespoon pink and/or black peppercorns, coarsely cracked

1 Preheat oven to 325°. If desired, score ham in a diamond pattern by making shallow diagonal cuts at 1-inch intervals. Place ham, flat side down, on a rack in a shallow roasting pan. Insert an oven-going meat thermometer into the thickest portion of the meat, making sure bulb does not touch bone. Bake in preheated oven for 1½ hours. Meanwhile, prepare Raspberry Sauce.

2 Spoon or brush some Raspberry Sauce over the ham. Bake ham for 15 to 30 minutes more or until thermometer registers 135°F, spooning or brushing once or twice with additional sauce. Remove from oven. Sprinkle with coarsely cracked peppercorns. Cover ham with foil; let stand for 15 minutes before carving. (The temperature of the meat will rise 5°F during standing.)

3 Just before serving, carve the ham. Reheat any remaining Raspberry Sauce until bubbly; pass with ham.

Raspberry Sauce: In a small saucepan combine 1½ cups seedless raspberry preserves; 2 tablespoons white vinegar; 2 to 3 canned chipotle chile peppers in adobo sauce, drained and chopped;* and 1½ teaspoons bottled minced garlic (3 cloves). Bring just to boiling; reduce heat. Simmer, uncovered, for 5 minutes, stirring frequently. Makes 1¾ cups.

***Note:** Because chile peppers contain volatile oils that can burn your skin and eyes, avoid direct contact with them as much as possible. When working with chile peppers, wear plastic or rubber gloves. If your bare hands do touch the peppers, wash your hands and nails well with soap and warm water.

Nutrition Facts per serving: 470 cal., 15 g total fat (5 g sat. fat), 179 mg chol., 144 mg sodium, 21 g carbo., 0 g fiber, 58 g pro.

FRUITED BAKED HAM

Prep: 10 minutes

Roast: 1½ hours

. . . .

Oven: 325°F

Makes: 12 to 16 servings

1	3- to 4-pound boneless cooked smoked ham
1½	cups cherry preserves
¾	cup apricot preserves
3	tablespoons orange juice

1 Preheat oven to 325°. Line a shallow roasting pan with foil. If desired, score top of ham in a diamond pattern by making shallow diagonal cuts at 1-inch intervals. Place ham in prepared pan. Insert an oven-going meat thermometer in center of ham. Roast, uncovered, in preheated oven for 1½ to 2¼ hours or until thermometer registers 140°F.

2 Meanwhile, for sauce, in a medium saucepan combine cherry preserves, apricot preserves, and orange juice. Heat through. For the last 20 minutes of baking, spoon about ½ cup of the sauce mixture over the ham. Slice ham and serve with remaining sauce.

Nutrition Facts per serving: 375 cal., 12 g total fat (4 g sat. fat), 65 mg chol., 1,513 mg sodium, 45 g carbo., 1 g fiber, 20 g pro.

PEACH-MUSTARD GLAZED HAM

Prep: 10 minutes
Grill: 12 minutes

Makes: 4 servings

2	tablespoons brown sugar
2	tablespoons spicy brown mustard
1/3	cup peach or apricot nectar
1	1-pound cooked ham slice, cut 3/4 to 1 inch thick
4	medium peaches, peeled and halved lengthwise
2	small green and/or red sweet peppers, each cut crosswise into 4 rings

1 Preheat grill. For glaze, in a small bowl combine brown sugar and mustard. Gradually whisk in the peach nectar until smooth. To prevent ham from curling, make shallow cuts around the edge at 1-inch intervals. Brush one side of the ham slice with the glaze.

2 Place ham, glazed side down, on the greased rack of an uncovered grill directly over medium-hot heat. Grill for 6 minutes. Turn ham. Top with peach halves and sweet pepper rings. Brush ham, peaches, and sweet peppers with remaining glaze. Grill for 6 to 10 minutes more or until heated through, brushing occasionally with glaze.

Nutrition Facts per serving: 284 cal., 7 g total fat (2 g sat. fat), 60 mg chol., 1,468 mg sodium, 31 g carbo., 3 g fiber, 26 g pro.

HAM & ASPARAGUS PASTA

Start to Finish:

20 minutes

· · · · · · · · · · · · · · · · · · · ·

Makes: 4 servings

4	cups dried bow ties, rotini (corkscrew), or other medium pasta
1	10-ounce package frozen cut asparagus or broccoli
8	ounces sliced cooked ham, cut into thin strips
1	8-ounce container soft-style cream cheese with chives and onion
⅓	cup milk

1 Cook the pasta according to package directions, adding the frozen asparagus for the last 5 minutes and the ham the last minute of the cooking time. Drain and return to the pan.

2 In a 2-cup measure stir cream cheese into milk; add to the pasta mixture in the pan. Stir gently over medium heat until heated through.

Nutrition Facts per serving: 505 cal., 24 g total fat (12 g sat. fat), 140 mg chol., 905 mg sodium, 45 g carbo., 1 g fiber, 25 g pro.

DENVER POTATO CASSEROLE

Prep: 20 minutes
Bake: 65 minutes

Oven: 350°F
Makes: 4 servings

4   medium Yukon gold potatoes, thinly sliced (1⅓ pounds total)
8   ounces cooked ham, cubed
1   medium green sweet pepper, chopped
1   small sweet yellow onion, chopped
1   cup shredded Colby and Monterey Jack cheese (4 ounces)

1 Preheat oven to 350°. Grease a 2-quart square baking dish; layer half of the potatoes, half of the ham, half of the sweet pepper, half of the onion, and half of the cheese in prepared baking dish. Repeat with the remaining ham, sweet pepper, and onion. Top with the remaining potatoes.

2 Bake, covered, in preheated oven for 45 minutes. Uncover and bake about 15 minutes more or until potatoes are tender. Sprinkle with remaining half of the cheese. Bake, uncovered, about 5 minutes more or until cheese is melted.

Nutrition Facts per serving: 315 cal., 12 g total fat (6 g sat. fat), 56 mg chol., 1,010 mg sodium, 27 g carbo., 3 g fiber, 24 g pro.

CREAMY MACARONI-&-CHEESE HAM BAKE

Prep: 25 minutes
Bake: 30 minutes

Oven: 375°F
Makes: 4 servings

1	7$\frac{1}{4}$-ounce package macaroni and cheese dinner mix
1$\frac{1}{2}$	cups cubed cooked ham or chopped cooked chicken (about 8 ounces)
1	cup cream-style cottage cheese
$\frac{1}{2}$	cup dairy sour cream
1	teaspoon dried minced onion
$\frac{1}{4}$	teaspoon black pepper
$\frac{1}{4}$	cup fine dry bread crumbs
1	tablespoon butter or margarine, melted
1	teaspoon dried parsley, crushed (optional)

1 Preheat oven to 375°. Prepare macaroni and cheese mix according to package directions, except do not add salt to water. Stir ham, cottage cheese, sour cream, dried minced onion, and pepper into prepared macaroni and cheese. Transfer to a 1$\frac{1}{2}$-quart casserole.

2 In a small bowl combine bread crumbs, melted butter, and, if desired, parsley. Sprinkle over casserole.

3 Bake in preheated oven about 30 minutes or until heated through.

Nutrition Facts per serving: 434 cal., 18 g total fat (9 g sat. fat), 63 mg chol., 1,462 mg sodium, 43 g carbo., 1 g fiber, 25 g pro.

SHORTCUT HAM QUICHE

Prep: 15 minutes
Bake: 38 minutes

Oven: 375°F
Makes: 4 to 6 servings

1	8-ounce package (8) refrigerated crescent rolls
1	cup diced cooked ham (5 ounces)
4	ounces Havarti dill cheese, shredded (1 cup)
2	eggs
1	5-ounce can evaporated milk ($2/3$ cup)
$1/2$	teaspoon Dijon-style mustard
$1/3$	cup sliced almonds, toasted (optional)

1 Preheat oven to 375°. Grease a 9-inch pie plate. Unroll crescent rolls and press into bottom and onto side of the prepared pie plate. If desired, mark the edge of the pastry with the tines of a fork. Bake in preheated oven for 8 minutes. Remove from oven.

2 Sprinkle ham and cheese over the pastry. In a small bowl beat eggs with a wire whisk; whisk in evaporated milk and mustard. Pour egg mixture over ham and cheese. Cover edge of pastry with foil. Bake in the 375° oven for 30 to 35 minutes or until a knife inserted near the center comes out clean. If desired, sprinkle with almonds. Let stand for 5 minutes before serving.

Nutrition Facts per serving: 471 cal., 32 g total fat (6 g sat. fat), 172 mg chol., 1,152 mg sodium, 27 g carbo., 0 g fiber, 22 g pro.

HAM & BROCCOLI-TOPPED SPUDS

Prep: 10 minutes
Bake: 40 minutes

. . . .

Oven: 425°F
Makes: 4 servings

4   medium baking potatoes (6 to 8 ounces each)
2   10-ounce packages frozen cut broccoli in cheese sauce
2   cups chopped cooked ham
½   teaspoon caraway seeds

1 Preheat oven to 425°. Scrub potatoes thoroughly; pat dry. Prick potatoes with a fork. (If desired, for soft skins, rub potatoes with shortening or wrap each potato in foil.) Bake potatoes in preheated oven for 40 to 60 minutes or until tender. Roll each potato gently under your hand. Cut a crisscross in each potato top.

2 Meanwhile, heat broccoli in pouches according to package directions. Pour contents of pouches into a medium saucepan. Add ham and caraway seeds; heat through. To serve, top potatoes with broccoli mixture.

Nutrition Facts per serving: 338 cal., 10 g total fat (3 g sat. fat), 44 mg chol., 1,713 mg sodium, 38 g carbo., 6 g fiber, 24 g pro.

HAM & CHEESE CALZONES

Prep: 15 minutes
Bake: 15 minutes

....

Oven: 400°F
Makes: 4 servings

1	10-ounce package refrigerated pizza dough (for 1 crust)
¼	cup coarse-grain mustard
6	ounces sliced Swiss or provolone cheese
8	ounces cooked ham, cubed (1½ cups)
½	teaspoon caraway seeds

1 Preheat oven to 400°. Line a baking sheet with foil; lightly grease foil. Unroll pizza dough. On a lightly floured surface, roll or pat dough into a 15×10-inch rectangle. Cut dough in half crosswise and lengthwise to make 4 rectangles. Spread mustard over rectangles. Divide half of the cheese among rectangles, placing cheese on half of each rectangle and cutting or tearing to fit as necessary. Top with ham and sprinkle with caraway seeds. Top with remaining cheese. Brush edges with water. For each calzone, fold dough over filling to opposite edge, stretching slightly if necessary. Seal edges with the tines of a fork.

2 Place calzones on the prepared baking sheet. Prick tops to allow steam to escape. Bake in preheated oven about 15 minutes or until golden. Let stand for 5 minutes before serving.

Nutrition Facts per serving: 421 cal., 21 g total fat (10 g sat. fat), 72 mg chol., 1,390 mg sodium, 28 g carbo., 1 g fiber, 30 g pro.

LAMB CHOPS JALAPEÑO

Prep: 15 minutes
Grill: 12 minutes

Makes: 4 servings

8   lamb rib or loin chops, cut 1 inch thick (about 2½ pounds total)
½   teaspoon salt
½   teaspoon black pepper
½   teaspoon ground cinnamon
1   8-ounce can crushed pineapple (juice pack), undrained
⅓   to ½ cup jalapeño pepper jelly
½   cup lemon juice
2   teaspoons yellow mustard
     Hot cooked couscous (optional)

1 Preheat grill. Trim fat from meat. For rub, in a small bowl combine salt, black pepper, and cinnamon. Sprinkle rub evenly over both sides of each chop; rub in with your fingers. Set aside.

2 For glaze, in a small saucepan combine undrained pineapple, jalapeño jelly, lemon juice, and mustard. Bring to boiling; reduce heat. Simmer, uncovered, for 10 minutes, stirring occasionally.

3 Place chops on the rack of uncovered grill directly over medium heat. Grill to desired doneness, turning once halfway through grilling. (Allow 12 to 14 minutes for medium-rare doneness [145°F] or 15 to 17 minutes for medium doneness [160°F].) Set aside 1 cup of the glaze. Brush chops with remaining glaze during the last 5 minutes of grilling; discard any remaining glaze used as a brush-on. Serve meat with reserved glaze. If desired, serve with couscous.

Nutrition Facts per serving: 430 cal., 16 g total fat (6 g sat. fat), 139 mg chol., 437 mg sodium, 29 g carbo., 1 g fiber, 43 g pro.

LAMB & PEPPERS

Start to Finish:

25 minutes

Makes: 4 servings

8	lamb rib chops or loin chops, cut 1 inch thick (about 2 pounds total)
3	small green, red, and/or yellow sweet peppers, cut into 1-inch pieces
1	tablespoon snipped fresh oregano
1	teaspoon bottled minced garlic (2 cloves)
1	tablespoon olive oil or cooking oil
¼	cup sliced pitted green or ripe olives

1 Preheat broiler. Trim fat from chops. Place chops on the unheated rack of a broiler pan. Broil 3 to 4 inches from the heat for 10 to 15 minutes or until medium doneness (160°F), turning once halfway through broiling. Transfer chops to a serving platter.

2 Meanwhile, in a large skillet cook sweet peppers, oregano, and garlic in hot oil for 8 to 10 minutes or until sweet peppers are crisp-tender. Add olives. Cook and stir until heated through. Spoon over chops.

Nutrition Facts per serving: 216 cal., 13 g total fat (3 g sat. fat), 64 mg chol., 264 mg sodium, 4 g carbo., 1 g fiber, 20 g pro.

LAMB CHOPS WITH CRANBERRY RELISH

Prep: 15 minutes
Broil: 10 minutes

Makes: 4 servings

½ cup purchased cranberry-orange relish

¼ cup chopped pecans, toasted

2 tablespoons orange juice

2 teaspoons snipped fresh rosemary or ½ teaspoon dried rosemary, crushed

8 lamb loin chops, cut ¾ inch thick (about 2 ½ pounds total)

Salt

Black pepper

1 In a small bowl combine cranberry-orange relish, pecans, orange juice, and rosemary. Set aside.

2 Trim fat from chops. Place chops on the unheated rack of a broiler pan. Season generously with salt and pepper. Broil chops 3 to 4 inches from the heat for 9 to 11 minutes or until medium doneness (160°F), turning once. Spread relish mixture over chops. Broil for 1 minute more.

Nutrition Facts per serving: 324 cal., 13 g total fat (3 g sat. fat), 100 mg chol., 172 mg sodium, 18 g carbo., 1 g fiber, 33 g pro.

PAN-SEARED LAMB CHOPS WITH MINT SALAD

Start to Finish:

30 minutes

....

Makes: 4 servings

¼   cup snipped fresh mint

¼   cup snipped fresh flat-leaf parsley

¼   cup crumbled feta cheese (1 ounce)

¼   cup chopped pecans, toasted

8   lamb rib chops or loin chops, cut 1 inch thick (about 2 pounds total)

2   teaspoons olive oil

¼   teaspoon salt

⅛   teaspoon black pepper

   Olive oil (optional)

   Lemon juice (optional)

   Mixed salad greens (optional)

1 In a small bowl combine mint, parsley, feta cheese, and pecans; set aside.

2 Trim fat from chops. Rub chops with the 2 teaspoons oil, the salt, and pepper. Preheat a heavy, large skillet over medium-high heat until very hot. Add chops. Cook over medium-high heat for 8 to 10 minutes or until medium-rare doneness (145°F), turning once halfway through cooking.

3 To serve, sprinkle chops with mint mixture. If desired, drizzle additional oil and/or lemon juice over mint mixture and serve with salad greens.

Nutrition Facts per serving: 252 cal., 17 g total fat (5 g sat. fat), 72 mg chol., 311 mg sodium, 2 g carbo., 1 g fiber, 22 g pro.

HONEY-MUSTARD LAMB CHOPS

Prep: 10 minutes
Broil: 10 minutes

Makes: 4 servings

8   small lamb loin chops, cut 1 inch thick (about 1½ pounds total)
2   medium zucchini and/or yellow summer squash, quartered lengthwise
    Salt
    Black pepper
2   tablespoons Dijon-style mustard
2   tablespoons honey
1   tablespoon snipped fresh rosemary or 1 teaspoon dried rosemary, crushed

1 Preheat broiler. Trim fat from chops. Season chops and zucchini with salt and pepper. Arrange chops and zucchini, cut sides down, on the unheated rack of a broiler pan. In a small bowl stir together mustard, honey, and rosemary. Brush some of the mustard mixture on top of the chops.

2 Broil chops and zucchini 3 to 4 inches from the heat for 5 minutes. Turn chops and zucchini; brush remaining mustard mixture on the chops and zucchini. Broil for 5 to 10 minutes more or until lamb is medium doneness (160°F) and zucchini is tender.

Nutrition Facts per serving: 181 cal., 5 g total fat (2 g sat. fat), 60 mg chol., 302 mg sodium, 12 g carbo., 1 g fiber, 20 g pro.

LAMB BURGERS WITH FETA & MINT

Prep: 15 minutes
Grill: 14 minutes

. . . .

Makes: 4 servings

1½   pounds ground lamb or ground beef
4   lettuce leaves
4   kaiser rolls, split and toasted
½   cup crumbled feta cheese with peppercorns (2 ounces)
4   tomato slices
1   tablespoon snipped fresh mint

1 Shape ground meat into four patties ¾ inch thick. Place patties on the greased rack of an uncovered grill directly over medium heat. Grill for 14 to 18 minutes or until done (160°F),* turning once.

2 Place lettuce on bottoms of rolls. Top with patties, feta cheese, tomato slices, mint, and tops of rolls.

*Note: The internal color of a burger is not a reliable doneness indicator. A lamb or beef patty cooked to 160°F is safe, regardless of color. To measure the doneness of a patty, insert an instant-read thermometer through the side of the patty to a depth of 2 to 3 inches.

Nutrition Facts per serving: 554 cal., 30 g total fat (13 g sat. fat), 130 mg chol., 615 mg sodium, 32 g carbo., 1 g fiber, 38 g pro.

FISH & SEAFOOD

SIMPLE SALSA FISH

Start to Finish:

15 minutes

· · · · · · · · · · · · · · · · · · ·

Makes: 4 servings

1	pound fresh or frozen skinless orange roughy or red snapper fillets, ½- to 1-inch thickness
⅓	cup bottled salsa
½	teaspoon bottled minced garlic (1 clove)
1	14-ounce can vegetable broth
1	cup quick-cooking couscous
¼	cup thinly sliced green onions or coarsely chopped fresh cilantro
	Lime or lemon wedges

1 Thaw fish, if frozen. Rinse fish; pat dry with paper towels. Set aside. In a small bowl combine salsa and garlic; set aside.

2 In a medium saucepan bring broth to boiling. Stir in couscous; cover and remove from heat. Let stand about 5 minutes or until liquid is absorbed. Stir in green onions.

3 Meanwhile, grease the unheated rack of a broiler pan. Measure thickness of fish. Place fish on rack. Broil about 4 inches from the heat just until fish flakes easily when tested with a fork. (Allow 4 to 6 minutes per ½-inch thickness of fish.) If fillets are 1 inch thick or more, turn once halfway through broiling. Spoon salsa mixture over fish; broil about 1 minute more or until salsa is heated through.

4 Arrange fish on couscous mixture. Serve with lime wedges.

Nutrition Facts per serving: 295 cal., 3 g total fat (0 g sat. fat), 42 mg chol., 549 mg sodium, 39 g carbo., 7 g fiber, 30 g pro.

FISH WITH BLACK BEAN SAUCE

Start to Finish:

25 minutes

- - - - - - - - - - - - - - - - - - - -

Makes: 6 servings

1½   pounds fresh or frozen skinless sea bass or orange roughy fillets, cut into 6 portions

1   15-ounce can black beans, rinsed and drained

3   tablespoons bottled teriyaki sauce

2   tablespoons bottled hoisin sauce

     Nonstick cooking spray

     Hot cooked rice

1 Thaw fish, if frozen. Rinse fish; pat dry with paper towels. In a blender container or food processor bowl combine the drained beans, teriyaki sauce, and hoisin sauce. Cover and blend or process until nearly smooth.

2 Lightly coat an unheated 12-inch skillet with cooking spray. Preheat over medium-high heat. Carefully place fish portions in skillet; cook about 4 minutes or until brown, turning once. Add bean mixture to fish. Bring to boiling; reduce heat to medium. Simmer, covered, about 8 minutes or until fish flakes easily when tested with a fork.

3 To serve, spoon some of the sauce onto plate; place fish portion on the sauce. Serve remaining sauce with hot cooked rice.

Nutrition Facts per serving: 276 cal., 3 g total fat (1 g sat. fat), 46 mg chol., 617 mg sodium, 35 g carbo., 4 g fiber, 28 g pro.

ORANGE-SAUCED FISH WITH BROCCOLI

Prep: 15 minutes

Microwave: 12 minutes

Makes: 4 servings

1	pound fresh or frozen fish fillets, 1/2- to 3/4-inch thickness
1	10-ounce package frozen chopped broccoli
1	tablespoon water
1	cup water
1/2	cup orange marmalade
1/4	teaspoon salt
1	cup quick-cooking couscous
	Salt
	Black pepper
1	tablespoon butter or margarine
2	teaspoons lemon juice

1 Thaw fish, if frozen. Rinse fish; pat dry with paper towels. Cut into 4 serving-size portions; set aside.

2 Place broccoli and the 1 tablespoon water in a microwave-safe 2-quart square baking dish. Cover with vented plastic wrap. Microwave on 100% power (high) for 4 to 6 minutes or until crisp-tender, giving the dish a half-turn and stirring broccoli halfway through cooking.

3 Stir the 1 cup water, 2 tablespoons of the orange marmalade, and the 1/4 teaspoon salt into the broccoli. Stir in couscous. Spread couscous mixture evenly in dish. Arrange fish on the couscous mixture, folding under any thin edges; sprinkle fish with additional salt and pepper.

4 Cover with vented plastic wrap. Microwave on 100% power (high) for 7 to 9 minutes or until fish flakes easily when tested with a fork, giving the dish a half-turn halfway through cooking.

5 For sauce, in a small microwave-safe bowl combine remaining marmalade, the butter, and lemon juice. Microwave on high about 1 minute or until butter melts and sauce is bubbly. Stir sauce; drizzle over fish.

Nutrition Facts per serving: 420 cal., 5 g total fat (2 g sat. fat), 62 mg chol., 312 mg sodium, 66 g carbo., 5 g fiber, 29 g pro.

SESAME-COATED TILAPIA SALAD

Start to Finish:

20 minutes

Makes: 4 servings

1	pound fresh or frozen tilapia fillets
1/4	cup all-purpose flour
1/4	cup sesame seeds
1/2	teaspoon black pepper
2/3	cup bottled honey-Dijon salad dressing
2	tablespoons cooking oil
1	5-ounce package baby spinach and red leaf lettuce or baby spinach with radicchio

1 Thaw fish, if frozen. Rinse fish; pat dry with paper towels. Cut fish into 4 serving-size pieces.

2 In a shallow bowl combine the flour, sesame seeds, and pepper. Transfer 2 tablespoons of the salad dressing to a small bowl. Brush all sides of the fish pieces with the 2 tablespoons salad dressing. Firmly press both sides of each fish piece into sesame mixture.

3 In a 12-inch skillet heat oil over medium heat. Cook coated fish in hot oil about 6 minutes or until fish flakes easily when tested with a fork, turning once.

4 Divide spinach mixture among 4 dinner plates; top each with a fish piece. Drizzle with the remaining salad dressing.

Nutrition Facts per serving: 418 cal., 30 g total fat (3 g sat. fat), 0 mg chol., 247 mg sodium, 16 g carbo., 4 g fiber, 22 g pro.

SALMON WITH PESTO MAYONNAISE

. . . .

Makes: 4 servings

4   5- to 6-ounce skinless, boneless fresh or frozen salmon fillets

2   tablespoons crumbled firm-textured bread

¼   cup mayonnaise or salad dressing

3   tablespoons purchased basil pesto

1   tablespoon grated Parmesan cheese

1 Thaw fish, if frozen. Rinse fish; pat dry with paper towels. Preheat broiler. Place the bread crumbs in a shallow baking pan. Broil 4 inches from heat for 1 to 2 minutes or until lightly toasted, stirring once. Set bread crumbs aside.

2 Measure thickness of fish. Grease the unheated rack of a broiler pan; place fish on rack, tucking under any thin edges. Broil 4 inches from heat just until fish flakes easily when tested with a fork. (Allow 4 to 6 minutes per ½-inch thickness of fish.) If fillets are 1 inch thick or more, turn over halfway through broiling.

3 Meanwhile, in a small bowl stir together mayonnaise and pesto; set aside. Combine toasted bread crumbs and Parmesan cheese. Spoon mayonnaise mixture over fillets. Sprinkle with crumb mixture. Broil for 1 to 2 minutes more or until crumbs are lightly browned.

Nutrition Facts per serving: 363 cal., 24 g total fat (3 g sat. fat), 84 mg chol., 309 mg sodium, 5 g carbo., 0 g fiber, 31 g pro.

EASY CITRUS SALMON STEAKS

Prep: 10 minutes
Broil: 8 minutes

· · · · · · · · · · · · · · · · · · · ·

Makes: 2 servings

1   fresh or frozen salmon steak, cut 1 inch thick (about 8 ounces total)
1   teaspoon finely shredded lemon peel or orange peel
1   tablespoon lemon juice or orange juice
⅛   teaspoon black pepper
½   teaspoon bottled minced garlic (1 clove)
    Nonstick cooking spray
1   tablespoon sliced green onion
1   medium orange, peeled and sliced crosswise

1 Thaw fish, if frozen. Rinse fish; pat dry with paper towels. Preheat broiler. In a small bowl stir together lemon peel, lemon, pepper, and garlic.

2 Coat the unheated rack of a broiler pan with nonstick cooking spray. Place fish on rack. Brush with half of the juice mixture. Broil 4 inches from the heat for 5 minutes. Using a wide spatula, carefully turn fish. Brush with the remaining juice mixture. Broil for 3 to 7 minutes more or until fish flakes easily when tested with a fork.

3 To serve, cut the fish into 2 portions and sprinkle with green onion. Serve with orange slices.

Nutrition Facts per serving: 226 cal., 10 g total fat (2 g sat. fat), 70 mg chol., 54 mg sodium, 9 g carbo., 2 g fiber, 25 g pro.

GARDEN-PATCH FISH DINNER

Prep: 20 minutes
Bake: 25 minutes

Oven: 350°F
Makes: 6 servings

1½	pounds fresh or frozen skinless salmon fillets, cut into 6 serving-size portions
1	20-ounce package refrigerated mashed potatoes
¼	cup plain yogurt
¼	teaspoon salt
¼	teaspoon black pepper
3	tablespoons olive oil
½	cup snipped fresh basil
3	cups frozen green soybeans (shelled edamane) or peas, thawed
1	cup grape tomatoes or small cherry tomatoes
¼	teaspoon salt
¼	teaspoon black pepper

1 Thaw fish, if frozen. Rinse fish; pat dry with paper towels. Preheat oven to 350°. In a medium bowl stir together mashed potatoes, yogurt, ¼ teaspoon salt, and ¼ teaspoon pepper. Set aside.

2 In a large skillet heat oil over medium-low heat. Add basil. Cook and stir for 3 minutes. Add soybeans; cook and stir about 5 minutes more or until almost tender (if using peas, cook only for 1 minute).

3 With a slotted spoon, remove soybeans from skillet and divide among six 12- to 16-ounce casseroles or au gratin dishes. Divide tomatoes among the casseroles. Place fish on top of bean-tomato mixture. Sprinkle fish with ¼ teaspoon salt and ¼ teaspoon pepper. Brush with some of the basil-oil mixture from the skillet. Divide the potato mixture among the casseroles, spooning into a mound on one side of the fish in each casserole.

4 Bake, uncovered, in preheated oven about 25 minutes or until fish flakes easily when tested with a fork.

Nutrition Facts per serving: 470 cal., 21 g total fat (3 g sat. fat), 59 mg chol., 439 mg sodium, 30 g carbo., 7 g fiber, 42 g pro.

SALMON SCALLOPS WITH TARRAGON CREAM

Start to Finish:

20 minutes

....

Makes: 3 servings

12	ounces fresh or frozen salmon fillets or steaks
1	9-ounce package refrigerated fettuccine
2	cups thinly sliced zucchini, yellow summer squash, and/or red sweet pepper
1	teaspoon cooking oil
²/₃	cup milk
3	tablespoons reduced-fat cream cheese (Neufchâtel)
1	tablespoon snipped fresh tarragon, basil, or dill, or 1 teaspoon dried tarragon or basil, crushed, or 1 teaspoon dried dill
¼	teaspoon black pepper

1 Thaw fish, if frozen. Skin fish, if necessary. Rinse fish; pat dry with paper towels. Cut fish into 1-inch pieces. Set aside.

2 Cook pasta according to package directions, adding vegetables to pasta for the last minute of cooking. Drain and keep warm.

3 Meanwhile, in a large nonstick skillet heat oil over medium-high heat. Add fish pieces; cook, stirring gently, for 3 to 5 minutes or until fish flakes easily when tested with fork. Remove fish from skillet. Add milk, cream cheese, herb, and pepper to skillet. Cook and whisk until cream cheese is melted and sauce is smooth. Return fish to skillet. Cook and stir gently until heated through. Serve over fettuccine and vegetables.

Nutrition Facts per serving: 535 cal., 21 g total fat (6 g sat. fat), 171 mg chol., 172 mg sodium, 50 g carbo., 3 g fiber, 37 g pro.

PESCE ITALIANO

Start to Finish:

30 minutes

Makes: 2 servings

2   fresh or frozen salmon, tuna, or swordfish steaks, ³/₄-inch thickness (about 12 ounces)

1   cup dried penne pasta

1   teaspoon Creole seasoning

1   cup sliced fresh mushrooms

¹/₃   cup dry white wine

2   tablespoons purchased basil pesto

1   tablespoon lemon juice

2   teaspoons drained capers

1   tablespoon olive oil

1 Thaw fish, if frozen. Rinse fish; pat dry with paper towels. In a large saucepan cook the pasta in lightly salted boiling water for 4 minutes; drain and set aside. (Pasta will not be tender.)

2 Meanwhile, sprinkle both sides of the fish steaks with the Creole seasoning; set aside. (If using salt-free Creole seasoning, sprinkle fish with ¹/₄ teaspoon salt.) In a medium bowl combine the partially cooked pasta, the mushrooms, wine, pesto, lemon juice, and capers; set aside.

3 In a large skillet heat oil over medium-high heat. Add fish steaks; cook for 2 minutes, turning once. Reduce heat to medium. Spoon pasta mixture around fish steaks in the skillet. Bring to boiling; reduce heat to medium. Simmer, covered, over medium heat for 6 to 9 minutes or until fish flakes easily when tested with a fork.

Nutrition Facts per serving: 627 cal., 30 g total fat (5 g sat. fat), 109 mg chol., 352 mg sodium, 36 g carbo., 2 g fiber, 46 g pro.

BROILED HALIBUT WITH DIJON CREAM

Start to Finish:

15 minutes

....

Makes: 4 servings

4	fresh or frozen halibut steaks, cut 1 inch thick (1 to 1½ pounds)
1	teaspoon Greek-style or Mediterranean seasoning blend
¼	teaspoon coarsely ground black pepper
¼	cup dairy sour cream
¼	cup creamy Dijon-style mustard blend
1	tablespoon milk
½	teaspoon dried oregano, crushed

1 Preheat broiler. Thaw fish, if frozen. Rinse fish; pat dry with paper towels. Grease the unheated rack of a broiler pan; place fish on rack. Sprinkle fish with Greek-style seasoning and pepper.

2 Broil fish 4 inches from the heat for 8 to 12 minutes or until fish flakes easily when tested with a fork, turning once halfway through broiling. Invert fish onto serving platter.

3 Meanwhile, for sauce, in a small bowl combine sour cream, mustard blend, milk, and oregano. Serve sauce over fish.

Nutrition Facts per serving: 168 cal., 5 g total fat (2 g sat. fat), 42 mg chol., 300 mg sodium, 4 g carbo., 0 g fiber, 24 g pro.

GINGER SCALLION FISH

Start to Finish:

20 minutes

. . . .

Makes: 4 servings

4   4-ounce fresh or frozen skinless sea bass or other firm-fleshed white fish fillets, ¾- to 1-inch thickness

⅔   cup thinly sliced scallions or green onions

4   teaspoons lemon juice or dry sherry

2   teaspoons grated fresh ginger

1   teaspoon bottled minced garlic (2 cloves)

2   teaspoons bottled fish sauce or reduced-sodium soy sauce

1   small fresh jalapeño chile pepper, seeded and finely chopped*

1 Thaw fish, if frozen. Rinse fish; pat dry with paper towels. In a small bowl stir together scallions, 2 teaspoons of the lemon juice, the ginger, and garlic.

2 Arrange fish fillets in a single layer in a microwave-safe shallow baking dish, tucking under any thin edges. Spoon scallion mixture over fish. Cover dish with vented plastic wrap. Microwave on 100% power for 3 to 5 minutes or until fish flakes easily when tested with a fork, giving the dish a half-turn halfway through cooking.

3 Using a slotted spatula, transfer fish to 4 dinner plates. In a small bowl stir together fish sauce, jalapeño pepper, and remaining 2 teaspoons lemon juice or sherry; drizzle over fish.

***Note:** Because chile peppers contain volatile oils that can burn your skin and eyes, avoid direct contact with them as much as possible. When working with chile peppers, wear plastic or rubber gloves. If your bare hands do touch the peppers, wash your hands and nails well with soap and warm water.

Nutrition Facts per serving: 121 cal., 2 g total fat (1 g sat. fat), 46 mg chol., 312 mg sodium, 3 g carbo., 1 g fiber, 22 g pro.

CRUNCHY CATFISH & ZUCCHINI

Prep: 15 minutes
Bake: 12 minutes

· · · · · · · · · · · · · · · · · · · ·

Oven: 425°F
Makes: 4 servings

1	pound fresh or frozen catfish fillets
1	medium zucchini or yellow summer squash
4	cups cornflakes
1	cup bottled ranch salad dressing
2	teaspoons bottled hot pepper sauce

1 Thaw fish, if frozen. Grease a 15×10×1-inch baking pan; set aside. Rinse fish; pat dry with paper towels. Bias-cut fish into 1-inch-wide strips. Cut the zucchini in half crosswise; cut each half lengthwise into 6 wedges.

2 Preheat oven to 425°. Place the cornflakes in a large resealable plastic bag; seal bag. Crush cornflakes slightly; set aside. In a large bowl combine the ranch dressing and hot pepper sauce. Set aside half of the dressing mixture to use as a dipping sauce. Add catfish and zucchini strips to remaining dressing mixture in bowl; stir gently to coat.

3 Add one-third of the zucchini and one-third of the fish to the bag with the crushed cornflakes. Seal and shake to coat. Remove zucchini and fish; place in a single layer in prepared baking pan. Repeat with remaining zucchini and fish.

4 Bake in preheated oven for 12 to 15 minutes or until fish flakes easily when tested with a fork and coating is golden. Serve with reserved dressing mixture.

Nutrition Facts per serving: 545 cal., 40 g total fat (7 g sat. fat), 58 mg chol., 779 mg sodium, 24 g carbo., 0 g fiber, 20 g pro.

EASY BAKED FISH

Prep: 10 minutes
Bake: 18 minutes

· ·

Oven: 425°F
Makes: 4 servings

½   cup packaged herb-seasoned stuffing mix, finely crushed
2   tablespoons butter, melted
2   7.6-ounce packages frozen Caesar Parmesan or grill-flavored fish portions (4 portions total)
2   teaspoons lemon juice

1 Preheat oven to 425°. In a small bowl combine dry stuffing mix and melted butter, tossing until well mixed.

2 Lightly grease a 2-quart rectangular baking dish; place frozen fish portions in prepared baking dish. Sprinkle with lemon juice. Sprinkle crumb mixture over fish.

3 Bake in preheated oven for 18 to 20 minutes or until fish flakes easily when tested with a fork.

Nutrition Facts per serving: 183 cal., 9 g total fat (4 g sat. fat), 76 mg chol., 401 mg sodium, 6 g carbo., 1 g fiber, 18 g pro.

SMOKED SALMON PASTA

. . . .

Makes: 4 to 6 servings

8 ounces dried bow ties or mini lasagna pasta

1 cup whipping cream

½ teaspoon seafood seasoning blend

8 ounces smoked salmon, flaked, with skin and bones removed
if present

½ cup drained bottled roasted red sweet peppers, cut into bite-size
strips

1 In a large saucepan cook pasta according to package directions.

2 Meanwhile, in a medium saucepan combine whipping cream and seasoning; cook over medium heat until bubbly. Continue to cook, uncovered, about 5 minutes or until thickened, stirring occasionally.

3 Stir in salmon and roasted red pepper strips; heat through. Drain pasta; return to pan. Add salmon mixture to pasta. Toss to coat.

Nutrition Facts per serving: 489 cal., 26 g total fat (14 g sat. fat), 95 mg chol., 552 mg sodium, 45 g carbo., 2 g fiber, 19 g pro.

SALMON CAESAR SALAD

Start to Finish:

15 minutes

. . . .

Makes: 3 servings

1   10-ounce package Caesar salad (includes lettuce, dressing, croutons, and cheese)*

1   small yellow, red, or green sweet pepper, cut into thin strips

1   small cucumber, quartered lengthwise and sliced

6   ounces smoked, poached, or canned salmon, skinned, boned, and broken into chunks (1 cup)

½   of a lemon, cut into 3 wedges

1 In a large bowl combine the lettuce and dressing from the packaged salad, the sweet pepper strips, and cucumber; toss gently to coat.

2 Add salmon and the croutons and cheese from the packaged salad; toss gently to mix. Divide among 3 dinner plates. Before serving, squeeze juice from a lemon wedge over each salad.

*Note: If you can't find packaged Caesar salad, substitute 5 cups torn mixed salad greens, ⅓ cup purchased croutons, 3 tablespoons bottled Caesar or ranch salad dressing, and 2 tablespoons grated Parmesan cheese.

Nutrition Facts per serving: 199 cal., 11 g total fat (1 g sat. fat), 16 mg chol., 564 mg sodium, 10 g carbo., 2 g fiber, 14 g pro.

SALMON-SAUCED BISCUITS

Start to Finish:

30 minutes

. . . .

Makes: 4 servings

4	frozen individual ready-to-bake biscuits or 4 English muffins, split
1	10-ounce container refrigerated Alfredo pasta sauce
1	9- to 10-ounce package frozen cut asparagus, thawed
1	4-ounce can (drained weight) mushroom stems and pieces, drained
1	teaspoon lemon juice
¼	teaspoon dried dill
1	6-ounce can skinless, boneless salmon, drained and flaked
1	tablespoon dry sherry

1 Bake biscuits according to package directions. Cool biscuits slightly; split biscuits.

2 Meanwhile, in a medium saucepan combine Alfredo pasta sauce, thawed asparagus, mushrooms, lemon juice, and dill. Cook and stir over medium heat until bubbly and heated through. Remove from heat; stir in salmon and sherry.

3 Spoon salmon mixture over biscuits.

Nutrition Facts per serving: 498 cal., 33 g total fat (3 g sat. fat), 59 mg chol., 1,158 mg sodium, 31 g carbo., 3 g fiber, 18 g pro.

SALMON SHORTCAKES

Prep: 15 minutes
Cook: 9 minutes

· ·

Makes: 4 servings

1   egg
2   tablespoons mayonnaise or salad dressing
1   14³/₄-ounce can salmon, drained, flaked, and skin and bones removed
³/₄   cup soft bread crumbs
1   green onion, chopped
1   tablespoon butter or margarine
4   purchased buttermilk biscuits or one 10.8-ounce package refrigerated large flaky biscuits (5), baked*
1   recipe Herbed Mayonnaise

1 In a large bowl whisk together egg and mayonnaise; stir in salmon, bread crumbs, and green onion. Form the mixture into eight ³/₄-inch-thick patties.

2 In a large skillet melt butter over medium heat. Cook patties in hot butter about 9 minutes or until brown, turning once.

3 Split biscuits. Top biscuit halves with salmon patties; spoon Herbed Mayonnaise over patties.

Herbed Mayonnaise: In a small bowl stir together ¹/₄ cup mayonnaise, 1 tablespoon snipped fresh dill, and 1 tablespoon milk. Add enough additional milk, 1 teaspoon at a time, to make of drizzling consistency. Makes about ¹/₃ cup.

*Note: If desired, you may warm already baked biscuits in the oven or microwave before serving.

Nutrition Facts per serving: 528 cal., 37 g total fat (9 g sat. fat), 129 mg chol., 1,129 mg sodium, 23 g carbo., 1 g fiber, 26 g pro.

TUNA ALFREDO CASSEROLE

Prep: 20 minutes
Bake: 10 minutes

. . . .

Oven: 425°F
Makes: 6 servings

3   cups dried rigatoni or penne pasta

1   cup fresh pea pods

1   10-ounce container refrigerated Alfredo pasta sauce or four-cheese pasta sauce or 1¼ cups bottled Alfredo pasta sauce or four-cheese pasta sauce

3   tablespoons milk

2   tablespoons purchased dried tomato pesto

1   12-ounce can solid white tuna (water pack), drained and broken into chunks

¼   cup finely shredded Parmesan cheese (1 ounce)

1 Preheat oven to 425°. In a Dutch oven cook pasta according to package directions, adding the pea pods during the last minute of cooking. Drain well; return to Dutch oven.

2 Meanwhile, in a medium bowl combine Alfredo sauce, milk, and pesto. Add to pasta, stirring gently to coat. Gently fold in tuna.

3 Transfer pasta mixture to a 2-quart oval baking dish. Sprinkle with Parmesan cheese. Bake in preheated oven for 10 to 15 minutes or until heated through and just until cheese is melted.

Nutrition Facts per serving: 414 cal., 20 g total fat (2 g sat. fat), 51 mg chol., 516 mg sodium, 33 g carbo., 1 g fiber, 23 g pro.

TUNA SPINACH BRAID

Prep: 25 minutes
Bake: 18 minutes

. . . .

Oven: 375°F
Makes: 4 to 6 servings

1   10-ounce package frozen chopped spinach, thawed and well drained

1   9$\frac{1}{4}$-ounce can chunk white tuna (water pack), drained and flaked

1   cup light ricotta cheese or cream-style cottage cheese, drained

$\frac{1}{2}$ cup grated Parmesan cheese (2 ounces)

$\frac{1}{2}$ teaspoon bottled minced garlic (1 clove)

1   8-ounce package refrigerated crescent rolls (8)

3   thick slices provolone cheese (3 ounces)

     Chopped tomato (optional)

     Grated Parmesan cheese (optional)

1 Preheat oven to 375°. For filling, in a medium bowl stir together spinach, tuna, ricotta cheese, the $\frac{1}{2}$ cup Parmesan cheese, and the garlic; set aside.

2 Unroll and separate crescent roll dough into 4 rectangles. On an ungreased baking sheet or shallow baking pan, place rectangles together, overlapping edges slightly to form a 14×10-inch rectangle. Firmly press edges and perforations together to seal.

3 Spread filling in a 3$\frac{1}{2}$-inch-wide strip, lengthwise down the center of dough. Top with provolone, cutting cheese as necessary to cover the filling.

4 Make cuts in dough at 1-inch intervals on both long sides of rectangle just to the edge of the filling. Fold dough strips diagonally over filling, overlapping strips and alternating from side to side to give a braided appearance.

5 Bake in preheated oven for 18 to 20 minutes or until golden. Serve warm. If desired, serve with chopped tomatoes and additional grated Parmesan cheese.

Nutrition Facts per serving: 507 cal., 28 g total fat (11 g sat. fat), 69 mg chol., 1,208 mg sodium, 29 g carbo., 2 g fiber, 38 g pro.

SALMON-SOUR CREAM TURNOVERS

Prep: 15 minutes
Bake: 25 minutes

. . . .

Oven: 375°F
Makes: 4 servings

1	15-ounce package folded refrigerated unbaked piecrusts (2 crusts)
1	tablespoon all-purpose flour
⅓	cup dairy sour cream dip with chives
2	6-ounce cans skinless, boneless salmon, drained and flaked
½	cup chopped celery
¼	cup finely chopped red or green sweet pepper
	Milk
1	teaspoon sesame seeds

1 Preheat oven to 375°. Let piecrusts stand at room temperature for 15 minutes as directed on package.

2 Meanwhile, in a medium bowl stir flour into the sour cream dip. Fold in salmon, celery, and sweet pepper.

3 Unfold piecrusts. Spread half of the salmon mixture onto one half of each piecrust, spreading to within 1 inch of the edges. Moisten edges with water. Carefully lift and fold piecrusts in half over filling; turn edges under. Seal edges with the tines of a fork. Cut slits in tops of turnovers to allow steam to escape. Brush tops of turnovers with milk; sprinkle with sesame seeds. Transfer turnovers to a large baking sheet.

4 Bake in preheated oven for 25 to 30 minutes or until pastry is golden. Let stand for 5 minutes before removing from baking sheet.

Nutrition Facts per serving: 658 cal., 36 g total fat (15 g sat. fat), 80 mg chol., 996 mg sodium, 57 g carbo., 1 g fiber, 20 g pro.

CURRIED TUNA CUPS

Start to Finish:
15 minutes

....

Makes: 4 servings

1½ cups purchased creamy coleslaw

1 small tomato, seeded and chopped

1 teaspoon curry powder

1 6-ounce can tuna, drained and flaked

4 large butterhead (Bibb or Boston) lettuce leaves

¼ cup chopped peanuts

Dairy sour cream dip with chives (optional)

1 In a small bowl stir together coleslaw, tomato, and curry powder. Fold in tuna.

2 To serve, spoon the tuna mixture into lettuce leaves. Sprinkle with peanuts. If desired, top with dip.

Nutrition Facts per serving: 148 cal., 7 g total fat (1 g sat. fat), 21 mg chol., 213 mg sodium, 9 g carbo., 2 g fiber, 14 g pro.

TUNA SALAD WITH A TWIST

Start to Finish:

15 minutes

Makes: 4 servings

1   12-ounce can solid white tuna (water pack), drained

⅓   cup bottled creamy Italian salad dressing

¼   cup chopped green or red sweet pepper

4   butterhead (Boston or Bibb) lettuce leaves

2   sourdough, sesame, or plain bagels, halved and toasted

1 In a medium bowl combine drained tuna, salad dressing, and sweet pepper.

2 Place lettuce leaves on the cut sides of the toasted bagel halves. Spoon tuna mixture over the lettuce leaves.

Nutrition Facts per serving: 276 cal., 10 g total fat (2 g sat. fat), 38 mg chol., 902 mg sodium, 22 g carbo., 1 g fiber, 24 g pro.

SWEET-&-SOUR SHRIMP

Start to Finish:

15 minutes

....

Makes: 4 servings

1	12-ounce package frozen peeled, deveined shrimp
1/3	cup bottled stir-fry sauce
1/4	cup pineapple-orange juice*
	Nonstick cooking spray
3	cups assorted fresh stir-fry vegetables (from produce department)

1 Thaw shrimp. Rinse shrimp; pat dry with paper towels. Set aside. In a small bowl combine stir-fry sauce and pineapple-orange juice; set aside.

2 Coat an unheated nonstick wok or large skillet with cooking spray. (Add oil during cooking, if necessary.) Preheat wok over medium-high heat.

3 Add vegetables to wok; stir-fry for 3 to 5 minutes or until crisp-tender. Remove vegetables from wok. Add shrimp; stir-fry for 2 to 3 minutes or until shrimp turn opaque. Push shrimp to side of wok.

4 Add sauce mixture to wok. Return vegetables to wok. Toss gently to coat. Cook and stir about 1 minute more or until heated through.

*Note: If you can't find pineapple-orange juice, substitute orange juice or apple juice.

Nutrition Facts per serving: 119 cal., 1 g total fat (0 g sat. fat), 131 mg chol., 666 mg sodium, 11 g carbo., 2 g fiber, 17 g pro.

SPANISH-STYLE RICE WITH SEAFOOD

Start to Finish:

25 minutes

. . . .

Makes: 4 servings

1	5.6- to 6.2-ounce package Spanish-style rice mix
1¾	cups water
1	tablespoon butter or margarine
	Several dashes bottled hot pepper sauce
1	12-ounce package frozen peeled, deveined shrimp
1	cup loose-pack frozen peas
1	medium tomato, chopped

1 In a large skillet stir together rice mix, the water, butter, and hot pepper sauce. Bring to boiling; reduce heat. Simmer, covered, for 5 minutes.

2 Stir shrimp into rice mixture. Return to boiling; reduce heat. Simmer, covered, for 2 to 3 minutes more or until shrimp turn opaque. Remove from heat. Stir in peas. Cover and let stand for 10 minutes. Sprinkle with tomato before serving.

Nutrition Facts per serving: 282 cal., 5 g total fat (2 g sat. fat), 137 mg chol., 897 mg sodium, 36 g carbo., 3 g fiber, 23 g pro.

SHRIMP OVER RICE

Start to Finish:

25 minutes

. . . .

Makes: 4 servings

1   cup uncooked instant rice

3   cups water

1   12-ounce package frozen peeled, deveined shrimp

1   15½-ounce jar chunky-style meatless spaghetti sauce (about 2 cups)

¼   cup dry red wine

¼   teaspoon Worcestershire sauce
     Several dashes bottled hot pepper sauce

1 Prepare rice according to package directions. Set aside.

2 Meanwhile, in a large saucepan bring the water to boiling. Add shrimp to water. Return to boiling; reduce heat. Simmer, uncovered, for 1 to 3 minutes or until shrimp turn opaque. Drain in a colander.

3 In the same large saucepan combine spaghetti sauce, red wine, Worcestershire sauce, and hot pepper sauce. Bring to boiling. Stir in shrimp; heat through. Serve shrimp mixture over rice.

Nutrition Facts per serving: 246 cal., 2 g total fat (0 g sat. fat), 129 mg chol., 657 mg sodium, 34 g carbo., 3 g fiber, 21 g pro.

SHRIMP ALFREDO FOR TWO

1½   cups water

½   cup milk

2   tablespoons butter or margarine

1   4.4-ounce package noodles with Alfredo-style sauce

1   medium zucchini, thinly sliced (1½ cups)

6   ounces frozen peeled, deveined, cooked shrimp, thawed, or 6 ounces chunk-style imitation crabmeat

1 In a medium saucepan combine the water, milk, and butter. Bring to boiling. Stir in noodle mix. Return to boiling; reduce heat. Simmer, uncovered, for 5 minutes.

2 Stir in zucchini. Return to a gentle boil; cook, uncovered, about 3 minutes more or until noodles are tender.

3 Gently stir in shrimp. Heat through. Remove from heat; let stand for 3 to 5 minutes or until slightly thickened.

Nutrition Facts per serving: 486 cal., 21 g total fat (12 g sat. fat), 264 mg chol., 1,279 mg sodium, 44 g carbo., 2 g fiber, 30 g pro.

SAUCY SHRIMP OVER POLENTA

Start to Finish:

25 minutes

....

Makes: 6 servings

18	fresh or frozen peeled and deveined, cooked shrimp, tails removed (about 8 ounces)
1	16-ounce tube refrigerated cooked polenta, cut crosswise into 12 slices
1	tablespoon cooking oil
2	cups loose-pack frozen whole kernel corn
4	medium Roma tomatoes, chopped (about 1½ cups)
3	tablespoons balsamic vinegar
1	teaspoon dried thyme, crushed
½	teaspoon ground cumin
¼	teaspoon salt

1 Thaw shrimp, if frozen. Rinse shrimp; pat dry with paper towels. Set aside. In a large skillet cook polenta slices in hot oil for 5 to 8 minutes or until golden, turning once. Transfer to a serving platter; keep warm.

2 In the same large skillet combine corn, tomatoes, balsamic vinegar, thyme, cumin, and salt. Cook and stir about 5 minutes or until heated through. Stir in shrimp. Cook and stir until heated through.

3 Using a slotted spoon, spoon shrimp mixture over polenta slices.

Nutrition Facts per serving: 196 cal., 3 g total fat (1 g sat. fat), 74 mg chol., 483 mg sodium, 30 g carbo., 4 g fiber, 12 g pro.

CURRIED SHRIMP ON RICE

Start to Finish:

25 minutes

. . . .

Makes: 4 servings

1 10-ounce container refrigerated Alfredo pasta sauce

2 to 3 teaspoons curry powder

12 ounces peeled and deveined, cooked medium shrimp*
    Hot cooked rice

¼ cup slivered almonds, toasted

1 In a large saucepan combine Alfredo sauce and curry powder. If necessary, stir in 1 or 2 tablespoons water to thin sauce. Cook and stir over medium heat just boiling.

2 Add shrimp. Cook and stir for 2 to 3 minutes more or until heated through. Serve shrimp mixture over rice; sprinkle with almonds.

***Note:** If tails are present on the shrimp, remove them before using.

Nutrition Facts per serving: 550 cal., 29 g total fat (1 g sat. fat), 206 mg chol., 426 mg sodium, 41 g carbo., 2 g fiber, 32 g pro.

EASY SEAFOOD QUICHE

Prep: 15 minutes
Bake: 52 minutes

. . . .

Oven: 450°F/350°F
Makes: 8 servings

½ of a 15-ounce package folded refrigerated unbaked piecrust (1 crust)

6 eggs

1 cup cream-style cottage cheese

1 cup shredded Italian cheese blend (4 ounces)

1 6- to 8-ounce package flake-style imitation crabmeat

3 green onions, thinly sliced

1 Preheat oven to 450°. Let piecrust stand at room temperature for 15 minutes as directed on package. Meanwhile, grease a 9-inch pie plate. Line prepared pie plate with piecrust; fold under edge. Crimp as desired. Line unpricked piecrust with a double thickness of foil.

2 Bake in preheated oven for 8 minutes. Remove foil. Bake for 4 to 5 minutes more or until pastry is set and dry. Remove from oven; reduce oven temperature to 350°.

3 For filling, in a medium bowl beat eggs with a fork; stir in cottage cheese, shredded cheese, flaked imitation crabmeat, and green onions. Pour into prebaked piecrust.

4 Bake in the 350° oven for 40 to 45 minutes or until a knife inserted near the center comes out clean. If necessary, cover edge of piecrust with foil during baking to prevent overbrowning. Let stand for 10 minutes before serving.

Nutrition Facts per serving: 266 cal., 16 g total fat (7 g sat. fat), 205 mg chol., 440 mg sodium, 14 g carbo., 0 g fiber, 16 g pro.

ROCKEFELLER-STYLE CRAB

Prep: 15 minutes
Bake: 30 minutes

. . . .

Oven: 400°F
Makes: 4 servings

2   12-ounce packages frozen spinach soufflé, thawed

2   6½-ounce cans refrigerated, pasteurized crabmeat, drained and broken into large flakes

2   cups packaged herb-seasoned dry stuffing mix

¼   teaspoon bottled hot pepper sauce

2   tablespoons butter, melted

1 Preheat oven to 400°. In a large bowl combine thawed spinach soufflé, crabmeat, 1½ cups of the dry stuffing mix, and the hot pepper sauce. Spread in an ungreased 1-quart au gratin dish.

2 In a small bowl combine remaining ½ cup dry stuffing mix and the melted butter; sprinkle over spinach mixture.

3 Bake in preheated oven about 30 minutes or until heated through.

Nutrition Facts per serving: 433 cal., 20 g total fat (7 g sat. fat), 263 mg chol., 1,516 mg sodium, 36 g carbo., 3 g fiber, 27 g pro.

SOUPS & STEWS

OVEN STEW

Prep: **15** minutes
Bake: **2** hours

· · · · · · · · · · · · · · · · · · · ·

Oven: 350°F
Makes: 6 servings

1	pound beef stew meat (1-inch cubes)
¼	teaspoon salt
¼	teaspoon black pepper
1	16-ounce package frozen stew vegetables
1	4½-ounce jar (drained weight) whole mushrooms, drained
1	10¾-ounce can condensed cream of celery soup
1	10¾-ounce can condensed beefy mushroom or cream of mushroom soup
1¼	cups water
¼	cup dry sherry (optional)

1 Preheat oven to 350°. Place meat in a 4-quart Dutch oven. Sprinkle with salt and pepper. Stir in stew vegetables and mushrooms. In a medium bowl combine celery soup, mushroom soup, the water, and, if desired, sherry; pour over stew. Stir to combine.

2 Cover and bake in preheated oven for 2 to 2½ hours or until meat and vegetables are tender. Stir. Cut up any large vegetable chunks before serving.

Nutrition Facts per serving: 199 cal., 6 g total fat (2 g sat. fat), 53 mg chol., 1,053 mg sodium, 15 g carbo., 2 g fiber, 20 g pro.

FRENCH ONION & BEEF SOUP

Start to Finish:

25 minutes

. . . .

Makes: 4 servings

3	tablespoons butter or margarine
1	medium onion, thinly sliced and separated into rings
2	10½-ounce cans condensed French onion soup
2½	cups water
8	ounces cooked beef, cubed (2 cups)
4	1-inch-thick slices French bread
½	cup shredded Gruyère or Swiss cheese (2 ounces)

1 Preheat broiler. In a large skillet melt butter over medium heat. Add onion; cook about 5 minutes or until very tender. Stir in French onion soup, the water, and cooked beef. Bring to boiling, stirring occasionally.

2 Meanwhile, place the bread slices on a baking sheet. Broil 4 inches from the heat about 1 minute or until toasted on one side. Top the toasted side of bread slices with shredded cheese; broil about 1 minute more or until cheese is melted.

3 To serve, ladle soup into soup bowls. Top with bread slices, cheese sides up.

Nutrition Facts per serving: 465 cal., 21 g total fat (10 g sat. fat), 82 mg chol., 1,701 mg sodium, 40 g carbo., 3 g fiber, 28 g pro.

MEATBALL STEW

Start to Finish:

30 minutes

Makes: 6 servings

2	14-ounce cans reduced-sodium beef broth
1	14½-ounce can diced tomatoes, undrained
½	cup water
2	medium carrots, diced
2	stalks celery, sliced
1	large onion, chopped
⅓	cup quick-cooking barley
1	teaspoon dried basil, crushed
1	bay leaf
1	16-ounce package frozen cooked meatballs (about 32 meatballs)

1 In a large saucepan or Dutch oven combine beef broth, undrained tomatoes, the water, carrots, celery, onion, barley, basil, and bay leaf. Bring to boiling over medium heat, stirring occasionally; reduce heat. Simmer, covered, for 5 minutes.

2 Add frozen meatballs. Return to boiling; reduce heat. Simmer, covered, about 5 minutes more or until meatballs are heated through and barley is tender, stirring once or twice. Discard bay leaf.

Nutrition Facts per serving: 330 cal., 22 g total fat (9 g sat. fat), 30 mg chol., 1,518 mg sodium, 21 g carbo., 5 g fiber, 13 g pro.

HURRY-UP BEEF-VEGETABLE STEW

. . . .

Makes: 5 servings

2	cups water
1	10¾-ounce can condensed golden mushroom soup
1	10¾-ounce can condensed tomato soup
½	cup dry red wine or beef broth
2	cups chopped cooked roast beef (about 10 ounces)
1	16-ounce package frozen sugar snap stir-fry vegetables or one 16-ounce package frozen cut broccoli
½	teaspoon dried thyme, crushed

1 In a 4-quart Dutch oven combine the water, mushroom soup, tomato soup, and wine. Stir in beef, frozen vegetables, and thyme.

2 Cook stew over medium heat until bubbly, stirring frequently. Continue cooking, uncovered, for 4 to 5 minutes or until vegetables are crisp-tender, stirring occasionally.

Nutrition Facts per serving: 231 cal., 4 g total fat (1 g sat. fat), 42 mg chol., 906 mg sodium, 21 g carbo., 4 g fiber, 20 g pro.

STUFFED GREEN PEPPER SOUP

Prep: 15 minutes
Cook: 20 minutes

Makes: 6 servings

8   ounces lean ground beef

2   14½-ounce cans diced tomatoes with green peppers and onions, undrained

3   cups water

1   14-ounce can beef broth

1   5.7-ounce package tomato basil risotto mix

1   medium green sweet pepper, chopped

1 In a large saucepan cook ground beef until meat is brown. Drain well. Stir undrained tomatoes, the water, broth, risotto mix and seasoning packet, and sweet pepper into meat in saucepan.

2 Bring to boiling; reduce heat. Simmer, covered, about 20 minutes or until rice is tender.

Nutrition Facts per serving: 214 cal., 5 g total fat (2 g sat. fat), 24 mg chol., 1,103 mg sodium, 32 g carbo., 3 g fiber, 11 g pro.

BISCUIT-TOPPED MEAT & BEAN STEW

Prep: 20 minutes
Bake: 15 minutes

. . . .

Oven: 375°F
Makes: 6 servings

1	pound ground beef, ground pork, and/or bulk sweet Italian sausage
1	15½-ounce can red kidney beans, rinsed and drained
1	14½-ounce can diced tomatoes, undrained
1	8-ounce can pizza sauce
1	tablespoon grated Parmesan cheese
1	tablespoon yellow cornmeal
1	teaspoon dried parsley, crushed
1	5-ounce package refrigerated biscuits (5)
2	tablespoons milk

1 Preheat oven to 375°. In a large skillet cook the ground meat until meat is brown. Drain off fat.

2 Stir beans, undrained tomatoes, and pizza sauce into meat in skillet. Cook and stir over medium heat until heated through. Transfer mixture to a 2-quart casserole.

3 Meanwhile, in a large plastic bag combine Parmesan cheese, cornmeal, and parsley. Quarter each biscuit. Dip biscuit pieces into milk. Place biscuit pieces in the plastic bag; shake to coat each biscuit piece.

4 Arrange biscuit pieces around outer edge of the casserole. Bake, uncovered, in preheated oven about 15 minutes or until biscuits are golden.

Nutrition Facts per serving: 329 cal., 14 g total fat (5 g sat. fat), 49 mg chol., 721 mg sodium, 30 g carbo., 5 g fiber, 23 g pro.

BROCCOLI-SWISS SOUP

Prep: 15 minutes
Cook: 10 minutes

Makes: 4 servings

2   14-ounce cans chicken broth
1   16-ounce package fresh broccoli florets
1   medium onion, chopped
2   teaspoons bottled roasted garlic
1   cup shredded Swiss cheese (4 ounces)
1   cup half-and-half or light cream
½   cup cubed ham
    Salt
    Black pepper

1 In a large saucepan combine broth, broccoli, onion, and garlic. Bring to boiling; reduce heat. Simmer, covered, about 10 minutes or until broccoli is very tender. In a blender container or food processor bowl blend or process the broccoli mixture, in 2 or 3 batches, until smooth.

2 Return to saucepan. Return to simmering. Add cheese; cook, stirring constantly, until melted. Stir in half-and-half or light cream and ham. Season to taste with salt and pepper.

Nutrition Facts per serving: 283 cal., 18 g total fat (10 g sat. fat), 58 mg chol., 1,213 mg sodium, 14 g carbo., 4 g fiber, 18 g pro.

MASHED POTATO SOUP

Start to Finish:

15 minutes

. . . .

Makes: 3 servings

1 20-ounce package refrigerated mashed potatoes

1 14-ounce can chicken broth

¼ cup sliced green onions

2 ounces Swiss, cheddar, or smoked Gouda cheese, shredded (½ cup)

   Dairy sour cream (optional)

1 In a medium saucepan combine mashed potatoes, broth, and green onions. Cook over medium-high heat just until mixture reaches boiling, whisking to make nearly smooth. Add cheese; whisk until cheese is melted. If desired, serve with sour cream.

Nutrition Facts per serving: 239 cal., 9 g total fat (4 g sat. fat), 17 mg chol., 917 mg sodium, 27 g carbo., 2 g fiber, 11 g pro.

GERMAN SAUSAGE CHOWDER

Start to Finish:

35 minutes

Makes: 6 to 8 servings

2 tablespoons butter or margarine

1 medium onion, chopped

1 stalk celery, chopped

2 tablespoons all-purpose flour

1 32-ounce box chicken broth

2 cups packaged shredded cabbage with carrot (coleslaw mix)

2 cups packaged refrigerated diced potatoes with onions

8 ounces kielbasa, cut into 1/2-inch-thick slices

1 teaspoon dried thyme, crushed

Salt

Black pepper

1 cup shredded Swiss cheese (4 ounces)

1 In a large saucepan melt butter over medium heat. Add onion and celery; cook until tender. Stir in flour; cook for 1 minute more. Stir in broth. Bring to boiling; cook until slightly thickened.

2 Stir coleslaw mix, potatoes, kielbasa, and thyme into broth mixture. Cook until cabbage is wilted and potatoes are heated through. Season to taste with salt and pepper. Top servings with Swiss cheese.

Nutrition Facts per serving: 317 cal., 22 g total fat (12 g sat. fat), 45 mg chol., 1,149 mg sodium, 17 g carbo., 2 g fiber, 13 g pro.

CORN & SAUSAGE CHOWDER

Start to Finish:

20 minutes

. . . .

Makes: 5 servings

1	20-ounce package refrigerated shredded potatoes
1	14-ounce can reduced-sodium chicken broth
1	10-ounce package frozen whole kernel corn
2	cups fat-free milk
1	12-ounce 97% fat-free cooked link sausage, halved lengthwise and sliced
1/3	cup sliced green onions
1/4	teaspoon black pepper
	Salt
	Fresh cilantro sprigs
	Green or red bottled hot pepper sauce (optional)

1 In a 4-quart Dutch oven combine potatoes, broth, and corn. Bring just to boiling; reduce heat. Simmer, covered, about 10 minutes or just until potatoes are tender, stirring occasionally. Using a potato masher, slightly mash potatoes. Stir in milk, sausage, green onions, and black pepper. Heat through. Season to taste with salt, cilantro, and, if desired, hot pepper sauce.

Nutrition Facts per serving: 264 cal., 3 g total fat (0 g sat. fat), 26 mg chol., 1,243 mg sodium, 42 g carbo., 3 g fiber, 19 g pro.

PIZZA SOUP

. . . .

Makes: 6 servings

1   cup chopped onion

1   cup chopped green sweet pepper

1   cup sliced fresh mushrooms

1   cup halved, sliced zucchini

1   14-ounce can beef broth

1   14½-ounce can Italian-style tomatoes, undrained and cut up

1   8-ounce can pizza sauce

4   ounces cooked smoked sausage links, thinly sliced

½   teaspoon pizza seasoning

½   cup shredded reduced-fat mozzarella cheese (2 ounces)

1 In a medium saucepan combine onion, sweet pepper, mushrooms, zucchini, and ¼ cup of the beef broth. Bring to boiling; reduce heat. Simmer, covered, for 5 minutes.

2 Stir in the remaining beef broth, the undrained tomatoes, pizza sauce, sausage, and pizza seasoning. Simmer for 5 to 10 minutes more or until vegetables are tender. Top each serving with cheese.

Nutrition Facts per serving: 163 cal., 9 g total fat (3 g sat. fat), 18 mg chol., 919 mg sodium, 12 g carbo., 2 g fiber, 10 g pro.

RANGE-TOP SAUSAGE SOUP

Start to Finish:

25 minutes

. . . .

Makes: 3 or 4 servings

1   7-ounce package frozen maple-flavored brown-and-serve sausage links or original brown-and-serve sausage links (10 links)

1   15-ounce can Great Northern beans

1   cup sliced cauliflower florets

½   cup water

1   8-ounce can pizza sauce

1 Cut each of the sausage links into thirds. In a medium saucepan cook the sausage pieces over medium-high heat about 7 minutes or until brown. Stir in the undrained beans, cauliflower, and the water.

2 Bring to boiling; reduce heat. Simmer, covered, for 8 to 10 minutes or until cauliflower is tender. Stir in pizza sauce; heat through.

Nutrition Facts per serving: 469 cal., 30 g total fat (10 g sat. fat), 58 mg chol., 1,501 mg sodium, 31 g carbo., 8 g fiber, 21 g pro.

CHICKEN TORTILLA SOUP

Prep: 20 minutes

Cook: 15 minutes

Makes: 6 servings

1	2- to 2¼-pound deli-roasted chicken
2	14-ounce cans chicken broth with roasted garlic
1	15-ounce can chopped tomatoes and green chile peppers, undrained
1	11-ounce can whole kernel corn with sweet peppers, drained
1	small fresh jalapeño chile pepper, seeded and finely chopped*
1	teaspoon ground cumin
2	tablespoons snipped fresh cilantro
1	tablespoon lime juice
	Tortilla chips with lime or regular tortilla chips, broken

1 Remove chicken meat from the frame of the deli-roasted chicken. Shred enough of the chicken meat to measure 2 cups; set aside. Reserve any remaining chicken meat for another use.

2 In a large saucepan combine chicken broth, undrained tomatoes, corn, jalapeño, and cumin. Bring to boiling; reduce heat. Simmer, covered, for 10 minutes. Stir in shredded chicken, cilantro, and lime juice. Heat through. Top each serving with tortilla chips.

***Note:** Because chile peppers contain volatile oils that can burn your skin and eyes, avoid direct contact with them as much as possible. When working with chile peppers, wear plastic or rubber gloves. If your bare hands do touch the peppers, wash your hands and nails well with soap and warm water.

Nutrition Facts per serving: 183 cal., 5 g total fat (1 g sat. fat), 43 mg chol., 1,080 mg sodium, 18 g carbo., 2 g fiber, 16 g pro.

CHICKEN WITH VEGETABLES SOUP

Start to Finish:

25 minutes

Makes: 4 servings

2   14-ounce cans chicken broth

2   cups frozen stir-fry vegetables (any combination)

1   9-ounce package refrigerated or frozen chopped, cooked chicken breast

1   tablespoon soy sauce

1   to 2 teaspoons hot chili sauce

½   teaspoon toasted sesame oil

¼   teaspoon ground ginger

1   3-ounce package ramen noodles, broken

2   tablespoons sliced green onion

1 In a large saucepan combine broth, frozen vegetables, chicken, soy sauce, chili sauce, sesame oil, and ginger. Bring to boiling; reduce heat. Simmer, covered, for 5 minutes.

2 Stir in ramen noodles (discard seasoning packet). Return to boiling; reduce heat. Simmer, covered, about 3 minutes more or until vegetables and noodles are tender. Top each serving with green onion.

Nutrition Facts per serving: 251 cal., 7 g total fat (2 g sat. fat), 74 mg chol., 1,126 mg sodium, 20 g carbo., 2 g fiber, 26 g pro.

CHICKEN VEGETABLE SOUP

Start to Finish:

25 minutes

. . . .

Makes: 4 servings

1   16-ounce package loose-pack frozen Italian vegetables (zucchini, carrots, cauliflower, lima beans, and Italian beans)

1   14½-ounce can Italian-style stewed tomatoes, undrained

1   12-ounce can vegetable juice

1   cup chicken broth

1½   cups chopped cooked chicken (about 8 ounces)

1 In a large saucepan combine frozen vegetables, undrained tomatoes, vegetable juice, and chicken broth.

2 Bring to boiling; reduce heat. Simmer, covered, about 10 minutes or until vegetables are tender. Stir in chicken. Heat through.

Nutrition Facts per serving: 206 cal., 5 g total fat (1 g sat. fat), 47 mg chol., 784 mg sodium, 18 g carbo., 4 g fiber, 18 g pro.

PASTA & BEAN CHICKEN SOUP

Start to Finish:
25 minutes

Makes: 5 servings

3½	cups reduced-sodium chicken broth
1	19-ounce can white kidney beans (cannellini beans) or one 15-ounce can Great Northern beans, rinsed and drained
1	14½-ounce can diced tomatoes with onion and garlic or diced tomatoes with basil, oregano, and garlic, undrained
2	cups chopped cooked chicken (about 10 ounces)
1½	cups thinly sliced carrots
1	cup water
1	cup dried ditalini or tiny bow ties (4 ounces)
¼	cup purchased pesto

1 In a large saucepan combine broth, beans, undrained tomatoes, chicken, carrots, the water, and pasta.

2 Bring to boiling; reduce heat. Simmer, covered, about 10 minutes or until pasta is tender yet still firm. Stir in pesto.

Nutrition Facts per serving: 323 cal., 12 g total fat (1 g sat. fat), 46 mg chol., 914 mg sodium, 33 g carbo., 5 g fiber, 25 g pro.

CURRIED CHICKEN-&-CORN CHOWDER

Start to Finish:

20 minutes

. . . .

Makes: 4 servings

1	17-ounce can cream-style corn
2	cups milk
1	10³/₄-ounce can condensed cream of chicken soup
³/₄	cup chopped green or red sweet pepper
1	tablespoon dried minced onion
2	to 3 teaspoons curry powder
1	10-ounce can chunk-style chicken or 1¹/₂ cups frozen diced cooked chicken (about 8 ounces)
	Coarsely chopped peanuts (optional)

1 In a large saucepan stir together corn, milk, chicken soup, sweet pepper, dried minced onion, and curry powder. Bring to boiling, stirring frequently.

2 Stir in the undrained canned chicken; cook about 2 minutes or until heated through. If desired, sprinkle with peanuts.

Nutrition Facts per serving: 324 cal., 11 g total fat (4 g sat. fat), 49 mg chol., 1,201 mg sodium, 39 g carbo., 3 g fiber, 24 g pro.

BEER-CHILI BEAN SOUP

Start to Finish:

20 minutes

. . . .

Makes: 4 servings

1	15-ounce can hot-style chili beans with chili gravy, undrained
1	12-ounce can beer (1½ cups)
1	11¼-ounce can condensed chili beef soup
1½	cups chopped cooked turkey (about 8 ounces)
1	cup hot water
1	teaspoon dried minced onion
1	teaspoon Worcestershire sauce
½	teaspoon garlic powder
	Shredded cheddar cheese
	Dairy sour cream (optional)

1 In a large saucepan combine undrained chili beans, beer, soup, turkey, the water, onion, Worcestershire sauce, and garlic powder.

2 Bring to boiling; reduce heat. Simmer, uncovered, for 5 minutes. Top each serving with cheese and, if desired, sour cream.

Nutrition Facts per serving: 353 cal., 10 g total fat (5 g sat. fat), 57 mg chol., 1,154 mg sodium, 35 g carbo., 12 g fiber, 27 g pro.

SMOKED TURKEY CHUCKWAGON SOUP

Makes: 4 servings

2	14-ounce cans reduced-sodium chicken broth
1	15-ounce can white hominy, drained
1	11-ounce can condensed tomato rice soup
2	cups chopped smoked turkey (about 10 ounces)
½	cup chopped yellow sweet pepper
⅓	cup bottled salsa
1	teaspoon ground cumin
1½	cups crushed tortilla chips (2½ ounces)
	Dairy sour cream (optional)

1 In a large saucepan combine broth, hominy, soup, turkey, sweet pepper, salsa, and cumin. Bring to boiling; reduce heat. Simmer, uncovered, about 5 minutes or until sweet pepper is tender.

2 Ladle soup into serving bowls. Top each serving with tortilla chips and, if desired, sour cream.

Nutrition Facts per serving: 318 cal., 10 g total fat (2 g sat. fat), 38 mg chol., 2,013 mg sodium, 39 g carbo., 5 g fiber, 20 g pro.

POTATO-SAUSAGE CHOWDER

Start to Finish:

35 minutes

· ·

Makes: 4 or 5 servings

4	cups water

4   cups water

1   4.7-ounce package dry roasted garlic potato mix or dry sour cream and chives potato mix

8   ounces cooked smoked turkey sausage, halved lengthwise and sliced

2   cups loose-pack frozen mixed vegetables (such as broccoli, green beans, pearl onions, and red sweet peppers)

2   cups half-and-half, light cream, or milk

Salt

Black pepper

1 Bring the water to boiling in a 3-quart saucepan. Add the dry potatoes from the packaged mix; set aside the sauce mix packet. Return to boiling; reduce heat. Simmer, covered, for 10 minutes.

2 Add the sausage slices and frozen vegetables to the potato mixture in the saucepan. Return to boiling; reduce heat. Cover and cook for 5 minutes more.

3 In a medium bowl whisk together the reserved sauce mix and the half-and-half. Stir into potato mixture in saucepan. Cook and stir until slightly thickened and bubbly. Cook and stir for 1 minute more. Season to taste with salt and pepper.

Nutrition Facts per serving: 372 cal., 21 g total fat (10 g sat. fat), 82 mg chol., 1,223 mg sodium, 33 g carbo., 2 g fiber, 16 g pro.

TURKEY SAUSAGE & BEAN SOUP

Start to Finish:

30 minutes

. . . .

Makes: 4 servings

2   15-ounce cans Great Northern or white kidney beans (cannellini beans), rinsed and drained

1   10³/₄-ounce can condensed cream of celery soup

8   ounces cooked smoked turkey sausage, halved lengthwise and sliced

1¹/₂   cups milk

1   teaspoon dried minced onion

1   teaspoon bottled minced garlic (2 cloves) or ¹/₄ teaspoon garlic powder

¹/₂   teaspoon dried thyme, crushed

¹/₈   to ¹/₄ teaspoon black pepper

1 In a large saucepan combine beans, soup, turkey sausage, milk, onion, garlic, thyme, and pepper.

2 Bring to boiling over medium-high heat, stirring occasionally; reduce heat. Simmer, covered, for 10 minutes, stirring occasionally.

Nutrition Facts per serving: 434 cal., 11 g total fat (3 g sat. fat), 54 mg chol., 1,129 mg sodium, 57 g carbo., 11 g fiber, 29 g pro.

SEAFOOD CHOWDER

Start to Finish:

25 minutes

· · · · · · · · · · · · · · · ·

Makes: 4 servings

12   ounces fresh or frozen fish fillets (such as salmon, orange roughy, or cod)

3   cups loose-pack frozen diced hash brown potatoes with onions and peppers

1   cup water

1   12-ounce can evaporated milk*

1   10³/₄-ounce can condensed cream of shrimp or cream of potato soup

¹/₃   of a 3-ounce can cooked bacon pieces (¹/₃ cup)

2   teaspoons snipped fresh dill or ³/₄ teaspoon dried dill

¹/₄   teaspoon black pepper

1   2-ounce jar diced pimiento, drained

Fresh dill (optional)

1 Thaw fish, if frozen.** Rinse fish; pat dry with paper towels. Cut fish into 1-inch pieces. Set aside.

2 Meanwhile, in a large saucepan combine hash brown potatoes and the water. Bring to boiling; reduce heat. Simmer, covered, about 5 minutes or until tender.

3 Stir in evaporated milk, soup, bacon, dill, and pepper. Return to boiling. Add fish and pimiento; reduce heat. Simmer, covered, for 3 to 5 minutes more or until fish flakes easily when tested with a fork.

4 If desired, garnish each serving with additional fresh dill.

***Note:** Cut about 5 grams of fat per serving by using fat-free evaporated milk.

****Note:** To quickly thaw fish, place unwrapped fish in a microwave-safe 2-quart square baking dish. Cover and cook on 30% power (medium-low) for 5 to 6 minutes, turning and separating fillets after 3 minutes. When thawed, the fish should be pliable and cold on the outside, but still slightly icy in the center of the thick areas.

Nutrition Facts per serving: 366 cal., 15 g total fat (7 g sat. fat), 86 mg chol., 1,045 mg sodium, 27 g carbo., 2 g fiber, 30 g pro.

SALMON-BROCCOLI CHOWDER

Start to Finish:

20 minutes

Makes: 4 servings

2¹/₂   cups milk

1   10³/₄-ounce can condensed broccoli-cheese soup or condensed cream of chicken soup

³/₄   cup shredded sharp cheddar cheese or process American cheese (3 ounces)

1   cup loose-pack frozen cut broccoli

¹/₂   cup loose-pack frozen whole kernel corn

1   15-ounce can salmon, drained, flaked, and skin and bones removed

1 In a medium saucepan stir together milk and soup. Stir in cheese, broccoli, and corn.

2 Cook and stir just until mixture boils. Stir in salmon. Heat through.

Nutrition Facts per serving: 401 cal., 22 g total fat (10 g sat. fat), 65 mg chol., 1,257 mg sodium, 19 g carbo., 2 g fiber, 31 g pro.

SALMON CONFETTI CHOWDER

Start to Finish:

25 minutes

Makes: 4 servings

2	cups frozen pepper stir-fry vegetables (yellow, green, and red peppers and onion)
2	tablespoons finely chopped, seeded fresh jalapeño chile pepper*
1	tablespoon butter or margarine
2	tablespoons all-purpose flour
2	cups fat-free milk
1	cup fat-free half-and-half
2	cups refrigerated diced potatoes with onions
1	15-ounce can salmon, drained, flaked, and skin and bones removed
¼	cup snipped fresh watercress
½	teaspoon finely shredded lemon peel
½	teaspoon salt
½	teaspoon black pepper

1 In a large saucepan stir-fry vegetables and jalapeño pepper in hot butter for 3 to 5 minutes or until tender. Stir in flour. Stir in milk and half-and-half. Cook and stir until slightly thickened. Cook and stir for 2 minutes more.

2 Stir in diced potatoes, salmon, watercress, lemon peel, salt, and black pepper. Cook and stir until heated through.

***Note:** Because chile peppers contain volatile oils that can burn your skin and eyes, avoid direct contact with them as much as possible. When working with chile peppers, wear plastic or rubber gloves. If your bare hands do touch the peppers, wash your hands and nails well with soap and warm water.

Nutrition Facts per serving: 349 cal., 10 g total fat (2 g sat. fat), 61 mg chol., 1,174 mg sodium, 33 g carbo., 3 g fiber, 29 g pro.

TUNA TORTELLINI SOUP

Start to Finish:

20 minutes

· · · · · · · · · · · · · · · · · · · ·

Makes: 6 servings

3   cups milk

2   10³/₄-ounce cans condensed cream of potato soup

1   cup loose-pack frozen peas

1   teaspoon dried basil, crushed

1   9-ounce package refrigerated cheese tortellini

1   12-ounce can tuna (water pack), drained and flaked

¹/₃   cup dry white wine

1 In a large saucepan combine milk, soup, peas, and basil; bring just to boiling. Add tortellini. Simmer gently, uncovered, for 6 to 8 minutes or until tortellini is tender, stirring frequently to prevent sticking.

2 Stir in tuna and white wine. Heat through.

Nutrition Facts per serving: 351 cal., 9 g total fat (4 g sat. fat), 59 mg chol., 1,267 mg sodium, 38 g carbo., 2 g fiber, 27 g pro.

QUICK ASIAN SHRIMP SOUP

Start to Finish:

15 minutes

Makes: 4 servings

2$^{1}/_{2}$ cups water

2   10$^{1}/_{2}$-ounce cans condensed chicken with rice soup

2   cups loose-pack frozen broccoli stir-fry vegetables (broccoli, carrots, onions, red peppers, celery, water chestnuts, and mushrooms)

1   tablespoon soy sauce

$^{1}/_{2}$ teaspoon ground ginger

8   ounces peeled and deveined, cooked medium shrimp*

1 In a large saucepan combine the water and soup. Bring to boiling.

2 Stir in frozen vegetables, soy sauce, and ginger. Return to boiling; reduce heat. Simmer, uncovered, for 3 to 5 minutes or until vegetables are tender. Stir in shrimp; heat through.

*Note: If tails are present on the shrimp, remove them before using.

Nutrition Facts per serving: 166 cal., 4 g total fat (1 g sat. fat), 117 mg chol., 1,571 mg sodium, 15 g carbo., 1 g fiber, 17 g pro.

CLAM CHOWDER

Prep: **15** minutes

Cook: **15** minutes

Makes: 4 to 6 servings

2   10³⁄₄-ounce cans condensed cream of celery soup

2   cups frozen loose-pack diced hash brown potatoes with onion and peppers

1   8-ounce bottle clam juice

1   6¹⁄₂-ounce can minced clams, undrained

2   teaspoons Worcestershire sauce

1   teaspoon dried thyme, crushed

1   cup half-and-half or light cream

3   slices packaged ready-to-serve cooked bacon, chopped

     Black pepper (optional)

1 In a large saucepan combine soup, hash browns, clam juice, undrained clams, Worcestershire sauce, and thyme. Bring to boiling; reduce heat. Simmer, covered, about 15 minutes or until potatoes are tender, stirring frequently.

2 Stir in half-and-half; heat through. Sprinkle each serving with bacon. If desired, season to taste with pepper.

Nutrition Facts per serving: 383 cal., 20 g total fat (9 g sat. fat), 62 mg chol., 1,410 mg sodium, 29 g carbo., 3 g fiber, 19 g pro.

NACHO CORN SOUP

Start to Finish:

15 minutes

Makes: 4 servings

2 cups milk

1 11-ounce can whole kernel corn with sweet peppers, drained

1 11-ounce can condensed nacho cheese soup

1/2 of a 4-ounce can diced green chile peppers (2 tablespoons)

1 tablespoon dried minced onion

1/4 teaspoon ground cumin

1/4 teaspoon dried oregano, crushed

Tortilla chips, broken (optional)

1 In a large saucepan stir together milk, corn, soup, chile peppers, onion, cumin, and oregano. Cook over medium heat, stirring frequently, until heated through.

2 If desired, top each serving with tortilla chips.

Nutrition Facts per serving: 219 cal., 8 g total fat (4 g sat. fat), 20 mg chol., 898 mg sodium, 29 g carbo., 4 g fiber, 10 g pro.

MEATLESS MAIN DISHES

ASIAN NOODLE BOWL

Start to Finish:
25 minutes

Makes: 4 servings

8 ounces dried buckwheat soba noodles, udon noodles, or vermicelli noodles

2 cups vegetable broth

½ cup bottled peanut sauce

2 cups frozen Chinese-style stir-fry vegetables with seasonings

½ cup dry-roasted peanuts, chopped

1 Cook the noodles according to package directions. Drain noodles but do not rinse. Set aside. In the same saucepan combine broth and peanut sauce. Bring to boiling. Stir in frozen vegetables and cooked noodles. Return to boiling; reduce heat. Simmer for 2 to 3 minutes or until vegetables are heated through.

2 Divide noodles and broth among 4 bowls. Sprinkle with peanuts.

Nutrition Facts per serving: 403 cal., 15 g total fat (2 g sat. fat), 0 mg chol., 1,326 mg sodium, 59 g carbo., 4 g fiber, 15 g pro.

CHEESY TORTELLINI & VEGETABLES

Start to Finish:

20 minutes

Makes: 4 servings

1   6-ounce package dried cheese-filled tortellini

1   16-ounce package loose-pack frozen broccoli, cauliflower, and carrots

1¼   cups milk

½   of a 1.8-ounce envelope white sauce mix (about 3 tablespoons)

6   ounces Havarti cheese with dill, cubed

1 Cook tortellini according to package directions, adding the frozen vegetables the last 5 minutes of cooking; drain.

2 Meanwhile, for sauce, in a small saucepan whisk together milk and white sauce mix. Bring to boiling; reduce heat. Cook and stir for 1 minute. Remove from heat. Add cheese, stirring until melted. Pour sauce over vegetable mixture. Toss lightly.

Nutrition Facts per serving: 453 cal., 24 g total fat (1 g sat. fat), 59 mg chol., 1,004 mg sodium, 38 g carbo., 4 g fiber, 22 g pro.

LINGUINE WITH GORGONZOLA SAUCE

Start to Finish:

20 minutes

. . . .

Makes: 4 servings

1   9-ounce package refrigerated linguine
1   pound fresh asparagus, trimmed and cut into 1-inch pieces, or one 10-ounce package frozen cut asparagus
1   cup half-and-half or light cream
1   cup crumbled Gorgonzola or other blue cheese (4 ounces)
¼   teaspoon salt
2   tablespoons chopped walnuts, toasted

1 Cook linguine and asparagus according to package directions for the linguine; drain. Return linguine and asparagus to pan.

2 Meanwhile, in a medium saucepan combine half-and-half, ³⁄₄ cup of the Gorgonzola cheese, and the salt. Bring to boiling over medium heat; reduce heat. Simmer, uncovered, for 3 minutes, stirring frequently.

3 Pour sauce over linguine mixture; toss gently to coat. Transfer to a warm serving dish. Sprinkle with remaining Gorgonzola cheese and the walnuts.

Nutrition Facts per serving: 399 cal., 20 g total fat (11 g sat. fat), 111 mg chol., 590 mg sodium, 39 g carbo., 3 g fiber, 18 g pro.

RIGATONI & VEGETABLES ALFREDO

Start to Finish:

25 minutes

. . . .

Makes: 6 servings

6	ounces dried rigatoni or mostaccioli pasta
1	small eggplant, cut into $3/4$-inch pieces (about 12 ounces)
1	medium onion, chopped
2	tablespoons cooking oil
1	medium zucchini or yellow summer squash, quartered lengthwise and cut into $1/2$-inch pieces
1	10-ounce container refrigerated light Alfredo pasta sauce
$1/2$	teaspoon garlic salt
2	medium tomatoes, seeded and chopped
$1/2$	cup shredded Asiago cheese (2 ounces)
1	tablespoon snipped fresh basil

1 Cook pasta according to package directions; drain.

2 Meanwhile, in a 12-inch skillet cook eggplant and onion in hot oil for 3 minutes. Add zucchini; cook for 2 to 3 minutes more or until zucchini is crisp-tender. Stir in Alfredo sauce and garlic salt. Stir in cooked pasta; heat through.

3 Transfer pasta mixture to a serving dish. Top with chopped tomatoes, Asiago cheese, and basil.

Nutrition Facts per serving: 332 cal., 15 g total fat (5 g sat. fat), 27 mg chol., 695 mg sodium, 40 g carbo., 3 g fiber, 12 g pro.

SAUCY PIZZA SKILLET DINNER

Start to Finish:

30 minutes

Makes: 4 servings

1	6.4-ounce package lasagna dinner mix
3	cups water
1	4-ounce can (drained weight) mushroom stems and pieces, undrained
½	cup chopped green sweet pepper
½	cup sliced pitted ripe olives (optional)
½	cup shredded mozzarella cheese (2 ounces)

1 If the noodles in the dinner mix are large, break them into bite-size pieces. In a large skillet combine noodles and seasoning from dinner mix, the water, undrained mushrooms, and sweet pepper.

2 Bring to boiling, stirring occasionally; reduce heat. Simmer, covered, about 13 minutes or until pasta is tender. Uncover and cook for 2 to 3 minutes more or until sauce is of desired consistency.

3 If desired, sprinkle with olives. Top with cheese. Remove from heat; let stand for 1 to 2 minutes or until cheese melts.

Nutrition Facts per serving: 318 cal., 14 g total fat (5 g sat. fat), 28 mg chol., 1,774 mg sodium, 37 g carbo., 3 g fiber, 14 g pro.

SWEET BEANS & NOODLES

Start to Finish:

30 minutes

Makes: 4 servings

8	ounces dried linguine
1½	cups loose-pack frozen green soybeans (shelled edamame)
1	cup purchased shredded carrots
1	10-ounce container refrigerated Alfredo pasta sauce
2	teaspoons snipped fresh rosemary

1 Cook the linguine according to package directions, adding the soybeans and carrots the last 10 minutes of cooking. Drain and return to pan.

2 Add Alfredo sauce and rosemary to linguine mixture in pan; toss to combine. Heat through.

Nutrition Facts per serving: 544 cal., 27 g total fat (1 g sat. fat), 35 mg chol., 280 mg sodium, 57 g carbo., 5 g fiber, 20 g pro.

TWO-CHEESE MACARONI BAKE

Prep: 20 minutes
Bake: 45 minutes

....

Oven: 375°F
Makes: 8 servings

2	cups dried elbow macaroni (8 ounces)
4	eggs
2½	cups milk
8	ounces feta cheese with basil and tomato or plain feta cheese, crumbled
¾	cup cream-style cottage cheese
½	teaspoon salt

1 Preheat oven to 375°. Grease a 2-quart square baking dish; set aside. Cook macaroni according to package directions. Drain well. Place macaroni in prepared baking dish. In a medium bowl beat eggs with a fork; stir in milk, feta cheese, cottage cheese, and salt. Pour over macaroni in dish.

2 Bake in preheated oven for 45 minutes. Let macaroni stand for 10 minutes before serving.

Nutrition Facts per serving: 266 cal., 11 g total fat (6 g sat. fat), 140 mg chol., 609 mg sodium, 25 g carbo., 1 g fiber, 15 g pro.

MEDITERRANEAN COUSCOUS WITH TOFU

Start to Finish:

15 minutes

Makes: 4 servings

1   5.7-ounce package curry-flavored or roasted garlic and olive oil flavored couscous mix

½   of a 12- to 16-ounce package extra-firm tofu (fresh bean curd), well drained

1   tablespoon olive oil

½   cup sliced pitted ripe olives or sliced pitted Greek black olives

½   cup crumbled feta cheese or finely shredded Parmesan cheese (2 ounces)

1 Prepare couscous according to package directions, except omit oil. Meanwhile, cut tofu into ½-inch cubes. Pat tofu dry with paper towels.

2 In a large skillet heat oil over medium-high heat. Add tofu; stir-fry for 5 to 7 minutes or until tofu is brown. Stir tofu and olives into couscous. Transfer to a serving dish. Top with cheese.

Nutrition Facts per serving: 259 cal., 10 g total fat (4 g sat. fat), 17 mg chol., 763 mg sodium, 33 g carbo., 3 g fiber, 11 g pro.

GARLIC COUSCOUS WITH EGGS & SALSA

Start to Finish:

25 minutes

....

Makes: 4 servings

1   5.8-ounce package roasted garlic and olive oil-flavored, toasted pine nut-flavored, or tomato-lentil-flavored couscous mix, or ²/₃ cup quick-cooking couscous

1   cup chopped tomato

1   cup chopped zucchini

2   teaspoons olive oil

1   teaspoon balsamic vinegar

½   teaspoon bottled minced garlic (1 clove)

1   tablespoon butter or margarine

4   beaten eggs

    Salt

    Black pepper

1 Prepare couscous according to package directions.

2 Meanwhile, for salsa, in a small bowl stir together tomato, zucchini, oil, balsamic vinegar, and garlic; set aside.

3 In a medium skillet melt butter over medium-high heat. Pour in eggs; reduce heat to medium. Cook eggs, without stirring, until eggs begin to set on the bottom and around edge.

4 Using a spatula, lift and fold the partially cooked eggs so the uncooked portion flows underneath. Continue cooking for 2 to 3 minutes or until eggs are cooked through but are still glossy and moist. Remove from heat. Stir eggs into couscous. Season to taste with salt and pepper. Serve with salsa.

Nutrition Facts per serving: 289 cal., 11 g total fat (3 g sat. fat), 221 mg chol., 496 mg sodium, 35 g carbo., 2 g fiber, 12 g pro.

VEGETARIAN DELIGHT

Prep: 30 minutes
Cook: 30 minutes

Makes: 4 servings

⅓	cup chopped onion
1	teaspoon olive oil
2	medium zucchini, halved lengthwise and sliced
2	medium carrots, chopped
1	cup water
1	teaspoon bottled minced garlic (2 cloves)
1	15-ounce can garbanzo beans (chickpeas), rinsed and drained
1	14½-ounce can low-sodium diced tomatoes, undrained
1	14½-ounce can Cajun-style stewed tomatoes, undrained
1	tablespoon sugar
	Dash cayenne pepper
	Hot cooked couscous or brown rice

1 In a large saucepan cook onion in hot oil for 5 minutes. Stir in zucchini, carrots, ¼ cup of the water, and the garlic. Cook and stir for 3 minutes.

2 Stir in remaining ¾ cup water, the drained garbanzo beans, undrained diced tomatoes, undrained stewed tomatoes, sugar, and cayenne pepper. Bring to boiling; reduce heat. Simmer, uncovered, about 20 minutes or until desired consistency.

3 Serve over hot cooked couscous.

Nutrition Facts per serving: 388 cal., 4 g total fat (1 g sat. fat), 0 mg chol., 740 mg sodium, 79 g carbo., 11 g fiber, 12 g pro.

SAUCY BEANS WITH RICE

Prep: **25** minutes
Cook: **15** minutes

Makes: 6 servings

1	medium onion, chopped
1/2	teaspoon bottled minced garlic (1 clove)
1	tablespoon olive oil
2	cups bottled salsa
1	15-ounce can black beans, rinsed and drained
1	15-ounce can Great Northern beans, rinsed and drained
1	14 1/2-ounce can diced tomatoes, undrained
2	tablespoons snipped fresh cilantro or 1 teaspoon dried cilantro, crushed
	Hot cooked rice or pasta
	Dairy sour cream (optional)

1 In a large saucepan cook onion and garlic in hot oil about 5 minutes or until tender. Stir in salsa, drained black and Great Northern beans, and undrained tomatoes. Bring to boiling; reduce heat. Simmer, covered, for 15 minutes, stirring occasionally. Stir in cilantro; heat through.

2 Ladle bean mixture into bowls over hot cooked rice. If desired, serve with sour cream.

Nutrition Facts per serving: 274 cal., 3 g total fat (0 g sat. fat), 0 mg chol., 1,041 mg sodium, 52 g carbo., 8 g fiber, 11 g pro.

BEANS, BARLEY & TOMATOES

Start to Finish:

30 minutes

· · · · · · · · · · · · · · · · · · · ·

Makes: 4 servings

1 14-ounce can vegetable broth or chicken broth

1 teaspoon Greek seasoning or garam masala

1 cup loose-pack frozen green soybeans (shelled edamame)

³⁄₄ cup quick-cooking barley

¹⁄₂ cup purchased shredded carrots

4 cups fresh spinach leaves

4 small to medium tomatoes, sliced

1 In a medium saucepan bring broth and Greek seasoning to boiling. Add soybeans and barley. Return to boiling; reduce heat. Simmer, covered, for 12 minutes. Stir carrots into barley mixture.

2 Meanwhile, divide spinach among 4 dinner plates. Arrange tomato slices on spinach. Using a slotted spoon, spoon barley mixture over tomatoes. (Or drain barley mixture; spoon over tomatoes.)

Make-Ahead Directions: Prepare as above through step 1. Cover and chill barley mixture for up to 24 hours. Arrange spinach and tomatoes as above. Spoon chilled barley mixture over tomatoes.

Nutrition Facts per serving: 171 cal., 3 g total fat (0 g sat. fat), 0 mg chol., 484 mg sodium, 33 g carbo., 10 g fiber, 9 g pro.

BLACK BEAN & CORN QUESADILLAS

Start to Finish:
20 minutes

. . . .

Oven: 300°F
Makes: 4 servings

1	8-ounce package shredded four-cheese Mexican blend cheese (2 cups)
8	8-inch flour tortillas
1½	cups bottled black bean and corn salsa
1	medium avocado, seeded, peeled, and chopped
	Dairy sour cream

1 Preheat oven to 300°. Divide cheese evenly among tortillas, sprinkling cheese over half of each tortilla. Top each tortilla with 1 tablespoon of the salsa. Divide avocado among tortillas. Fold tortillas in half, pressing gently.

2 Heat a large skillet over medium-high heat for 2 minutes; reduce heat to medium. Cook 2 of the quesadillas for 2 to 3 minutes or until lightly browned and cheese is melted, turning once. Remove quesadillas from skillet; place on a baking sheet. Keep warm in preheated oven. Repeat with remaining quesadillas, cooking 2 at a time.

3 Cut quesadillas into wedges. Serve with sour cream and remaining 1 cup salsa.

Nutrition Facts per serving: 512 cal., 33 g total fat (14 g sat. fat), 55 mg chol., 940 mg sodium, 38 g carbo., 4 g fiber, 18 g pro.

CAJUN BEANS OVER CORN BREAD

Prep: 10 minutes
Bake: 20 minutes

Makes: 4 servings

1	8½-ounce package corn muffin mix
1	medium green sweet pepper, chopped
1	tablespoon cooking oil
1	15- to 16-ounce can Great Northern beans, rinsed and drained
1	14½-ounce can diced tomatoes with garlic and onion, undrained
1	teaspoon instant chicken bouillon granules
¼	teaspoon black pepper
¼	to ½ teaspoon bottled hot pepper sauce
½	cup shredded cheddar cheese (2 ounces)

1 Prepare and bake corn muffin mix according to package directions for corn bread. Cool corn bread slightly.

2 Meanwhile, in a medium saucepan cook sweet pepper in hot oil just until tender. Add drained beans, undrained tomatoes, bouillon granules, black pepper, and hot pepper sauce. Bring to boiling; reduce heat. Simmer, covered, for 10 minutes.

3 Cut corn bread into 4 portions and place on dinner plates or in shallow bowls. Spoon bean mixture over corn bread. Sprinkle each portion with cheese.

Nutrition Facts per serving: 485 cal., 17 g total fat (4 g sat. fat), 70 mg chol., 1,563 mg sodium, 68 g carbo., 6 g fiber, 17 g pro.

CHIPOTLE BEAN ENCHILADAS

Prep: 25 minutes
Bake: 40 minutes

. . . .

Oven: 350°F
Makes: 5 servings

10	6-inch corn tortillas
1	15-ounce can pinto beans or black beans, rinsed and drained
1	tablespoon canned chipotle pepper in adobo sauce, chopped
1	8-ounce package shredded four-cheese Mexican blend cheese (2 cups)
2	10-ounce cans enchilada sauce

1 Preheat oven to 350°. Grease a 2-quart rectangular baking dish; set aside. Stack the tortillas and wrap tightly in foil. Bake in preheated oven about 10 minutes or until warm.

2 Meanwhile, for filling, in a medium bowl combine drained beans, chipotle pepper, 1 cup of the cheese, and $1/2$ cup of the enchilada sauce. Spoon about $1/4$ cup of the filling onto one edge of each tortilla. Starting at the edge with the filling, roll up each tortilla.

3 Arrange tortillas, seam sides down, in prepared baking dish. Top with remaining enchilada sauce. Cover with foil.

4 Bake in the 350° oven about 25 minutes or until heated through. Remove foil. Sprinkle with remaining cheese. Bake, uncovered, about 5 minutes more or until cheese is melted.

Nutrition Facts per serving: 487 cal., 19 g total fat (8 g sat. fat), 40 mg chol., 1,091 mg sodium, 63 g carbo., 14 g fiber, 23 g pro.

TOMATO, MOZZARELLA & POLENTA PLATTER

Start to Finish:
20 minutes

Makes: 4 servings

1   large head butterhead (Boston or Bibb) lettuce

8   ounces fresh mozzarella cheese, sliced

2   medium red tomatoes, cut into wedges

2   medium yellow tomatoes, sliced

$\frac{1}{4}$ cup fresh basil leaves

2   teaspoons olive oil

1   16-ounce tube refrigerated cooked polenta, cut into $\frac{3}{4}$-inch thick slices

$\frac{1}{3}$ cup kalamata olives

$\frac{1}{4}$ cup bottled red wine vinegar and oil salad dressing

1 Line a platter with butterhead lettuce leaves. (Or make a basket of the head of butterhead lettuce by removing center leaves.) Arrange mozzarella, tomatoes, and basil leaves on the lettuce, leaving room for polenta slices.

2 In a large nonstick skillet heat oil over medium heat. Cook polenta slices in hot oil for 4 to 6 minutes or until warm and lightly browned, turning once. Arrange polenta and olives on lettuce. Serve with salad dressing.

Nutrition Facts per serving: 395 cal., 25 g total fat (9 g sat. fat), 44 mg chol., 928 mg sodium, 30 g carbo., 5 g fiber, 16 g pro.

POLENTA WITH MUSHROOMS & ASPARAGUS

Start to Finish:

30 minutes

. . . .

Makes: 4 servings

1	cup instant or quick-cooking polenta
1	tablespoon olive oil
1	small onion, chopped
1	8-ounce package sliced fresh mushrooms (such as crimini, shiitake, or oyster) (3 cups)
1	pound fresh asparagus spears, trimmed and cut into 1-inch pieces or one 10-ounce package frozen cut asparagus
1½	teaspoons bottled minced garlic (3 cloves)
⅓	cup dry white wine, Marsala, vegetable broth, or chicken broth
¼	teaspoon salt
⅓	cup chopped walnuts or pecans or pine nuts, toasted
¼	cup finely shredded Parmesan cheese (1 ounce)

1 Prepare polenta according to package directions. Cover and keep warm.

2 Meanwhile, in a large skillet heat oil over medium heat. Add onion to oil in skillet; cook until tender. Add mushrooms, asparagus, and garlic; cook about 4 minutes or until almost tender. Stir in wine and salt. Cook over medium-high heat for 1 minute.

3 To serve, divide polenta among 4 serving bowls. Spoon the mushroom mixture over polenta. Sprinkle with nuts and Parmesan cheese.

Nutrition Facts per serving: 426 cal., 12 g total fat (1 g sat. fat), 5 mg chol., 220 mg sodium, 64 g carbo., 10 g fiber, 14 g pro.

ZUCCHINI QUICHE

Prep: 20 minutes
Bake: 40 minutes

....

Oven: 350°F
Makes: 6 servings

4	eggs
3	cups finely shredded zucchini
1	cup packaged biscuit mix
½	cup grated Parmesan cheese (2 ounces)
2	ounces Gruyère or Swiss cheese, shredded (½ cup)
¼	cup cooking oil
4	green onions, cut diagonally into 1-inch-long pieces
2	tablespoons snipped fresh dill or 1½ teaspoons dried dill
1	Recipe Tomato Dill Relish

1 Preheat oven to 350°. Grease a 9-inch quiche dish. In a large bowl beat eggs with a fork. Stir in zucchini, biscuit mix, cheeses, oil, green onions, and dill. Pour into prepared quiche dish.

2 Bake in preheated oven for 40 to 45 minutes or until a knife inserted near the center comes out clean.

3 Meanwhile, prepare Tomato Dill Relish.

4 Let quiche stand for 10 minutes before serving. Serve quiche with Tomato Dill Relish.

Tomato Dill Relish: In a medium bowl stir together 1½ cups seeded chopped tomato (about 2 large), 1½ teaspoons snipped fresh dill or ½ teaspoon dried dill, and ⅛ teaspoon salt. Cover and chill until ready to serve.

Nutrition Facts per serving: 313 cal., 21 g total fat (7 g sat. fat), 158 mg chol., 527 mg sodium, 18 g carbo., 2 g fiber, 13 g pro.

THREE-CHEESE SPINACH PIE

Prep: 15 minutes

Bake: 45 minutes

Cool: 15 minutes

Oven: 375°F

Makes: 8 servings

1	15-ounce package folded refrigerated unbaked piecrust (2 crusts)
4	eggs
1	15-ounce carton ricotta cheese
4	ounces Asiago cheese, finely shredded (1 cup)
¼	cup grated Parmesan cheese (1 ounce)
¾	teaspoon coarsely ground black pepper
1	teaspoon dried basil, crushed
1	10-ounce package frozen chopped spinach, thawed and well drained
¼	cup seasoned fine dry bread crumbs
¼	cup oil-packed dried tomatoes, drained and coarsely chopped

1 Preheat oven to 375°. Let piecrusts stand at room temperature for 15 minutes as directed on package. Meanwhile, beat 1 of the eggs with a fork; set aside. In a large bowl beat remaining 3 eggs with a fork; add cheeses, pepper, and basil, stirring well. Stir in spinach, bread crumbs, and tomatoes.

2 Line a 9-inch pie plate with 1 of the piecrusts; brush generously with some of the reserved egg. Spread cheese mixture evenly in crust. Top with second piecrust. Fold edges under to seal. Flute as desired. Brush with remaining reserved egg. Cut slits in top crust.

3 Bake in preheated oven for 45 minutes. If necessary to prevent overbrowning, cover edge with foil for the last 20 minutes of baking. Cool on a wire rack for 15 minutes before serving.

Nutrition Facts per serving: 472 cal., 30 g total fat (15 g sat. fat), 160 mg chol., 603 mg sodium, 33 g carbo., 1 g fiber, 16 g pro.

SOUTHWESTERN QUICHE

Prep: 15 minutes
Bake: 40 minutes

. . . .

Oven: 350°F
Makes: 6 servings

³/₄	cup shredded cheddar cheese (3 ounces)
¹/₂	cup shredded Monterey Jack cheese (2 ounces)
1	9-inch frozen unbaked deep-dish piecrust, thawed
3	eggs
1¹/₂	cups half-and-half or light cream
1	4-ounce can diced green chile peppers, drained
1	2¹/₄-ounce can sliced ripe olives, drained
2	tablespoons chopped green onion
¹/₄	teaspoon salt
¹/₄	teaspoon black pepper
	Dairy sour cream (optional)
	Bottled salsa (optional)

1 Preheat oven to 350°. In a small bowl combine cheeses; sprinkle evenly into the piecrust.

2 In a medium bowl beat eggs with a whisk. Stir in half-and-half, chile peppers, olives, green onion, salt, and black pepper. Pour over cheese.

3 Bake in preheated oven for 40 to 45 minutes or until a knife inserted near center comes out clean. Let stand for 15 minutes before serving. If desired, serve with sour cream and salsa.

Nutrition Facts per serving: 332 cal., 25 g total fat (11 g sat. fat), 152 mg chol., 573 mg sodium, 15 g carbo., 1 g fiber, 12 g pro.

GARDENER'S PIE

Prep: 15 minutes
Bake: 45 minutes

. . . .

Oven: 350°F
Makes: 4 servings

1	16-ounce package loose-pack frozen vegetable medley (any combination), thawed
1	11-ounce can condensed cheddar cheese soup
½	teaspoon dried thyme, crushed
1	20-ounce package refrigerated mashed potatoes
1	cup shredded smoked cheddar cheese (4 ounces)

1 Preheat oven to 350°. In a 1½-quart casserole combine vegetables, soup, and thyme. Stir mashed potatoes to soften. Carefully spread potatoes on vegetable mixture to cover surface.

2 Bake, covered, in preheated oven for 30 minutes. Uncover and bake about 15 minutes more or until heated through, topping with cheese the last 5 minutes of baking. Serve in shallow bowls.

Nutrition Facts per serving: 349 cal., 17 g total fat (8 g sat. fat), 39 mg chol., 1,031 mg sodium, 40 g carbo., 4 g fiber, 15 g pro.

VEGETARIAN SLOPPY JOES

Prep: 15 minutes
Cook: 25 minutes

Makes: 8 to 10 servings

1   cup chopped onion

1   large green sweet pepper, chopped

1   tablespoon cooking oil

1½ cups refrigerated or frozen precooked and crumbled ground meat substitute (soy protein)

1   10¾-ounce can tomato puree

1   cup water

⅓   cup bottled barbecue sauce

1   tablespoon yellow mustard

1   tablespoon soy sauce (optional)

2   teaspoons chili powder

1   teaspoon bottled minced garlic (2 cloves)

8   to 10 hamburger buns, toasted

1 In a large skillet cook onion and sweet pepper in hot oil for 5 to 7 minutes or until tender. Stir in ground meat substitute, tomato puree, the water, barbecue sauce, mustard, soy sauce (if desired), chili powder, and garlic.

2 Bring to boiling; reduce heat. Simmer, uncovered, for 20 minutes, stirring occasionally. Serve on buns.

Nutrition Facts per serving: 248 cal., 9 g total fat (3 g sat. fat), 20 mg chol., 485 mg sodium, 30 g carbo., 3 g fiber, 11 g pro.

SPINACH CALZONES

Prep: 30 minutes
Bake: 10 minutes

. . . .

Oven: 450°F
Makes: 4 servings

1	10-ounce package frozen chopped spinach
2	eggs
1	8-ounce can pizza sauce
¼	cup grated Parmesan cheese (1 ounce)
1	teaspoon dried basil, crushed
⅛	teaspoon garlic powder
1	10-ounce package refrigerated pizza dough (for 1 crust)
1	cup shredded mozzarella cheese (4 ounces)
	Cooking oil
1	tablespoon grated Parmesan cheese (1 ounce)

1 Cook spinach according to package directions. Drain, squeezing out excess liquid. In a medium bowl beat eggs with a fork. Stir in spinach, ¼ cup of the pizza sauce, the ¼ cup Parmesan cheese, basil, and garlic powder.

2 Preheat oven to 450°. Grease baking sheet; set aside. Unroll refrigerated pizza dough. On a lightly floured surface, press dough into a 15×10-inch rectangle. Cut dough into quarters. Divide mozzarella cheese among pizza dough quarters, sprinkling onto one-half of each quarter. Evenly spoon spinach mixture on cheese. Fold dough over mixture; seal edges. Place calzones on prepared baking sheet. Brush with oil. Sprinkle with the 1 tablespoon Parmesan cheese. Cut small slits in top of each calzone.

3 Bake in preheated oven for 10 to 15 minutes or until golden. In a small saucepan cook and stir remaining pizza sauce until heated through. Serve warmed pizza sauce with calzones.

Nutrition Facts per serving: 378 cal., 16 g total fat (6 g sat. fat), 136 mg chol., 1,120 mg sodium, 35 g carbo., 3 g fiber, 22 g pro.

ALFREDO & SWEET PEPPER PIZZA

Prep: 15 minutes
Bake: 10 minutes

....

Oven: 425°F
Makes: 4 servings

1 16-ounce Italian bread shell (Boboli)

½ of a 10-ounce container refrigerated Alfredo pasta sauce (about ⅔ cup)

½ teaspoon dried Italian seasoning, crushed

1 8-ounce package shredded four-cheese pizza cheese (2 cups)

1 16-ounce package frozen pepper stir-fry vegetables (yellow, green, and red peppers and onion), thawed and well drained

1 Preheat oven to 425°. Place bread shell on an ungreased baking sheet. In a small bowl stir together Alfredo sauce and Italian seasoning. Spread Alfredo sauce mixture over bread shell.

2 Sprinkle 1 cup of the cheese on the bread shell. Top with vegetables. Sprinkle with remaining 1 cup cheese. Bake in preheated oven about 10 minutes or until heated through.

Nutrition Facts per serving: 626 cal., 30 g total fat (8 g sat. fat), 63 mg chol., 1,136 mg sodium, 60 g carbo., 3 g fiber, 30 g pro.

SLOW COOKER

SO-EASY PEPPER STEAK

Prep: 15 minutes

Cook: 10 to **12** hours
(low) or 5 to 6 hours (high)

Makes: 8 servings

2   pounds boneless beef round steak, cut ³/₄ to 1 inch thick
     Salt
     Black pepper
1   14¹/₂-ounce can Cajun, Mexican, or Italian-style stewed tomatoes, undrained
¹/₃   cup tomato paste with Italian seasoning
¹/₂   teaspoon bottled hot pepper sauce
1   16-ounce package frozen pepper stir-fry vegetables (yellow, green, and red peppers and onion)
     Hot cooked noodles or mashed potatoes

1 Trim fat from meat. Cut meat into 8 serving-size pieces. Lightly sprinkle meat with salt and black pepper. Place meat in a 3¹/₂- or 4-quart slow cooker. In a medium bowl combine undrained tomatoes, tomato paste, and hot pepper sauce. Pour over meat. Top with frozen vegetables.

2 Cover and cook on low-heat setting for 10 to 12 hours or on high-heat setting for 5 to 6 hours.

3 Serve over hot cooked noodles or mashed potatoes.

Nutrition Facts per serving: 303 cal., 6 g total fat (2 g sat. fat), 80 mg chol., 416 mg sodium, 29 g carbo., 2 g fiber, 30 g pro.

GINGER BEEF WITH BROCCOLI

Prep: 20 minutes

Cook: 8 to **10** hours
(low) or 4 to 5 hours (high)
plus 15 minutes (high)

....

Makes: 6 servings

6	medium carrots, cut into 1-inch pieces
2	medium onions, cut into wedges
1½	pounds beef round steak, cut into ½-inch bias-sliced strips
1	tablespoon minced fresh ginger
1	teaspoon bottled minced garlic (2 cloves)
½	cup water
2	tablespoons reduced-sodium soy sauce
1	¾-ounce envelope beef gravy mix
4	cups broccoli florets
	Hot cooked rice

1 In a 3½- or 4-quart slow cooker place carrots, onions, beef strips, ginger, and garlic. In a small bowl stir together the water, soy sauce, and beef gravy mix. Pour over meat and vegetables in slow cooker.

2 Cover and cook on low-heat setting for 8 to 10 hours or on high-heat setting for 4 to 5 hours.

3 If using low-heat setting, turn slow cooker to high-heat setting. Stir in broccoli. Cover and cook about 15 minutes more or until broccoli is crisp-tender. Serve over hot cooked rice.

Nutrition Facts per serving: 327 cal., 6 g total fat (2 g sat. fat), 54 mg chol., 476 mg sodium, 37 g carbo., 4 g fiber, 31 g pro.

POT ROAST WITH CHIPOTLE-FRUIT SAUCE

Prep: 15 minutes

Cook: 10 to **11** hours (low) or 5 to 5 ½ hours (high)

Makes: 8 servings

1   3-pound boneless beef chuck pot roast

2   teaspoons garlic-pepper seasoning

1   7-ounce package dried mixed fruit

½   cup water

1   tablespoon finely chopped canned chipotle peppers in adobo sauce

1   tablespoon cold water

2   teaspoons cornstarch

1 Sprinkle both sides of roast with garlic-pepper seasoning. If necessary, cut roast to fit into a 3½- or 4-quart slow cooker. Place roast in slow cooker. Add fruit, the ½ cup water, and the chipotle peppers.

2 Cover and cook on low-heat setting for 10 to 11 hours or on high-heat setting for 5 to 5½ hours.

3 Transfer roast and fruit to a serving platter. Cover and keep warm.

4 For sauce, transfer cooking liquid to a bowl or measuring cup; skim off fat. In a medium saucepan combine the 1 tablespoon cold water and the cornstarch; add cooking liquid. Cook and stir until thickened and bubbly; cook and stir for 2 minutes more. Thinly slice roast. To serve, spoon sauce over sliced meat and fruit.

Nutrition Facts per serving: 275 cal., 6 g total fat (2 g sat. fat), 101 mg chol., 378 mg sodium, 17 g carbo., 1 g fiber, 37 g pro.

MUSHROOM-SAUCED POT ROAST

Prep: 20 minutes

Cook: 10 to **12** hours
(low) or 5 to 6 hours (high)

Makes: 5 or 6 servings

1	1$\frac{1}{2}$-pound boneless beef chuck eye roast, chuck pot roast, eye round roast, or round rump roast
4	medium potatoes (about 1$\frac{1}{2}$ pounds), quartered
1	16-ounce package frozen tiny whole carrots
1	4-ounce can (drained weight) mushroom stems and pieces, drained
$\frac{1}{2}$	teaspoon dried tarragon or basil, crushed
$\frac{1}{4}$	teaspoon salt
1	10$\frac{3}{4}$-ounce can condensed golden mushroom soup

1 Trim fat from roast. If necessary, cut roast to fit into a 3$\frac{1}{2}$- to 4$\frac{1}{2}$-quart slow cooker. Set aside.

2 In the slow cooker combine potatoes, frozen carrots, mushrooms, tarragon, and salt. Add roast. Pour mushroom soup over mixture in slow cooker.

3 Cover and cook on low-heat setting for 10 to 12 hours or on high-heat setting for 5 to 6 hours.

Nutrition Facts per serving: 338 cal., 8 g total fat (3 g sat. fat), 62 mg chol., 817 mg sodium, 31 g carbo., 5 g fiber, 35 g pro.

BEEF & MUSHROOM BURGUNDY

Prep: 20 minutes

Cook: 8 to **10** hours
(low) or 4 to 5 hours (high)

. . . .

Makes: 6 servings

1$\frac{1}{2}$	pounds beef stew meat, trimmed and cut into 1-inch cubes
2	tablespoons cooking oil
8	ounces sliced fresh mushrooms (3 cups)
1	10$\frac{3}{4}$-ounce can condensed cream of celery soup or reduced-fat and reduced-sodium condensed cream of celery soup
1	10$\frac{3}{4}$-ounce can condensed cream of mushroom soup or reduced-fat and reduced-sodium condensed cream of mushroom soup
$\frac{3}{4}$	cup Burgundy wine
$\frac{1}{2}$	of a 2-ounce package (1 envelope) dry onion soup mix
	Hot cooked noodles or rice

1 In a large skillet brown stew meat, half at a time, in hot oil. Drain off fat.

2 In a 3$\frac{1}{2}$- to 5-quart slow cooker combine mushrooms, cream of celery soup, mushroom soup, Burgundy, and dry onion soup mix. Stir in stew meat.

3 Cover and cook on low-heat setting for 8 to 10 hours or on high-heat setting for 4 to 5 hours.

4 Serve over hot cooked noodles.

Nutrition Facts per serving: 435 cal., 18 g total fat (4 g sat. fat), 95 mg chol., 1,179 mg sodium, 32 g carbo., 2 g fiber, 31 g pro.

SALSA VERDE BEEF STEW

Prep: 30 minutes

Cook: 8 to **9** hours
(low) or 5 to 6 hours (high)

. . . .

Makes: 6 servings

1½   pounds boneless beef chuck pot roast

1   tablespoon cooking oil

4   medium potatoes, cut into 1-inch pieces

1   large onion, coarsely chopped

1   green sweet pepper, cut into ½-inch pieces

1   14½-ounce can Mexican-style stewed tomatoes, undrained

1   15- or 16-ounce can pinto beans, rinsed and drained

1   cup bottled mild or medium green salsa

1   teaspoon ground cumin

1   teaspoon bottled minced garlic (2 cloves)

6   flour tortillas, warmed

1 Trim fat from roast. Cut roast into 1-inch pieces. In a large skillet brown meat, half at a time, in hot oil over medium-high heat.

2 In a 3½- to 5-quart slow cooker combine meat, potatoes, onion, sweet pepper, undrained tomatoes, beans, salsa, cumin, and garlic.

3 Cover and cook on low-heat setting for 8 to 9 hours or on high-heat setting for 5 to 6 hours. Serve with warm tortillas.

Nutrition Facts per serving: 465 cal., 12 g total fat (3 g sat. fat), 72 mg chol., 709 mg sodium, 56 g carbo., 8 g fiber, 33 g pro.

SWEET & SOUR BEEF STEW

Prep: **10** minutes

Cook: **10** to **11** hours (low) or 5 to 5½ hours (high)

Makes: 6 to 8 servings

1½ pounds beef stew meat, cut into ¾- to 1-inch cubes

1 16-ounce package loose-pack frozen stew vegetables (3 cups)

2 10¾-ounce cans condensed beefy mushroom soup

½ cup bottled sweet and sour sauce

½ cup water

⅛ to ¼ teaspoon cayenne pepper

1 Place stew meat and frozen vegetables in a 3½- or 4-quart slow cooker. Stir in beefy mushroom soup, sweet and sour sauce, the water, and cayenne pepper.

2 Cover and cook on low-heat setting for 10 to 11 hours or on high-heat setting for 5 to 5½ hours.

Nutrition Facts per serving: 291 cal., 9 g total fat (3 g sat. fat), 62 mg chol., 1,019 mg sodium, 19 g carbo., 2 g fiber, 30 g pro.

REFRIED BEAN CHILI

Prep: 20 minutes

Cook: 6 to **8** hours
(low) or 3 to 4 hours (high)

. . . .

Makes: 8 to 10 servings

2 pounds ground beef

1 cup chopped onion

2 15- or 15$\frac{3}{4}$-ounce cans chili beans with chili gravy, undrained

1 16-ounce jar thick and chunky salsa

1 16-ounce can refried beans

1 12-ounce can beer or one 14-ounce can beef broth

2 tablespoons chili powder

1 tablespoon ground cumin

2 tablespoons lime juice

   Dairy sour cream (optional)

1 In a large skillet cook ground beef and onion until beef is brown and onion is tender, leaving some of the meat in larger pieces. Drain off fat.

2 Spoon beef mixture into a 5- to 6-quart slow cooker. Stir in undrained chili beans, salsa, refried beans, beer, chili powder, and cumin.

3 Cover and cook on low-heat setting for 6 to 8 hours or on high-heat setting for 3 to 4 hours. Stir in lime juice at the end of cooking.

4 If desired, top servings with sour cream.

Nutrition Facts per serving: 482 cal., 22 g total fat (8 g sat. fat), 86 mg chol., 960 mg sodium, 36 g carbo., 10 g fiber, 30 g pro.

BLACK-EYED PEA TACO SOUP

Prep: 15 minutes

Cook: 6 to **8** hours
(low) or 3 to 4 hours (high)

Makes: 8 servings

1   pound ground beef

1   15½-ounce can black-eyed peas, undrained

1   15-ounce can black beans, undrained

1   15- or 15¾-ounce can chili beans with chili gravy, undrained

1   15-ounce can garbanzo beans (chickpeas), undrained

1   14½-ounce can Mexican-style stewed tomatoes, undrained

1   11-ounce can whole kernel corn with sweet peppers, undrained

1   1¼-ounce package taco seasoning mix

     Dairy sour cream

     Bottled salsa

     Tortilla chips

1 In a 4-quart Dutch oven cook ground beef until brown. Drain off fat. Spoon beef into a 3½- or 4-quart slow cooker. Stir in undrained black-eyed peas, undrained black beans, undrained chili beans, undrained garbanzo beans, undrained tomatoes, and undrained corn. Stir in taco seasoning mix until well mixed.

2 Cover and cook on low-heat setting for 6 to 8 hours or on high-heat setting for 3 to 4 hours.

3 Serve with sour cream, salsa, and tortilla chips.

Nutrition Facts per serving: 409 cal., 13 g total fat (5 g sat. fat), 41 mg chol., 1,423 mg sodium, 52 g carbo., 12 g fiber, 26 g pro.

SPICY PEANUT PORK CHOPS

Prep: 20 minutes

Cook: 6 to **8** hours
(low) or 3 to 4 hours (high)

Makes: 8 servings

8 boneless pork chops, cut ³/₄ inch thick (about 2 pounds total)

1 tablespoon cooking oil

2 cups purchased shredded carrots

2 medium onions, chopped

1 14-ounce can light coconut milk

½ cup chicken broth

½ cup creamy peanut butter

½ teaspoon crushed red pepper

  Hot cooked basmati rice or shredded Chinese cabbage (napa)

1 In a large skillet brown pork chops, half at a time, in hot oil, turning once.

2 Place carrots and onions in a 3½- or 4-quart slow cooker. In a medium bowl combine coconut milk, chicken broth, peanut butter, and crushed red pepper; pour over vegetables. Place chops on top of vegetables.

3 Cover and cook on low-heat setting for 6 to 8 hours or on high-heat setting for 3 to 4 hours.

4 Serve with rice.

Nutrition Facts per serving: 500 cal., 18 g total fat (6 g sat. fat), 62 mg chol., 212 mg sodium, 47 g carbo., 3 g fiber, 32 g pro.

PORK CHOPS WITH ORANGE-DIJON SAUCE

Prep: 15 minutes

Cook: 6 to **7** hours (low) or 3 to 3½ hours (high)

Makes: 6 servings

6	boneless pork sirloin chops, cut 1 inch thick (about 2 pounds total)
	Salt
	Black pepper
½	teaspoon dried thyme, crushed
1	cup orange marmalade
⅓	cup Dijon-style mustard
¼	cup water

1 Sprinkle both sides of chops lightly with salt and pepper. Sprinkle chops with thyme. Place chops in a 3½- or 4-quart slow cooker. In a small bowl combine orange marmalade and mustard. Remove 2 tablespoons of the marmalade mixture; cover and refrigerate. Combine remaining marmalade mixture and the water. Pour over chops.

2 Cover and cook on low-heat setting for 6 to 7 hours or on high-heat setting for 3 to 3½ hours.

3 Transfer chops to a serving platter; discard cooking liquid. Spread reserved marmalade mixture over chops.

Nutrition Facts per serving: 277 cal., 5 g total fat (2 g sat. fat), 59 mg chol., 405 mg sodium, 35 g carbo., 0 g fiber, 20 g pro.

SOUTHWEST PORK CHOPS

Prep: 15 minutes

Cook: 5 hours (low) or 2½ hours (high) plus 30 minutes (high)

·····························

Makes: 6 servings

6   pork rib chops, cut ³/₄ inch thick (about 2½ pounds total)
1   15-ounce can Mexican-style or Tex-Mex-style chili beans, undrained
1¼   cups bottled salsa
1   cup fresh* or loose-pack frozen whole kernel corn
     Hot cooked rice
     Snipped fresh cilantro (optional)

1 Trim fat from chops. Place chops in a 3½- or 4-quart slow cooker. Add undrained chili beans and salsa.

2 Cover and cook on low-heat setting for 5 hours or on high-heat setting for 2½ hours.

3 If using low-heat setting, turn to high-heat setting. Stir in corn. Cover and cook for 30 minutes more. Serve over rice. If desired, sprinkle with snipped cilantro.

*Note: You can cut about 1 cup whole kernel corn from 2 medium size ears of fresh corn.

Test Kitchen Tip: If you want to cook this dish all day, substitute 8 boneless pork chops, cut ³/₄ inch thick (about 2 pounds total), for the 6 rib chops. (When cooked this long, chops with bone may leave bony fragments in the cooked mixture.) Cover and cook on low-heat setting for 9½ hours. Turn to high-heat setting. Stir in corn. Cover and cook for 30 minutes more. Serve over rice. If desired, sprinkle with snipped cilantro. Makes 8 servings.

Nutrition Facts per serving: 334 cal., 7 g total fat (2 g sat. fat), 77 mg chol., 716 mg sodium, 34 g carbo., 4 g fiber, 33 g pro.

APRICOT-GLAZED PORK ROAST

Prep: 15 minutes

Cook: 10 to **12** hours
(low) or 5 to 6 hours (high)

....

Makes: 6 to 8 servings

1   3- to 3½-pound boneless pork shoulder roast

1   18-ounce jar apricot preserves

1   large onion, chopped

¼   cup chicken broth

2   tablespoons Dijon-style mustard

    Hot cooked rice (optional)

1 Trim fat from roast. If necessary, cut roast to fit into a 3½- to 6-quart slow cooker. Place roast in slow cooker. In a small bowl combine apricot preserves, onion, chicken broth, and mustard; pour over roast.

2 Cover and cook on low-heat setting for 10 to 12 hours or on high-heat setting for 5 to 6 hours.

3 Transfer roast to a serving plate. Skim fat from sauce. Spoon some of the sauce over roast. If desired, serve remaining sauce with hot cooked rice.

Nutrition Facts per serving: 456 cal., 10 g total fat (3 g sat. fat), 93 mg chol., 184 mg sodium, 61 g carbo., 2 g fiber, 29 g pro.

PORK & SLAW BARBECUE ROLLS

Prep: 10 minutes

Cook: 10 to **12** hours (low) or 5 to 6 hours (high)

Makes: 16 servings

1	4- to 5-pound pork shoulder blade roast
³⁄₄	cup cider vinegar
2	tablespoons brown sugar
½	teaspoon salt
½	teaspoon crushed red pepper
¼	teaspoon black pepper
16	kaiser rolls, split and toasted
	Purchased deli coleslaw

1 Cut roast to fit into a 4- to 6-quart slow cooker; place meat in slow cooker. In a small bowl combine vinegar, brown sugar, salt, red pepper, and black pepper. Pour over meat.

2 Cover and cook on low-heat setting for 10 to 12 hours or on high-heat setting for 5 to 6 hours.

3 Transfer roast to a cutting board; reserve cooking juices. When cool enough to handle, cut meat off bones and coarsely chop. In a medium bowl combine meat and as much of the juices as desired to moisten. Spoon meat onto roll bottoms. Top with coleslaw. Add roll tops.

Nutrition Facts per serving: 272 cal., 6 g total fat (2 g sat. fat), 41 mg chol., 563 mg sodium, 34 g carbo., 1 g fiber, 18 g pro.

HOT PEPPER PORK SANDWICHES

Prep: 20 minutes

Cook: 11 to **12** hours
(low) or 5½ to 6 hours
(high)

· ·

Makes: 8 servings

1 2½- to 3-pound boneless pork shoulder roast

2 teaspoons fajita seasoning

2 10-ounce cans enchilada sauce

1 or 2 fresh jalapeño chile peppers, seeded (if desired) and finely chopped,* or 1 large green or red sweet pepper, cut into bite-size strips

8 kaiser rolls, split and toasted

1 Trim fat from roast. If necessary, cut roast to fit into a 3½- to 5-quart slow cooker. Place roast in slow cooker. Sprinkle meat with fajita seasoning. Add enchilada sauce and jalapeño or sweet pepper.

2 Cover and cook on low-heat setting for 11 to 12 hours or on high-heat setting for 5½ to 6 hours.

3 Transfer roast to a cutting board. Using 2 forks, pull meat apart into shreds. Stir shredded meat into sauce mixture in slow cooker. Using a slotted spoon, spoon shredded meat mixture into toasted kaiser rolls.

***Note:** Because chile peppers contain volatile oils that can burn your skin and eyes, avoid direct contact with them as much as possible. When working with chile peppers, wear plastic or rubber gloves. If your bare hands do touch the peppers, wash your hands and nails well with soap and warm water.

Nutrition Facts per serving: 316 cal., 9 g total fat (2 g sat. fat), 58 mg chol., 891 mg sodium, 34 g carbo., 2 g fiber, 23 g pro.

HOT HONEYED SPARERIBS

Prep: 20 minutes

Cook: 6 to **7** hours (low) or 3 to 3½ hours (high)

Makes: 10 to 12 appetizer servings

3½   to 4 pounds pork baby back ribs, cut into 1-rib portions

2   cups bottled picante sauce or salsa

½   cup honey

1   tablespoon quick-cooking tapioca

1   teaspoon ground ginger

1 Preheat broiler. Place ribs on the unheated rack of a broiler pan. Broil 6 inches from the heat about 10 minutes or until brown, turning once. Transfer ribs to a 3½- to 6-quart slow cooker.

2 For sauce, in a medium bowl combine picante sauce, honey, tapioca, and ginger. Pour sauce over ribs.

3 Cover and cook on low-heat setting for 6 to 7 hours or on high-heat setting for 3 to 3½ hours.

4 Skim fat from sauce. Serve sauce with ribs.

Nutrition Facts per serving: 215 cal., 6 g total fat (2 g sat. fat), 43 mg chol., 246 mg sodium, 18 g carbo., 0 g fiber, 20 g pro.

SOUTHERN HAM STEW

Prep: 20 minutes

Cook: 8 to **10** hours (low) or 4 to 5 hours (high) plus 10 minutes (high)

. . . .

Makes: 8 servings

1½   cups dry black-eyed peas (about 9½ ounces)

4   cups water

2   cups cubed cooked ham

1   15-ounce can white hominy, rinsed and drained

1   10-ounce package frozen cut okra

1   large onion, chopped

2   teaspoons bottled minced garlic (4 cloves)

1   to 2 teaspoons Cajun or Creole seasoning

¼   teaspoon black pepper

4½   cups water

4   cups chopped fresh collard greens or fresh spinach

1   14½-ounce can stewed tomatoes, undrained

1 Rinse black-eyed peas; drain. In a large saucepan combine black-eyed peas and the 4 cups water. Bring to boiling; reduce heat. Simmer, uncovered, for 10 minutes. Drain and rinse black-eyed peas.

2 In a 3½- to 6-quart slow cooker combine black-eyed peas, ham, hominy, frozen okra, onion, garlic, Cajun seasoning, and pepper. Stir in the 4½ cups water.

3 Cover and cook on low-heat setting for 8 to 10 hours or on high-heat setting for 4 to 5 hours.

4 If using low-heat setting, turn to high-heat setting. Stir in collard greens and undrained tomatoes. Cover and cook for 10 minutes more.

Nutrition Facts per serving: 245 cal., 5 g total fat (1 g sat. fat), 20 mg chol., 673 mg sodium, 35 g carbo., 7 g fiber, 16 g pro.

PLUM GOOD SAUSAGE & MEATBALLS

Prep: 10 minutes

Cook: 5 to **6** hours
(low) or 2½ to 3 hours
(high)

Makes: 16 appetizer
servings

1   18-ounce bottle barbecue sauce (1⅔ cups)

1   10- or 12-ounce jar plum jam or preserves

1   16-ounce link cooked jalapeño smoked sausage or smoked sausage,
cut into bite-size pieces

1   16- to 18-ounce package Italian-style or original flavor frozen cooked
meatballs (16), thawed

1 In a 3½- or 4-quart slow cooker combine barbecue sauce and jam. Add the
sausage and thawed meatballs.

2 Cover and cook on low-heat setting for 5 to 6 hours or on high-heat setting for
2½ to 3 hours.

Nutrition Facts per serving: 267 cal., 16 g total fat (6 g sat. fat), 38 mg chol., 898 mg sodium,
19 g carbo., 2 g fiber, 12 g pro.

SAUSAGE-HOMINY SUPPER

Prep: 15 minutes
Cook: 6 to **8** hours
(low) or 3 to 4 hours (high)

. . . .

Makes: 8 servings

2   pounds cooked smoked sausage links, cut into 1-inch pieces

3   15-ounce cans golden hominy, drained

1½ cups chopped onion

1   15-ounce can tomato sauce

1   cup coarsely chopped green sweet pepper

1   6-ounce can tomato juice

½   teaspoon dried oregano, crushed

1   cup shredded mozzarella cheese (4 ounces)

1 In a 4½- to 6-quart slow cooker combine sausage, hominy, onion, tomato sauce, sweet pepper, tomato juice, and oregano.

2 Cover and cook on low-heat setting for 6 to 8 hours or on high-heat setting for 3 to 4 hours.

3 Sprinkle each serving with cheese.

Nutrition Facts per serving: 571 cal., 39 g total fat (18 g sat. fat), 58 mg chol., 1,735 mg sodium, 36 g carbo., 6 g fiber, 21 g pro.

TEXAS TWO-STEP STEW

Prep: 20 minutes

Cook: 4 to **6** hours (low) or 2 to 3 hours (high) plus 1 hour (low) or 45 minutes (high)

. . . .

Makes: 6 servings

8   ounces bulk chorizo sausage

1   medium onion, chopped

1   15-ounce can Mexican-style or Tex-Mex-style chili beans, undrained

1   11-ounce can whole kernel corn with sweet peppers, drained

1   6-ounce package regular Spanish-style rice mix

6   cups water

1 In a medium skillet cook sausage and onion over medium heat until sausage is brown. Drain off fat. Transfer sausage mixture to a 3½- or 4-quart slow cooker. Stir in undrained chili beans, drained corn, and the seasoning packet contents of the rice mix, if present (set aside remaining rice mix). Pour the water over all.

2 Cover and cook on low-heat setting for 4 to 6 hours or on high-heat setting for 2 to 3 hours.

3 Stir in remaining rice mix. Cover and cook on low-heat setting for 1 hour more or on high-heat setting for 45 minutes more.

Nutrition Facts per serving: 371 cal., 16 g total fat (6 g sat. fat), 33 mg chol., 1,424 mg sodium, 43 g carbo., 5 g fiber, 16 g pro.

CRANBERRY CHICKEN

Prep: 15 minutes

Cook: 6 to **7** hours (low) or 3 to 3½ hours (high)

Makes: 6 servings

2	medium apples, cored and cut into wedges
1	medium onion, thinly sliced
6	skinless, boneless chicken breast halves (about 2 pounds total)
1	16-ounce can whole cranberry sauce
¼	cup frozen lemonade concentrate, thawed
2	tablespoons quick-cooking tapioca
2	tablespoons honey
¼	teaspoon salt
2	6- to 6¼-ounce packages long grain and wild rice mix

1 In a 3½- or 4-quart slow cooker combine apples and onion. Place chicken on top of apple mixture. In a medium bowl combine cranberry sauce, lemonade concentrate, tapioca, honey, and salt. Pour over chicken in slow cooker.

2 Cover and cook on low-heat setting for 6 to 7 hours or on high-heat setting for 3 to 3½ hours.

3 In a large saucepan prepare long grain and wild rice with seasoning packets according to package directions. Serve chicken and apple mixture over rice.

Nutrition Facts per serving: 565 cal., 2 g total fat (1 g sat. fat), 88 mg chol., 993 mg sodium, 96 g carbo., 4 g fiber, 40 g pro.

ANGEL CHICKEN

Prep: 15 minutes

Cook: 4 to **5** hours
(low)

Makes: 6 servings

6	skinless, boneless chicken breast halves (about 1½ pounds total)
¼	cup butter
1	0.7-ounce package Italian salad dressing mix
1	10¾-ounce can condensed golden mushroom soup
½	cup dry white wine
½	of an 8-ounce tub cream cheese with chives and onion
	Hot cooked angel hair pasta
	Snipped fresh chives (optional)

1 Place chicken in a 3½- or 4-quart slow cooker. In a medium saucepan melt butter. Stir in the dry Italian salad dressing mix. Add mushroom soup, white wine, and cream cheese, stirring until smooth. Pour over the chicken.

2 Cover and cook on low-heat setting for 4 to 5 hours.

3 Serve chicken and sauce over hot cooked pasta. If desired, sprinkle with snipped chives.

Nutrition Facts per serving: 405 cal., 17 g total fat (9 g sat. fat), 110 mg chol., 1,043 mg sodium, 26 g carbo., 1 g fiber, 32 g pro.

CASHEW CHICKEN

Prep: 15 minutes
Cook: 6 to **8** hours
(low) or 3 to 4 hours (high)

Makes: 6 servings

1   10³/₄-ounce can condensed golden mushroom soup

2   tablespoons soy sauce

¹/₂   teaspoon ground ginger

1¹/₂   pounds chicken breast tenderloins or skinless, boneless chicken breasts, cut lengthwise into 1-inch-wide strips

1   cup sliced fresh mushrooms or one 4-ounce can (drained weight), sliced mushrooms, drained

1   cup sliced celery

1   cup purchased shredded carrots

1   8-ounce can sliced water chestnuts, drained

¹/₂   cup cashews

    Hot cooked rice

1 In a 3¹/₂- or 4-quart slow cooker combine mushroom soup, soy sauce, and ginger. Stir in chicken, mushrooms, celery, carrots, and water chestnuts.

2 Cover and cook on low-heat setting for 6 to 8 hours or on high-heat setting for 3 to 4 hours.

3 Stir cashews into chicken mixture. Serve over hot cooked rice.

Nutrition Facts per serving: 364 cal., 9 g total fat (2 g sat. fat), 68 mg chol., 789 mg sodium, 38 g carbo., 3 g fiber, 33 g pro.

CHERRIED CHICKEN

Prep: 20 minutes

Cook: 5 to **6** hours (low) or 2½ to 3 hours (high)

Makes: 4 servings

2½   to 3 pounds chicken drumsticks, skinned

1   teaspoon herb-pepper seasoning

1   15- to 17-ounce can pitted dark sweet cherries, drained

1   12-ounce bottle chili sauce

½   cup packed brown sugar

1 Sprinkle chicken evenly with herb-pepper seasoning. Place chicken in a 3½- or 4-quart slow cooker. In a medium bowl combine cherries, chili sauce, and brown sugar. Pour over chicken.

2 Cover and cook on low-heat setting for 5 to 6 hours or on high-heat setting for 2½ to 3 hours.

3 Remove chicken to a serving platter. Skim fat from cherry mixture. Spoon some of the cherry mixture over chicken; pass remaining cherry mixture.

Nutrition Facts per serving: 410 cal., 5 g total fat (1 g sat. fat), 105 mg chol., 1,539 mg sodium, 63 g carbo., 7 g fiber, 31 g pro.

ALFREDO CHICKEN

Prep: 20 minutes

Cook: 6 to **7** hours (low) or 3 to 3½ hours (high)

Makes: 6 servings

3   pounds meaty chicken pieces (breast halves, thighs, and drumsticks), skinned
    Salt
    Black pepper
1   16-ounce jar light Parmesan Alfredo pasta sauce
1   9-ounce package frozen Italian green beans, thawed
3   cups hot cooked whole wheat pasta
    Finely shredded Parmesan cheese (optional)

1 Place chicken in a 3½- or 4-quart slow cooker. Sprinkle lightly with salt and pepper. Pour pasta sauce over chicken.

2 Cover and cook on low-heat setting for 6 to 7 hours or on high-heat setting for 3 to 3½ hours, adding green beans for the last 30 minutes of cooking.

3 Remove chicken and green beans to a serving platter. Stir cooked pasta into sauce in cooker; serve with the chicken and beans. If desired, sprinkle with Parmesan cheese.

Nutrition Facts per serving: 392 cal., 15 g total fat (7 g sat. fat), 123 mg chol., 680 mg sodium, 26 g carbo., 3 g fiber, 36 g pro.

SPICY CHICKEN WITH PEPPERS & OLIVES

Prep: 20 minutes

Cook: 6 to **7** hours (low) or 3 to 3½ hours (high)

Makes: 6 servings

2½   to 3 pounds meaty chicken pieces (breast halves, thighs, and drumsticks), skinned

Salt

Black pepper

1   small yellow sweet pepper, coarsely chopped

½   cup sliced, pitted ripe olives and/or pimiento-stuffed green olives

1   26-ounce jar spicy red pepper pasta sauce

Hot cooked whole wheat pasta (optional)

1 Place chicken in a 3½- or 4-quart slow cooker. Sprinkle lightly with salt and black pepper. Add sweet pepper and olives to slow cooker. Pour pasta sauce over chicken mixture in slow cooker.

2 Cover and cook on low-heat setting for 6 to 7 hours or on high-heat setting for 3 to 3 ½ hours.

3 If desired, serve chicken and sauce over hot cooked pasta.

Nutrition Facts per serving: 239 cal., 10 g total fat (2 g sat. fat), 77 mg chol., 592 mg sodium, 10 g carbo., 3 g fiber, 27 g pro.

EASY CHICKEN & RICE

Prep: **15** minutes

Cook: **5** to **6** hours (low) or 2½ to 3 hours (high) plus 10 minutes (high)

Makes: 4 servings

2	cups sliced fresh mushrooms
1	cup sliced celery
½	cup chopped onion
1½	teaspoons dried dill
¼	teaspoon black pepper
2	pounds chicken thighs, skinned and fat removed
1	10¾-ounce can condensed cream of mushroom or cream of chicken soup
¾	cup chicken broth
1½	cups uncooked instant rice

1 In a 3½- or 4-quart slow cooker combine mushrooms, celery, onion, dill, and pepper. Place chicken thighs on top of mushroom mixture. In a small bowl combine soup and chicken broth. Pour over chicken.

2 Cover and cook on low-heat setting for 5 to 6 hours or on high-heat setting for 2½ to 3 hours.

3 If using low-heat setting, turn slow cooker to high-heat setting. Stir uncooked rice into the mushroom mixture. Cover and cook for 10 minutes more.

Nutrition Facts per serving: 516 cal., 12 g total fat (3 g sat. fat), 108 mg chol., 840 mg sodium, 66 g carbo., 3 g fiber, 34 g pro.

CREAMY CHICKEN NOODLE SOUP

Prep: **15** minutes

Cook: **6** to **8** hours (low) or 3 to 4 hours (high) plus 20 to 30 minutes (high)

Makes: 6 to 8 servings

5	cups water
2	10¾-ounce cans condensed creamy chicken mushroom soup
2	cups chopped cooked chicken (about 10 ounces)
1	9- to 10-ounce package frozen mixed vegetables (cut green beans, corn, diced carrots, and peas)
1	teaspoon seasoned pepper or garlic-pepper seasoning
1½	cups dried egg noodles

1 In a 3½- or 4-quart slow cooker gradually stir the water into the soup. Stir or whisk until smooth. Stir in cooked chicken, frozen vegetables, and pepper.

2 Cover and cook on low-heat setting for 6 to 8 hours or on high-heat setting for 3 to 4 hours.

3 If using low-heat setting, turn slow cooker to high-heat setting. Stir in uncooked noodles. Cover and cook for 20 to 30 minutes more or just until noodles are tender.

Nutrition Facts per serving: 262 cal., 12 g total fat (3 g sat. fat), 63 mg chol., 908 mg sodium, 21 g carbo., 3 g fiber, 19 g pro.

MEXICAN-STYLE SAUSAGE & BEANS

Prep: 15 minutes

Cook: 6 to **7** hours (low) or 3 to 3½ hours (high)

Makes: 6 servings

1	pound smoked turkey sausage, sliced
1	15-ounce can white kidney beans (cannellini beans), rinsed and drained
1	15-ounce can black beans, rinsed and drained
1	15-ounce can red kidney beans, rinsed and drained
1½	cups loose-pack frozen whole kernel corn
1½	cups bottled salsa
1	cup chopped green sweet pepper
1	large onion, chopped
1½	teaspoons bottled minced garlic (3 cloves)
1	teaspoon ground cumin

1 In a 3½- or 4-quart slow cooker combine sausage, beans, corn, salsa, sweet pepper, onion, garlic, and cumin.

2 Cover and cook on low-heat setting for 6 to 7 hours or on high-heat setting for 3 to 3½ hours.

Nutrition Facts per serving: 307 cal., 8 g total fat (2 g sat. fat), 47 mg chol., 1,213 mg sodium, 47 g carbo., 12 g fiber, 28 g pro.

CAJUN SHRIMP & RICE

Prep: **20** minutes

Cook: **5** to **6** hours (low)
or 3 to 3½ hours (high)
plus 15 minutes (high)

Makes: 6 servings

1   28-ounce can tomatoes, undrained and cut up

1   14-ounce can chicken broth

1   cup chopped onion

1   cup chopped green sweet pepper

1   6- to 6¼-ounce package long grain and wild rice mix

¼   cup water

1   teaspoon bottled minced garlic (2 cloves)

½   teaspoon Cajun seasoning

1   pound cooked, peeled, and deveined shrimp

    Bottled hot pepper sauce (optional)

1 In a 3½- or 4-quart slow cooker combine tomatoes, chicken broth, onion, sweet pepper, rice mix with seasoning packet, the water, garlic, and Cajun seasoning.

2 Cover and cook on low-heat setting for 5 to 6 hours or on high-heat setting for 3 to 3½ hours.

3 If using low-heat setting, turn slow cooker to high-heat setting. Stir shrimp into rice mixture. Cover and cook for 15 minutes more. If desired, pass hot pepper sauce.

Nutrition Facts per serving: 223 cal., 2 g total fat (0 g sat. fat), 147 mg chol., 1,063 mg sodium, 32 g carbo., 3 g fiber, 21 g pro.

BAKED GOODS

ALMOST SOURDOUGH CHEESE BREAD

Prep: 30 minutes
Rise: 45 minutes
Bake: 30 minutes

. . . .

Oven: 350°F
Makes: 10 servings

1/3 cup warm water (110° to 115°F)

1 16-ounce package hot roll mix

1/4 cup dairy sour cream

1 egg

3 tablespoons cider vinegar

2 tablespoons butter, softened

1 tablespoon butter, melted

4 ounces cheese (such as cheddar, Monterey Jack, Monterey Jack with jalapeño peppers, Swiss, or American), shredded (1 cup)

1/4 cup chopped pecans or walnuts, toasted

1 tablespoon yellow cornmeal

1 In a large bowl combine the warm water and the yeast from hot roll mix; let stand for 5 minutes. Stir in the flour mixture from roll mix, the sour cream, egg, vinegar, and the 2 tablespoons softened butter, stirring until dough pulls away from the side of the bowl. Turn dough out onto a floured surface. Knead dough about 5 minutes or until smooth and elastic.

2 Cover dough; let rest for 5 minutes. On a lightly floured surface, roll dough to a 14×12-inch rectangle. Brush with the 1 tablespoon melted butter. Sprinkle with cheese and nuts. Starting from a short side, roll up into a spiral.

3 Grease a large baking sheet and sprinkle with cornmeal. Place loaf on prepared baking sheet. Cover and let rise in a warm place until almost double in size (about 45 minutes).

4 Meanwhile, preheat oven to 350°. Bake in preheated oven for 30 to 35 minutes or until golden and bread sounds hollow when lightly tapped. Cool slightly on wire rack. Serve warm.

Nutrition Facts per serving: 296 cal., 13 g total fat (6 g sat. fat), 47 mg chol., 383 mg sodium, 36 g carbo., 0 g fiber, 11 g pro.

ONION-CHEESE SUPPER BREAD

Prep: 15 minutes
Bake: 20 minutes

• •

Oven: 400°F
Makes: 8 servings

2	tablespoons butter or margarine
1/4	cup chopped onion
1	egg
1/4	cup milk
1 1/4	cups packaged biscuit mix
1	cup shredded American cheese or cheddar cheese (4 ounces)
2	teaspoons poppy seeds
	Cooked, thinly sliced onion (optional)

1 Preheat oven to 400°. Grease an 8×1 1/2-inch round baking pan; set aside.

2 In a small skillet melt 1 tablespoon of the butter over medium heat. Add chopped onion; cook until onion is tender.

3 In a small bowl whisk together egg and milk. Add to biscuit mix; stir just until moistened. Add the chopped onion mixture, half of the cheese, and half of the poppy seeds to biscuit mix mixture. Spread batter into prepared pan. Sprinkle with the remaining poppy seeds. Melt remaining 1 tablespoon butter; drizzle over batter in baking pan.

4 Bake in preheated oven for 10 minutes. Sprinkle top with remaining cheese. If desired, arrange cooked, thinly sliced onion on top. Bake about 10 minutes more or until a toothpick inserted near the center comes out clean. Serve warm.

Nutrition Facts per serving: 202 cal., 12 g total fat (6 g sat. fat), 49 mg chol., 528 mg sodium, 16 g carbo., 1 g fiber, 6 g pro.

EASY TAPENADE ROLLS

Prep: 20 minutes

Rise: 30 minutes

Bake: 15 minutes

Oven: 350°F

Makes: 12 rolls

⅓   cup purchased olive tapenade

¼   cup finely shredded or grated Romano cheese (1 ounce)

1   16-ounce package frozen white roll dough, (12) thawed

1   tablespoon butter, melted

2   tablespoons finely shredded or grated Romano cheese

1 Lightly grease an 11×7×1½-inch baking pan; set aside. In a small bowl combine tapenade and the ¼ cup cheese.

2 On a lightly floured surface, pat each thawed roll into a 3-inch circle. Place a rounded teaspoon of the tapenade mixture onto the center of each dough circle. Bring up edge of each roll and pinch to seal and enclose filling. Place filled rolls, seam sides down, in prepared pan. Cover and let rise in a warm place until nearly double in size (about 30 minutes). Meanwhile, preheat oven to 350°.

3 Brush tops of rolls with melted butter. Sprinkle with the 2 tablespoons cheese.

4 Bake in preheated oven for 15 to 20 minutes or until rolls are golden and sound hollow when lightly tapped. Remove rolls from pan. Cool on wire rack. Serve slightly warm or at room temperature.

Nutrition Facts per roll: 156 cal., 8 g total fat (2 g sat. fat), 5 mg chol., 365 mg sodium, 18 g carbo., 1 g fiber, 4 g pro.

COBBLESTONE-RANCH DINNER ROLLS

Prep: 40 minutes
Rise: 30 minutes
Bake: 20 minutes

Oven: 350°F
Makes: 12 rolls

Nonstick cooking spray
⅓ cup butter or margarine, melted
⅓ cup finely shredded Parmesan cheese
1 0.4-ounce envelope ranch salad dressing mix
1 16-ounce package frozen white roll dough (12 rolls), thawed
1 tablespoon yellow cornmeal

1 Coat a 9×1½-inch round baking pan with cooking spray; set aside. In a small bowl combine 3 tablespoons of the melted butter, the Parmesan cheese, and dry ranch dressing mix; set aside.

2 On a lightly floured surface, roll each thawed roll to a 3- to 4-inch circle. Place about 1 rounded teaspoon of the Parmesan mixture in the center of each dough circle; pull edges to center and pinch to seal, shaping into a round ball. Place balls in the prepared pan. Drizzle rolls with remaining melted butter. Sprinkle with cornmeal. Cover and let rise in a warm place until rolls are nearly double in size (30 to 45 minutes).

3 Meanwhile, preheat oven to 350°. Bake in preheated oven for 20 to 25 minutes or until golden. Carefully invert to remove rolls. Invert again onto a serving platter. Let stand for 15 minutes before serving.

Nutrition Facts per roll: 160 cal., 8 g total fat (4 g sat. fat), 16 mg chol., 261 mg sodium, 19 g carbo., 1 g fiber, 4 g pro.

CHEESE-COATED ROLLS

Prep: 20 minutes
Rise: 30 minutes
Bake: 30 minutes

Oven: 375°F
Makes: 12 rolls

1 cup shredded aged (dry) Monterey Jack cheese or Parmesan cheese (4 ounces)

2 teaspoons chili powder

2 16-ounce packages frozen white roll dough (12 rolls), thawed

1/3 cup butter, melted

1 Generously grease twelve 3½-inch (jumbo) muffin cups. Set aside.

2 In a small bowl stir together cheese and chili powder.

3 Roll each roll in butter; coat with cheese mixture. Place 2 rolls in each prepared muffin cup. Drizzle tops of rolls with any remaining butter mixture.

4 Cover and let rise in a warm place until rolls are nearly double in size (about 30 minutes).

5 Meanwhile, preheat oven to 375°. Bake in preheated oven about 30 minutes or until rolls sound hollow when lightly tapped. Immediately remove from muffin cups. Cool slightly on a wire rack. Serve warm.

Nutrition Facts per roll: 299 cal., 14 g total fat (5 g sat. fat), 18 mg chol., 415 mg sodium, 37 g carbo., 2 g fiber, 9 g pro.

CORN BREAD WITH DRIED TOMATOES

Prep: 20 minutes
Bake: 20 minutes

. . . .

Oven: 350°F
Makes: 9 servings

⅓	cup bulgur or cracked wheat
¼	cup dried tomato bits*
1¼	cups boiling water
¼	cup toasted wheat germ
1	8¼-ounce package corn muffin mix
¼	cup finely shredded Parmesan cheese (1 ounce)

1 Preheat oven to 350°. In a medium bowl combine bulgur wheat and tomato bits. Pour the boiling water over bulgur mixture. Let stand for 5 minutes. Drain well.

2 Meanwhile, grease an 8×8×2-inch baking pan; sprinkle bottom of pan with half of the wheat germ.

3 Prepare corn muffin mix according to package directions for corn bread. Stir drained bulgur and tomato mixture into batter along with the Parmesan cheese. Spread in prepared pan. Sprinkle with remaining wheat germ.

4 Bake in preheated oven for 20 to 25 minutes or until a toothpick inserted in center comes out clean. Serve warm.

*Note: If you can't purchase dried tomato bits, finely snip dried tomatoes.

Nutrition Facts per serving: 151 cal., 4 g total fat (1 g sat. fat), 26 mg chol., 269 mg sodium, 24 g carbo., 1 g fiber, 4 g pro.

BANANA-CINNAMON STREUSEL LOAF

Prep: 25 minutes
Bake: 45 minutes

Oven: 375°F
Makes: 1 loaf (12 to 14 slices)

- ⅓ cup all-purpose flour
- ⅓ cup packed brown sugar
- ½ teaspoon ground cinnamon
- ¼ cup cold butter
- ½ cup chopped pecans, toasted
- 1 14-ounce package banana quick bread mix

1 Preheat oven to 375°. Generously grease bottom and 1 inch up sides of a 9×5×3-inch loaf pan; set aside. For streusel mixture, in a medium bowl combine flour, brown sugar, and cinnamon. Using a pastry blender, cut in butter until crumbly. Stir in pecans; set aside.

2 Prepare banana quick bread mix according to package directions. Spoon half of the batter into prepared pan; sprinkle with half of the streusel mixture. Add remaining batter. Sprinkle with remaining streusel mixture.

3 Bake in preheated oven for 45 to 50 minutes or until a toothpick inserted near center comes out clean. Cool in pan on a wire rack for 10 minutes. Remove from pan; cool completely on wire rack. Wrap and store overnight before slicing.

Nutrition Facts per slice: 233 cal., 9 g total fat (3 g sat. fat), 11 mg chol., 234 mg sodium, 35 g carbo., 1 g fiber, 3 g pro.

JEWELED PUMPKIN LOAF

Prep: 15 minutes
Bake: 55 minutes

. . . .

Oven: 350°F
Makes: 1 large or 3 small loaves (16 to 24 servings)

½   cup apricot nectar

½   cup coarsely chopped dried apricots

⅓   cup coarsely chopped dried cranberries

⅔   cup water

3   tablespoons cooking oil

2   eggs

1   14-ounce package pumpkin quick bread mix

1   recipe Apricot Icing

1 Preheat oven to 350°. In a small bowl combine apricot nectar, apricots, and cranberries; let stand for 5 minutes. Grease the bottom and ½ inch up sides of an 8×4×2-inch loaf pan or three 5¾×3×2-inch loaf pans. Set aside.

2 In a large bowl whisk together the water, oil, and eggs; stir in bread mix. Using a wooden spoon, beat until well mixed. Stir in undrained dried fruit mixture. Spoon into prepared pan(s).

3 Bake in preheated oven for 55 to 65 minutes for large loaf, 30 to 35 minutes for smaller loaves, or until a toothpick inserted near center(s) comes out clean. Cool in pan(s) on wire rack for 10 minutes. Remove from pan(s). Cool completely on wire rack. For easier slicing, wrap and store overnight before slicing. Drizzle with Apricot Icing before slicing.

Apricot Icing: In a small bowl stir together ½ cup sifted powdered sugar and enough apricot nectar (2 to 3 teaspoons) to make of drizzling consistency.

Nutrition Facts per serving: 165 cal., 4 g total fat (1 g sat. fat), 27 mg chol., 152 mg sodium, 29 g carbo., 1 g fiber, 2 g pro.

CINNAMON GRANOLA LOAF

Prep: 20 minutes
Rise: 45 minutes
Bake: 25 minutes

Oven: 350°F
Makes: 12 servings

1   1-pound loaf frozen sweet or white bread dough, thawed

2   tablespoons butter, softened

3   tablespoons cinnamon sugar*

½   cup granola cereal (plain or with raisins), crushed

½   cup chopped almonds or pecans, toasted

1 Grease an 8×4×2-inch loaf pan; set aside.

2 On a lightly floured surface, roll the thawed bread dough to a 10×8-inch rectangle. Spread with 1 tablespoon of the softened butter. Sprinkle with 2 tablespoons of the cinnamon sugar. Sprinkle with crushed granola and nuts to within ½ inch of the edges. Roll up tightly starting from a short side. Pinch seam to seal. Place, seam side down, in prepared pan.

3 Cover and let rise in a warm place until nearly double in size (45 to 60 minutes).

4 Preheat oven to 350°. Bake in the preheated oven about 25 minutes or until bread sounds hollow when lightly tapped. Remove from pan to wire rack. Spread with remaining 1 tablespoon butter and sprinkle with remaining 1 tablespoon cinnamon sugar.

*Note: Look in the spice section of the supermarket for prepared cinnamon sugar. Or to make your own cinnamon sugar, in a small bowl stir together 3 tablespoons sugar and 1 teaspoon ground cinnamon.

Nutrition Facts per serving: 172 cal., 6 g total fat (2 g sat. fat), 5 mg chol., 208 mg sodium, 25 g carbo., 1 g fiber, 4 g pro.

STEP-SAVING SWEET POTATO BREAD

Prep: 15 minutes
Bake: 30 minutes

. . . .

Oven: 350°F
Makes: 4 mini loaves (16 slices total) or 1 large loaf (16 slices)

1	14- to 16-ounce package banana, cranberry, or cranberry orange quick bread mix
$^1/_2$	teaspoon ground cinnamon
$^1/_8$	teaspoon ground nutmeg
$^2/_3$	cup water
$^1/_2$	cup drained and mashed canned sweet potatoes
2	beaten eggs
2	tablespoons cooking oil
1	recipe Orange Icing

1 Preheat oven to 350°. Grease and lightly flour bottom(s) and 1 inch up the side(s) of four $4^1/_2\times2^1/_2\times1^1/_2$-inch loaf pans or one 8×4×2-inch loaf pan; set aside.

2 In a large bowl stir together quick bread mix, cinnamon, and nutmeg. Add the water, sweet potatoes, eggs, and oil. Stir just until moistened.

3 Pour batter into pan(s). Bake in preheated oven for 30 to 35 minutes for small pans, 55 to 60 minutes for large pan, or until a toothpick inserted near center(s) comes out clean.

4 Cool in the pan(s) on a wire rack for 10 minutes. Remove from pan(s); cool completely on wire rack. If desired, for easier slicing, wrap and store loave(s) overnight in a cool, dry place.

5 Before serving, drizzle loaves with Orange Icing.

Orange Icing: In a small bowl stir together $^1/_2$ cup powdered sugar and enough orange juice to make icing of drizzling consistency (1 to 2 teaspoons).

Nutrition Facts per slice: 143 cal., 3 g total fat (0 g sat. fat), 27 mg chol., 157 mg sodium, 25 g carbo., 1 g fiber, 2 g pro.

PARMESAN & PINE NUT FOCACCIA

Prep: 25 minutes
Rise: 30 minutes
Bake: 15 minutes

Oven: 375°F
Makes: 24 servings

Nonstick cooking spray
1   16-ounce package hot roll mix
1   egg
¼   cup olive oil
⅓   cup pine nuts
¼   cup grated Parmesan cheese (1 ounce)
1   teaspoon dried Italian seasoning, crushed

1 Lightly coat a 15×10×1-inch baking pan or a large baking sheet with cooking spray; set aside.

2 Prepare the hot roll mix according to package directions for the basic dough, using the 1 egg and substituting 2 tablespoons of the olive oil for the margarine called for on package. Stir pine nuts into the dough. Knead dough; allow to rest as directed.

3 Press dough into the prepared baking pan, or press dough into a 15×10-inch rectangle on the prepared baking sheet. With fingertips, press indentations every inch or so in dough. Brush remaining 2 tablespoons olive oil over dough.

4 In a small bowl stir together Parmesan cheese and Italian seasoning. Sprinkle over dough. Cover; let dough rise in a warm place until nearly double in size (about 30 minutes).

5 Preheat oven to 375°. Bake in preheated oven for 15 to 18 minutes or until golden. Cool for 10 minutes on a wire rack. Remove focaccia from pan or baking sheet; cool completely on wire rack.

Nutrition Facts per serving: 108 cal., 4 g total fat (1 g sat. fat), 10 mg chol., 128 mg sodium, 15 g carbo., 0 g fiber, 4 g pro.

CARAMELIZED ONION & BRIE FOCACCIA

Prep: 35 minutes
Rise: 25 minutes
Bake: 25 minutes

Oven: 400°F
Makes: 12 servings

1	16-ounce package hot roll mix
1	cup warm water (120°F to 130°F)
1	egg
2	tablespoons butter, softened
2	tablespoons butter
2	cups thinly sliced onion
2	teaspoons sugar
2	tablespoons balsamic vinegar or cider vinegar
1/4	cup sliced almonds
8	ounces Brie cheese (remove rind, if desired), thinly sliced

1 In a large bowl combine the flour mixture and yeast from hot roll mix. Stir in the warm water, egg, and 2 tablespoons softened butter, stirring until dough pulls away from side of bowl. Turn dough out onto floured surface. With floured hands, shape dough into a ball. Knead dough about 5 minutes or until smooth. (If necessary, sprinkle additional flour over surface to reduce stickiness.) Cover; let rest for 5 minutes.

2 Grease a 12-inch pizza pan or large baking sheet. Place dough on pizza pan or baking sheet. Press into a circle 12 inches in diameter. Cover loosely; let rise in a warm place until double in size (about 25 minutes).

3 Meanwhile, preheat oven to 400°. In a large skillet melt 2 tablespoons butter over medium-low heat. Add onion; cover and cook for 10 to 12 minutes or until onion is tender and slightly golden, stirring occasionally. Stir in sugar. Cook and stir, uncovered, for 1 minute. Add vinegar; cook, uncovered, for 5 minutes more, stirring occasionally. Remove from heat.

4 Uncover dough. With your fingers or a wooden spoon handle, make deep indentations in dough 1 inch apart. Bake in preheated oven for 10 minutes. Spoon onion mixture over partially baked dough. Sprinkle with almonds. Evenly arrange Brie pieces on top. Bake about 15 minutes more or until bottom crust, when carefully lifted, is evenly brown. Cool slightly. Cut into wedges. Serve warm.

Nutrition Facts per serving: 274 cal., 12 g total fat (6 g sat. fat), 47 mg chol., 417 mg sodium, 30 g carbo., 1 g fiber, 9 g pro.

CHECKERBOARD ROLLS

Prep: 20 minutes
Bake: 15 minutes

Oven: 375°F
Makes: 16 rolls

2   tablespoons poppy seeds

2   tablespoons sesame seeds

1   teaspoon lemon-pepper seasoning

2   tablespoons yellow cornmeal

2   tablespoons grated or finely shredded Parmesan cheese

3   tablespoons butter, melted

1   16-ounce package frozen white roll dough (12 rolls)

1 Grease a 9-inch square baking pan; set aside. In a shallow dish combine poppy seeds, sesame seeds, and lemon-pepper seasoning. In another shallow dish combine cornmeal and Parmesan cheese. Place butter in a third dish. Working quickly, roll dough pieces in butter, then in one of the seasoning mixtures to lightly coat. (Coat half of the rolls with one seasoning mixture and the remaining rolls with the other seasoning mixture.) Alternate rolls in prepared pan. Cover rolls with greased plastic wrap. Let thaw in refrigerator for at least 8 hours or up to 24 hours.

2 Remove pan from refrigerator; uncover and let stand at room temperature for 45 minutes. After 35 minutes, preheat oven to 375°.

3 Bake rolls in preheated oven for 15 to 20 minutes or until golden. Remove rolls from pan to wire rack. Cool slightly.

Nutrition Facts per roll: 137 cal., 5 g total fat (2 g sat. fat), 7 mg chol., 244 mg sodium, 19 g carbo., 1 g fiber, 4 g pro.

HAVE-A-BALL MINI ROLLS

Prep: 20 minutes
Rise: 30 minutes
Bake: 13 minutes

Oven: 350°F
Makes: 30 to 36 mini rolls

1   16-ounce frozen white or whole wheat bread dough, thawed
1   egg white
1   tablespoon water
    Fennel seeds, mustard seeds, and/or dill seeds

1 Lightly grease thirty to thirty-six 1¾-inch muffin cups or a baking sheet; set aside.

2 Divide dough into 30 to 36 pieces. Shape into small balls. Place rolls in prepared muffin cups or on prepared baking sheet.

3 Cover; let rise until nearly double in size (about 30 minutes). In a small bowl whisk together egg white and the water. Brush over rolls. Sprinkle generously with desired seeds.

4 Preheat oven to 350°. Bake in preheated oven for 13 to 15 minutes or until golden. Transfer rolls to wire racks. Serve warm.

Nutrition Facts per mini roll: 37 cal., 0 g total fat (0 g sat. fat), 0 mg chol., 2 mg sodium, 7 g carbo., 0 g fiber, 1 g pro.

GARLIC-CHEESE TWISTS

Prep: 30 minutes
Bake: 15 minutes

Oven: 375°F
Makes: 24 twists

¼   cup butter or margarine, softened
1   teaspoon bottled minced garlic (2 cloves)
½   teaspoon dried Italian seasoning, crushed
1   16-ounce loaf frozen bread dough, thawed
2   tablespoons pine nuts, toasted
½   cup finely shredded Parmesan cheese (2 ounces)
     Milk

1 Grease baking sheets; set aside. In a small bowl stir together butter, garlic, and Italian seasoning. Set aside.

2 On a lightly floured surface, roll bread dough into a 12-inch square. (If dough is too elastic, let rest for 5 to 10 minutes before rolling.) Spread butter mixture evenly over dough. Sprinkle with pine nuts, pressing into dough slightly. Sprinkle with cheese.

3 Fold dough into thirds. With a sharp knife or pastry wheel, cut dough crosswise into twenty-four ½-inch-wide strips. Twist each strip once; pinch ends to seal.

4 Place twists about 2 inches apart on prepared baking sheets. Cover and chill for at least 6 hours or up to 24 hours.

5 Preheat oven to 375°. Brush a little milk over each twist. Bake in preheated oven for 15 to 18 minutes or until golden. Serve warm.

Nutrition Facts per twist: 81 cal., 4 g total fat (2 g sat. fat), 7 mg chol., 154 mg sodium, 10 g carbo., 0 g fiber, 2 g pro.

ONION ROLLS

Prep: 25 minutes
Rise: 20 minutes
Bake: 20 minutes

. . . .

Oven: 375°F
Makes: 12 rolls

2	cups chopped onion
1	teaspoon dried basil, crushed
1	teaspoon paprika
⅛	teaspoon salt
1	tablespoon butter
1	tablespoon sugar
⅓	cup pine nuts, toasted
1	16-ounce package hot roll mix
1	tablespoon butter, melted

1 In a large skillet cook onion, basil, paprika, and salt in 1 tablespoon hot butter until onion is tender. Add sugar; cook and stir for 1 minute. Remove from heat and stir in pine nuts; cool slightly.

2 Prepare hot roll mix and let stand according to package directions. Grease a 13×9×2-inch baking pan; set aside.

3 To shape, on lightly floured surface, roll dough to a 12×8-inch rectangle. Spread the onion mixture over dough to within 1 inch of long edges. Roll up rectangle starting from a long side. Seal seams. Slice into 12 pieces. Place pieces, cut sides down, in prepared pan.

4 Cover dough loosely with plastic wrap, leaving room for rolls to rise. Let rise in a warm place until double in size (20 to 30 minutes). Uncover rolls.

5 Meanwhile, preheat oven to 375°. Bake in preheated oven for 20 to 25 minutes or until golden. Brush with 1 tablespoon melted butter. Serve warm.

Nutrition Facts per roll: 215 cal., 7 g total fat (2 g sat. fat), 22 mg chol., 293 mg sodium, 33 g carbo., 1 g fiber, 7 g pro.

PARMESAN PASTRY SPIRALS

Prep: 10 minutes
Bake: 12 minutes
Freeze: 30 minutes

. . . .

Oven: 350°F
Makes: about 24 spirals

½ of a 17.3-ounce package frozen puff pastry (1 sheet), thawed
1 tablespoon milk
⅓ cup grated Parmesan cheese

1 On a lightly floured surface, roll puff pastry sheet into a 14×10-inch rectangle. Brush pastry with some of the milk; sprinkle with Parmesan cheese. Starting at a short side, loosely roll up into a spiral, stopping at center; repeat, starting at other short side. (Roll-ups should meet in center. Do not coil tightly.) Wrap in plastic wrap; freeze for 30 minutes.

2 Preheat oven to 350°. Line 2 baking sheets with parchment paper; set aside. Unwrap roll and place on a cutting board. Brush with remaining milk. Cut pastry roll crosswise into ⅜-inch-thick slices. Place slices, cut sides down, on the prepared baking sheets, reshaping as necessary.

3 Bake in preheated oven for 12 to 14 minutes or until golden and crisp. Transfer to a wire rack; cool slightly. Serve warm.

Make-Ahead Directions: Prepare Parmesan Pastry Spirals as directed in step 1, except freeze spirals for up to 8 hours. Unwrap, cut, and bake as directed in steps 2 and 3.

Nutrition Facts per spiral: 50 cal., 4 g total fat (0 g sat. fat), 1 mg chol., 59 mg sodium, 4 g carbo., 0 g fiber, 1 g pro.

GARLIC DINNER ROLLS

Prep: 15 minutes
Bake: 13 minutes

. . . .

Oven: 375°F
Makes: 12 rolls

1	11-ounce package (12) refrigerated breadsticks
2	tablespoons purchased garlic butter spread, melted
½	cup shredded or grated Asiago or Romano cheese (2 ounces)
1	teaspoon dried parsley flakes
⅛	teaspoon cayenne pepper

1 Preheat oven to 375°. Line a large baking sheet with foil; set aside. On a lightly floured surface, separate dough into 12 breadsticks. Cut each piece lengthwise into three strips, leaving ¾ inch uncut at one end. For each roll, coil strips from cut end down toward uncut base, coiling outside strips away from the center and coiling the center strip either direction. If necessary, pinch slightly to hold shape. Transfer to prepared baking sheet.

2 Brush rolls with melted garlic butter spread. In a small bowl combine Asiago cheese, parsley, and cayenne pepper; generously sprinkle cheese mixture over rolls.

3 Bake in preheated oven for 13 to 15 minutes or until golden. Serve warm.

Nutrition Facts per roll: 112 cal., 5 g total fat (2 g sat. fat), 8 mg chol., 263 mg sodium, 12 g carbo., 0 g fiber, 3 g pro.

PARMESAN ROSETTES

Prep: 15 minutes
Bake: 15 minutes

Oven: 375°F
Makes: 12 rosettes

1	11-ounce package (12) refrigerated breadsticks
3	tablespoons grated Parmesan or Romano cheese
1	teaspoon sesame seeds
½	teaspoon dried Italian seasoning, crushed
¼	teaspoon garlic powder
2	tablespoons butter, melted

1 Preheat oven to 375°. Separate breadsticks and uncoil into individual pieces. On a lightly floured surface, roll each piece into a 12-inch-long rope.

2 Tie each rope in a loose knot, leaving 2 long ends. Tuck the top end of the rope under roll. Bring bottom end up and tuck into center of roll.

3 In a shallow dish combine Parmesan cheese, sesame seeds, Italian seasoning, and garlic powder. Brush top and sides of each rosette with melted butter. Carefully dip the top and sides of each rosette into the cheese mixture.

4 Place rosettes 2 to 3 inches apart on an ungreased baking sheet. Bake in preheated oven about 15 minutes or until golden. Serve warm.

Nutrition Facts per rosette: 135 cal., 5 g total fat (2 g sat. fat), 6 mg chol., 334 mg sodium, 18 g carbo., 1 g fiber, 4 g pro.

PARMESAN CORNMEAL SWIRLS

Prep: 15 minutes
Bake: 12 minutes

. . . .

Oven: 400°F
Makes: 8 swirls

1 11.5-ounce package (8) refrigerated corn bread twists
2 tablespoons bottled Italian salad dressing
⅓ cup finely shredded Parmesan or Romano cheese

1 Preheat oven to 400°. Grease a baking sheet; set aside. Carefully unroll corn bread twist dough on a sheet of waxed paper. Brush lightly with Italian salad dressing; sprinkle with cheese. Reroll dough. Separate along perforations to make 8 rolls. Place the rolls, cut sides down, on prepared baking sheet.

2 Bake in preheated oven about 12 minutes or until golden. Serve warm.

Nutrition Facts per swirl: 248 cal., 14 g total fat (6 g sat. fat), 16 mg chol., 730 mg sodium, 19 g carbo., 0 g fiber, 11 g pro.

CHEESE-GARLIC CRESCENTS

Prep: 15 minutes
Bake: 11 minutes

. . . .

Oven: 375°F
Makes: 8 crescents

1	8-ounce package (8) refrigerated crescent rolls
¼	cup semisoft cheese with garlic and herb
2	tablespoons finely chopped walnuts, toasted
	Nonstick cooking spray
	Milk
1	tablespoon seasoned fine dry bread crumbs

1 Preheat oven to 375°F. Unroll crescent rolls; divide into 8 triangles. In a small bowl stir together cheese and walnuts. Place a rounded teaspoon of the cheese mixture near the center of the wide end of each crescent roll. Roll up, starting at the wide end.

2 Lightly coat a baking sheet with nonstick cooking spray; place rolls, point sides down, on the prepared baking sheet. Brush tops lightly with milk; sprinkle with bread crumbs.

3 Bake crescents in preheated oven about 11 minutes or until bottoms are brown. Serve warm.

Nutrition Facts per crescent: 141 cal., 10 g total fat (3 g sat. fat), 6 mg chol., 254 mg sodium, 12 g carbo., 0 g fiber, 3 g pro.

GREEN ONION PARKER HOUSE BISCUITS

Prep: 10 minutes
Bake: 8 minutes

Oven: 400°F
Makes: 10 biscuits

1   5.2-ounce container semisoft cheese with garlic and herb
¼   cup sliced green onions
1   12-ounce package (10) refrigerated biscuits
1   egg yolk
1   tablespoon water
2   tablespoons grated Parmesan cheese
   Sliced green onions

1 Preheat oven to 400°. Grease a baking sheet; set aside. In a small bowl stir together semisoft cheese and the ¼ cup green onions; set aside.

2 Unwrap biscuits. Using your fingers, gently split the biscuits horizontally. Place the biscuit bottoms on prepared baking sheet. Spread about 1 tablespoon of the cheese mixture over each biscuit bottom. Replace biscuit tops.

3 In a small bowl whisk egg yolk and the water. Brush biscuit tops with egg yolk mixture. Sprinkle with Parmesan cheese and additional sliced green onions. Bake biscuits in preheated oven for 8 to 10 minutes or until golden. Serve warm.

Nutrition Facts per biscuit: 149 cal., 8 g total fat (5 g sat. fat), 23 mg chol., 394 mg sodium, 16 g carbo., 0 g fiber, 4 g pro.

CHEDDAR GARLIC BISCUITS

Prep: 10 minutes
Bake: 8 minutes

. . . .

Oven: 425°F
Makes: 10 to 12 biscuits

2	cups packaged biscuit mix
½	cup shredded cheddar cheese (2 ounces)
⅔	cup milk
¼	cup butter or margarine, melted
½	teaspoon garlic powder

1 Preheat oven to 425°. Grease a baking sheet; set aside.

2 In a large bowl combine biscuit mix and cheese; add milk. Stir to combine. Drop dough from a well-rounded tablespoon onto prepared baking sheet.

3 Bake in preheated oven for 8 to 10 minutes or until golden. In a small bowl combine melted butter and garlic powder; brush over hot biscuits. Serve warm.

Nutrition Facts per biscuit: 178 cal., 11 g total fat (5 g sat. fat), 21 mg chol., 402 mg sodium, 16 g carbo., 1 g fiber, 4 g pro.

LEMON-BASIL PULL-APARTS

Prep: 15 minutes
Bake: 30 minutes

Oven: 350°F
Makes: 6 to 8 servings

2   tablespoons butter, melted
1   16.3-ounce package (8) refrigerated large flaky biscuits
½   cup finely shredded Parmesan cheese (2 ounces)
1   teaspoon finely shredded lemon peel
1   teaspoon dried basil, crushed
¼   teaspoon onion powder
¼   teaspoon black pepper

1 Preheat oven to 350°. Place butter in a 9×5×3-inch loaf pan; tilt to coat bottom of pan.

2 Meanwhile, separate biscuits; snip each into 4 pieces. In a large plastic bag combine Parmesan cheese, lemon peel, basil, onion powder, and pepper. Add biscuits pieces, 3 or 4 at a time, to cheese mixture; shake to coat each piece. Place coated pieces in prepared loaf pan. Sprinkle with any remaining cheese mixture.

3 Bake in preheated oven for 30 minutes. Loosen edges; transfer to a serving plate. Cool slightly; serve warm.

Nutrition Facts per serving: 307 cal., 17 g total fat (6 g sat. fat), 16 mg chol., 860 mg sodium, 31 g carbo., 1 g fiber, 8 g pro.

HONEY & POPPY SEED BISCUITS

Prep: 15 minutes
Bake: 10 minutes

....

Oven: 450°F
Makes: 10 to 12 biscuits

½   cup cream-style cottage cheese
¼   cup milk
2   tablespoons honey
2¼   cups packaged biscuit mix
1   tablespoon poppy seeds

1 Preheat oven to 450°. In a food processor bowl or blender container combine cottage cheese, milk, and honey. Cover and process or blend until nearly smooth.

2 Prepare biscuit mix according to package directions for rolled biscuits, except substitute the pureed mixture and poppy seeds for the liquid called for in the directions.

3 Bake in preheated oven about 10 minutes or until bottoms are lightly browned.

Nutrition Facts per biscuit: 148 cal., 5 g total fat (1 g sat. fat), 3 mg chol., 394 mg sodium, 21 g carbo., 1 g fiber, 4 g pro.

PESTO BISCUITS

Prep: 20 minutes
Bake: 8 minutes

....

Oven: 450°F
Makes: 10 biscuits

2	cups all-purpose flour
3	tablespoons dry buttermilk powder or nonfat dry milk powder
2	teaspoons baking powder
1/2	teaspoon baking soda
1/4	teaspoon salt
1/3	cup butter-flavored shortening or regular shortening
2	tablespoons purchased pesto
1/2	cup water

1 Preheat oven to 450°. In a large bowl stir together flour, buttermilk powder, baking powder, baking soda, and salt. Using a pastry cutter, cut in shortening and pesto until mixture resembles coarse crumbs. Make a well in the center; add the water all at once. Stir just until dough clings together.

2 Turn out onto a lightly floured surface. Knead by folding and gently pressing dough for 10 to 12 strokes or until dough is nearly smooth. Roll or pat to 1/2-inch thickness. Cut with a 2 1/2-inch biscuit cutter, dipping cutter into flour between cuts. Place biscuits on an ungreased baking sheet.

3 Bake in preheated oven for 8 to 10 minutes or until golden.

Make-Ahead Directions: Prepare as directed. Wrap cooled biscuits in foil; place in airtight freezer containers or plastic freezer bags. Seal, label, and freeze for up to 1 month. To serve, preheat oven to 350°. Bake foil-wrapped biscuits in preheated oven for 15 to 20 minutes or until warm.

Nutrition Facts per biscuit: 173 cal., 8 g total fat (2 g sat. fat), 2 mg chol., 236 mg sodium, 20 g carbo., 1 g fiber, 4 g pro.

PUMPKIN RAISIN SCONES

Prep: 10 minutes
Bake: 12 minutes

Oven: 375°F
Makes: 8 scones

2   cups packaged biscuit mix
1/3   cup raisins or dried cranberries
1/4   cup granulated sugar
2   teaspoons pumpkin pie spice
1/2   cup canned pumpkin
1/4   cup milk
1   tablespoon coarse or granulated sugar
1   tablespoon very finely snipped crystallized ginger

1 Preheat oven to 375°. Grease a baking sheet; set aside. In a large bowl combine biscuit mix, raisins, the 1/4 cup granulated sugar, and the pumpkin pie spice. In a small bowl combine canned pumpkin and 3 tablespoons of the milk. Add pumpkin mixture all at once to dry mixture; stir until combined.

2 Turn out onto a lightly floured surface. Knead dough by folding and gently pressing dough for 10 to 12 strokes or until dough is nearly smooth.

3 Pat or lightly roll into a 7-inch circle. Cut into 8 wedges. Place wedges 1 inch apart on prepared baking sheet. In a small bowl combine the 1 tablespoon coarse sugar and the crystallized ginger. Brush dough wedges with remaining 1 tablespoon milk; sprinkle with crystallized ginger mixture.

4 Bake in preheated oven for 12 to 15 minutes or until a toothpick inserted near center comes out clean. Cool on wire rack. Serve warm.

Nutrition Facts per scone: 189 cal., 5 g total fat (1 g sat. fat), 1 mg chol., 377 mg sodium, 34 g carbo., 1 g fiber, 3 g pro.

HARVEST BRAN MUFFINS

Prep: **15** minutes
Bake: **15** minutes

Oven: 400°F
Makes: 12 muffins

1	14-ounce package oat bran muffin mix
⅓	cup finely shredded carrot
¼	cup snipped dried apples
¼	cup dried cranberries or coarsely chopped dried tart cherries
3	tablespoons finely chopped walnuts

1 Preheat oven to 400°. Grease twelve 2½-inch muffin cups; set aside.

2 Prepare muffin mix according to package directions; fold in carrot, apples, and cranberries. Divide evenly among prepared muffin cups. Sprinkle with nuts.

3 Bake in preheated oven for 15 to 18 minutes or until golden. Cool in pan on wire rack for 5 minutes; loosen edges and remove from muffin cups. Serve slightly warm or at room temperature.

Nutrition Facts per muffin: 161 cal., 4 g total fat (1 g sat. fat), 0 mg chol., 206 mg sodium, 28 g carbo., 2 g fiber, 3 g pro.

DESSERTS

SPICED RUM CAKE

Prep: 20 minutes
Bake: 35 minutes

. . . .

Oven: 350°F
Makes: 12 servings

1	package two-layer-size spice cake mix
1	cup milk
1/3	cup cooking oil
1/4	cup dairy sour cream
1/4	cup rum
4	eggs
1	teaspoon pumpkin pie spice
1	recipe Rum Glaze

1 Preheat oven to 350°. Grease and lightly flour a 10-inch fluted tube pan; set aside.

2 In a large mixing bowl combine cake mix, milk, oil, sour cream, rum, eggs, and pumpkin pie spice. Beat with an electric mixer on low speed just until moistened. Beat on medium speed for 2 minutes, scraping side of bowl occasionally. Pour batter into prepared pan.

3 Bake in preheated oven for 35 to 40 minutes or until a toothpick inserted near the center comes out clean. Cool in pan on a wire rack for 10 minutes. Remove cake from pan; cool completely on wire rack. Spoon Rum Glaze over cake.

Rum Glaze: In a small bowl combine 1 cup sifted powdered sugar, 1 tablespoon rum, and 1 teaspoon melted butter. Stir in enough water (1 to 2 teaspoons), 1 teaspoon at a time, to make of drizzling consistency.

Nutrition Facts per serving: 317 cal., 12 g total fat (3 g sat. fat), 75 mg chol., 307 mg sodium, 45 g carbo., 0 g fiber, 4 g pro.

ALMOND SNACK CAKE

Prep: 20 minutes
Bake: 30 minutes

Oven: 350°F
Makes: 8 servings

1	package one-layer-size chocolate or yellow cake mix
¼	cup packed brown sugar
½	cup almond butter or peanut butter
½	cup water
1	egg
½	cup almond toffee pieces
¼	cup chopped almonds or peanuts

1 Preheat oven to 350°. Grease and flour an 8×8×2-inch baking pan; set aside. In a large bowl combine cake mix and brown sugar; add almond butter. Beat with an electric mixer on low speed just until crumbly. Set aside ⅓ cup of the crumb mixture. Add the water and egg to remaining crumb mixture; beat on low speed for 30 seconds, scraping side of bowl constantly. Beat on high speed for 2 minutes. Stir in ¼ cup of the almond toffee pieces. Pour into prepared baking pan.

2 Bake in preheated oven for 20 minutes. Stir remaining ¼ cup almond toffee pieces and the almonds into the reserved crumb mixture; carefully sprinkle over cake. Bake for 10 to 20 minutes more or until a toothpick inserted into center comes out clean. Cool in pan on wire rack.

Nutrition Facts per serving: 366 cal., 22 g total fat (5 g sat. fat), 37 mg chol., 406 mg sodium, 41 g carbo., 2 g fiber, 6 g pro.

TRIPLE-NUT CHOCOLATE TORTE

Prep: 30 minutes
Bake: 30 minutes

. . . .

Oven: 350°F
Makes: 12 servings

1 package two-layer-size devil's food cake mix

³/₄ cup ground pecans, toasted

2 2.8-ounce packages milk chocolate or dark chocolate mousse dessert mix

¹/₂ cup chopped hazelnuts, toasted

¹/₂ cup slivered almonds, toasted and chopped

Sliced almonds, toasted (optional)

1 Preheat oven to 350°. Grease and lightly flour two 8×1¹/₂-inch round baking pans. Set aside.

2 Prepare cake mix according to package directions; fold in pecans. Divide half of the batter evenly between the prepared pans. Cover and refrigerate remaining batter while cakes bake.

3 Bake in preheated oven about 15 minutes or until a toothpick inserted in center comes out clean. Cool in pans on wire rack for 10 minutes. Remove from pans; cool completely on wire racks.

4 Wash pans; grease and lightly flour as in step 1. Divide remaining batter evenly between prepared pans. Bake and cool as directed in step 3.

5 Prepare mousse mixes according to package directions. Fold hazelnuts into half of the mousse and the chopped almonds into the other half of mousse.

6 Place 1 of the cake layers on a cake platter. Top with half of the hazelnut mousse mixture. Top with another cake layer and half of the almond mousse mixture. Repeat layers. Cover loosely and chill for at least 4 hours or up to 24 hours. If desired, sprinkle with sliced almonds.

Nutrition Facts per serving: 372 cal., 22 g total fat (5 g sat. fat), 3 mg chol., 374 mg sodium, 43 g carbo., 3 g fiber, 6 g pro.

LEMON-LIME CAKE

Prep: 25 minutes
Bake: 45 minutes

Oven: 350°F
Makes: 12 servings

1   package two-layer-size lemon cake mix
2   3-ounce packages cream cheese, softened
2   tablespoons butter, softened
1   tablespoon cornstarch
½   cup sweetened condensed milk
1   egg
3   teaspoons finely shredded lime peel
4   tablespoons lime juice
    Several drops green food coloring (optional)
1   cup sifted powdered sugar
    Water

1 Preheat oven to 350°. Generously grease and flour a 10-inch fluted tube pan; set aside.

2 Prepare cake mix according to package directions; pour batter into prepared pan. In a medium mixing bowl combine cream cheese, butter, and cornstarch; beat with an electric mixer on low to medium speed until smooth. Gradually beat in sweetened condensed milk, egg, 2 teaspoons of the lime peel, 3 tablespoons of the lime juice, and, if desired, green food coloring. Spoon cream cheese mixture evenly over batter in pan.

3 Bake in preheated oven about 45 minutes or until a toothpick inserted near the center comes out clean. Cool in pan on a wire rack for 10 minutes. Remove from pan. Cool completely on wire rack.

4 For icing, in a small bowl stir together powdered sugar, the remaining 1 teaspoon lime peel, the remaining 1 tablespoon lime juice, and, if desired, additional green food coloring. Stir in enough water (2 to 3 teaspoons) to make of drizzling consistency. Drizzle over cooled cake.

Nutrition Facts per serving: 321 cal., 12 g total fat (6 g sat. fat), 43 mg chol., 354 mg sodium, 52 g carbo., 0 g fiber, 4 g pro.

PRALINE CRUNCH CAKE

Prep: 25 minutes
Bake: 40 minutes

Oven: 350°F
Makes: 16 servings

2	tablespoons molasses
1	tablespoon instant coffee crystals
1	package 2-layer-size yellow cake mix
3	eggs
1/3	cup cooking oil
1/3	cup all-purpose flour
1	tablespoon packed brown sugar
1/2	teaspoon ground cinnamon
3	tablespoons butter
1/3	cup chopped pecans
1/4	cup butter, softened
3 1/2	cups sifted powdered sugar
1/4	cup half-and-half, light cream, or milk
1	teaspoon instant coffee crystals
1	teaspoon vanilla

1 Preheat oven to 350°. Grease 13×9×2-inch baking pan; set aside. Place molasses in a 2-cup glass measure; add water to make 1 1/3 cups total; stir. Transfer to mixing bowl. Add 1 tablespoon coffee crystals; stir to dissolve. Add cake mix, eggs, and oil. Beat with electric mixer on low until combined. Beat on medium for 2 minutes. Pour into prepared pan. Bake 30 minutes or until toothpick inserted in center comes out clean. Cool in pan on wire rack.

2 In a bowl stir together flour, brown sugar, and cinnamon. Using pastry blender, cut in 3 tablespoons butter. Stir in pecans. Knead with fingers to form small clumps. Spread in 15×10×1-inch baking pan. Bake in 350° oven 10 minutes or until golden. Transfer to foil to cool.

3 For frosting, in a mixing bowl beat 1/4 cup butter with electric mixer on medium 30 seconds. Add 1 cup powdered sugar; beat until combined. In a bowl stir together 1/4 cup half-and-half and 1 teaspoon coffee crystals until dissolved. Add to powdered sugar mixture along with vanilla. Beat until combined. Add remaining 2 1/2 cups powdered sugar, beating until smooth. Beat in additional half-and-half to make spreadable. Frost cake; sprinkle with pecan mixture.

Nutrition Facts per serving: 354 cal., 15 g total fat (5 g sat. fat), 56 mg chol., 272 mg sodium, 53 g carbo., 0 g fiber, 3 g pro.

CHOCOLATE CHIP ICE CREAM CAKE

Prep: **20** minutes
Freeze: **6** to **24** hours

· ·

Makes: 10 to 12 servings

1	3-ounce package cream cheese, softened
1	tablespoon sugar
1½	cups chocolate chip, strawberry, or vanilla ice cream
1	8- or 9-inch purchased angel food cake (15 or 16 ounces)
⅓	cup sliced fresh strawberries
⅓	cup chocolate fudge or strawberry ice cream topping

1 For filling, in a small bowl stir together cream cheese and sugar. In a medium bowl use a wooden spoon to stir ice cream just until it begins to soften; fold cream cheese mixture into ice cream. Place in freezer while preparing the cake.

2 Use a serrated knife to cut off the top ½ inch of the cake; set aside. Hold the knife parallel to the center hole of the cake and cut around the hole, leaving about ¾-inch thickness of cake around the hole. Cut around the outer edge of the cake, leaving an outer cake wall about ¾ inch thick. Use a spoon to remove center of cake, leaving about a ¾-inch-thick base. (Discard scooped-out cake.)

3 Spoon filling into hollowed cake. Arrange sliced strawberries on filling. Replace the top of the cake. Cover and freeze for at least 6 hours or up to 24 hours.

4 To serve, in a small saucepan heat ice cream topping until drizzling consistency; drizzle over cake. Slice cake with a serrated knife.

Nutrition Facts per serving: 219 cal., 7 g total fat (4 g sat. fat), 18 mg chol., 265 mg sodium, 37 g carbo., 0 g fiber, 5 g pro.

ANGEL FOOD CAKE WITH TROPICAL FRUITS

Prep: 20 minutes
Chill: 4 to **24** hours

. . . .

Makes: 8 servings

1/3	cup sugar
1	tablespoon cornstarch
3/4	cup milk
1	egg
1	egg yolk
3	tablespoons lime juice
1	tablespoon butter
1	drop green food coloring
2/3	cup plain yogurt
1/2	of a 9-inch purchased angel food cake or one 10 3/4-ounce package frozen pound cake, thawed
2	small red and/or gold papayas, sliced
2	medium kiwifruit, peeled and sliced
1	guava, cut into wedges (optional)

1 In a small saucepan combine sugar and cornstarch. Stir in milk. Cook and stir over medium heat until thickened and bubbly. Reduce heat. Cook and stir for 2 minutes more. In a small bowl beat the egg and egg yolk with a whisk. Gradually whisk about 1/2 cup of the hot milk mixture into the beaten egg mixture.

2 Return milk-egg mixture to saucepan. Cook and stir until nearly bubbly. Do not boil. Cook and stir for 2 minutes more. Remove from heat.

3 Stir in lime juice, butter, and food coloring. Cover surface of lime mixture with plastic wrap. Chill for 1 hour. Fold lime mixture into yogurt. Cover and chill for at least 3 hours or up to 24 hours.

4 To serve, cut angel food cake into 8 slices. Place 1 slice on each of 8 dessert plates. Spoon lime-yogurt mixture over cake slices. Top with sliced fruits. If desired, serve with guava wedges.

Nutrition Facts per serving: 188 cal., 4 g total fat (2 g sat. fat), 113 mg chol., 266 mg sodium, 34 g carbo., 2 g fiber, 5 g pro.

COFFEE ANGEL DESSERT

Prep: 20 minutes

Chill: 4 to **24** hours

. . . .

Makes: 4 servings

1	cup whipping cream
¼	cup sifted powdered sugar
⅓	cup coffee liqueur or brewed coffee
½	of an 8- to 10-inch angel food cake (about 7 ounces)
¼	cup shaved semisweet chocolate (1 ounce)

1 In a chilled medium mixing bowl combine whipping cream, powdered sugar, and 1 tablespoon of the liqueur; beat with chilled beaters of an electric mixer until stiff peaks form (tips stand straight). Set aside.

2 Cut cake into 1-inch cubes. Place half of the cake cubes in 4 parfait glasses or other tall glasses. Drizzle each with some of the remaining liqueur. Spoon half of the whipping cream mixture over cake in glasses. Sprinkle with some of the chocolate shavings. Repeat layers. Cover and chill for at least 4 hours or up to 24 hours.

Nutrition Facts per serving: 466 cal., 25 g total fat (15 g sat. fat), 82 mg chol., 396 mg sodium, 48 g carbo., 1 g fiber, 5 g pro.

NEAPOLITAN POUND CAKE

Prep: 30 minutes
Bake: 35 minutes

Oven: 350°F
Makes: 12 servings

1	16-ounce package pound cake mix
1/2	cup strawberry or seedless raspberry preserves
5	or 6 drops red food coloring
1/4	cup presweetened cocoa powder
1/2	cup canned chocolate frosting

1 Preheat oven to 350°. Generously grease and flour a 10-inch fluted tube pan or a 9×5×3-inch loaf pan.

2 Prepare cake mix according to package directions. Divide batter into thirds and place in 3 separate bowls. Stir preserves and red food coloring into 1 portion of the batter. Stir cocoa powder into another portion of the batter. Leave the remaining portion plain. Alternately drop batters by spoonfuls into prepared pan.

3 Bake in preheated oven for 35 to 40 minutes for the fluted tube pan or 60 to 70 minutes for the loaf pan or until a toothpick inserted in center of cake comes out clean. Cool in pan on wire rack for 10 minutes; loosen side and remove from pan. Cool completely on wire rack.

4 Place frosting in a small microwave-safe bowl; microwave on 100% power (high) for 10 to 20 seconds or just until drizzling consistency. Drizzle frosting over cake.

Nutrition Facts per serving: 223 cal., 5 g total fat (2 g sat. fat), 24 mg chol., 145 mg sodium, 43 g carbo., 1 g fiber, 2 g pro.

CINNAMON-SEARED POUND CAKE

Start to Finish:

20 minutes

. . . .

Makes: 6 servings

1   16-ounce carton frozen sliced strawberries in syrup, thawed

1   10³⁄₄-ounce package frozen pound cake, thawed

2   tablespoons butter or margarine, softened

¹⁄₂   teaspoon ground cinnamon

¹⁄₃   cup whipping cream, whipped

       Ground cinnamon

       Slivered almonds, toasted

1 Place undrained strawberries in a blender container. Cover; blend until smooth. Chill.

2 Cut a thin slice off each end of the pound cake. Cut remaining cake into 6 slices. In a small bowl stir together butter and the ¹⁄₂ teaspoon cinnamon. Spread butter-cinnamon mixture over a cut side of each cake slice.

3 Place cake slices, buttered sides down, on a griddle over medium heat; cook for 2 to 4 minutes or until golden, turning once.

4 To serve, divide strawberries among 6 dessert dishes. Top berries in each dish with a pound cake slice, buttered side up. Spoon on whipped cream and sprinkle with additional cinnamon. Top with almonds.

Nutrition Facts per serving: 360 cal., 20 g total fat (12 g sat. fat), 84 mg chol., 223 mg sodium, 44 g carbo., 2 g fiber, 3 g pro.

BROWNIE CARAMEL CHEESECAKE

Prep: 30 minutes
Bake: 60 minutes

. . . .

Oven: 350°F
Makes: 16 servings

1	8-ounce package brownie mix
1	egg
1	tablespoon water
1	14-ounce package vanilla caramels (about 48 caramels)
1	5-ounce can evaporated milk ($^2/_3$ cup)
3	8-ounce packages cream cheese, softened
1	14-ounce can sweetened condensed milk
3	eggs
$^1/_3$	cup chopped chocolate-covered toffee bar (one 1.4-ounce bar)

1 Preheat oven to 350°. Grease a 10-inch springform pan; set aside. For crust, in a medium bowl stir together brownie mix, the 1 egg, and the water. Spread into the bottom of prepared springform pan. Bake in preheated oven for 15 minutes.

2 Meanwhile, in a medium saucepan combine caramels and evaporated milk; cook and stir over medium-low heat until caramels are melted and smooth. Remove from heat. Remove $^1/_2$ cup of the melted caramel mixture; cover and refrigerate until serving time.

3 For filling, in a large mixing bowl beat cream cheese and sweetened condensed milk with an electric mixer on medium speed until combined. Add the 3 eggs, all at once, beating on low speed just until combined.

4 Pour filling over brownie layer. Drizzle remaining melted caramel mixture over filling. Swirl gently with a knife. Bake in preheated oven about 45 minutes or until center appears nearly set when gently shaken.

5 Cool in pan on a wire rack for 15 minutes. Loosen edge from side of pan; cool for 30 minutes more. Remove side of the pan; cool cheesecake completely. Cover; chill for at least 4 hours or up to 24 hours before serving. (Cake may crack where caramel mixture is swirled in.)

6 Before serving, heat reserved caramel mixture; drizzle over cheesecake. Sprinkle with chopped toffee bar.

Nutrition Facts per serving: 433 cal., 24 g total fat (14 g sat. fat), 111 mg chol., 316 mg sodium, 48 g carbo., 1 g fiber, 9 g pro.

MOCHA-CHIP CHEESECAKE

Prep: 15 minutes
Chill: 1 to **24** hours

Makes: 9 servings

1	11.1-ounce package cheesecake mix
1/3	cup butter or margarine, melted
1 1/4	cups milk
2	teaspoons instant coffee crystals
1/2	cup dairy sour cream
1/2	cup miniature semisweet chocolate pieces

1 In a small bowl stir together crust crumbs from the cheesecake mix and the melted butter. Press mixture into the bottom of an 8×8×2-inch baking pan.

2 In a large mixing bowl combine milk and coffee crystals; stir to dissolve coffee crystals. Add filling mix from the cheesecake mix. Beat with an electric mixer on medium speed just until combined. Add sour cream; beat on high speed for 3 minutes.

3 Stir in 1/4 cup of the chocolate pieces. Spread cheesecake mixture over crumb layer in baking pan. Sprinkle remaining 1/4 cup chocolate pieces on top. Cover and chill for at least 1 hour or up to 24 hours. To serve, cut into squares.

Nutrition Facts per serving: 323 cal., 17 g total fat (10 g sat. fat), 27 mg chol., 351 mg sodium, 37 g carbo., 1 g fiber, 5 g pro.

FOOL-YOUR-FAMILY PEACH PIE

Prep: **20** minutes
Bake: **50** minutes

Oven: 375°F
Makes: 8 servings

1 15-ounce package folded refrigerated unbaked piecrust (2 crusts)
1 21-ounce can peach pie filling
1½ cups fresh blueberries
⅓ cup slivered almonds, toasted
1 tablespoon milk
2 teaspoons coarse sugar or granulated sugar
   Sweetened whipped cream or vanilla ice cream (optional)

1 Preheat oven to 375°. Let piecrusts stand at room temperature for 15 minutes as directed on package. Meanwhile, in a large bowl stir together pie filling, blueberries, and almonds.

2 Line a 9-inch pie plate with 1 of the piecrusts; spoon in filling. Using a 1-inch round cutter, cut 3 holes in center of remaining piecrust; place on filled pie. Fold edge of top pastry under edge of bottom pastry. Crimp edge as desired. Brush top with milk; sprinkle with sugar. To prevent overbrowning, cover edge of pie with foil.

3 Bake in preheated oven for 25 minutes. Remove foil; bake for 25 to 30 minutes more or until filling is bubbly and pastry is golden. Cool on a wire rack.

4 If desired, serve pie with sweetened whipped cream.

Nutrition Facts per serving: 355 cal., 17 g total fat (6 g sat. fat), 10 mg chol., 212 mg sodium, 48 g carbo., 2 g fiber, 3 g pro.

RHUBARB PIE

Prep: 20 minutes
Bake: 45 minutes

Oven: 375°F
Makes: 8 servings

1   15-ounce package folded refrigerated unbaked piecrust (2 crusts)
¾   cup sugar
⅓   cup all-purpose flour
½   teaspoon ground cinnamon
6   cups fresh or frozen unsweetened sliced rhubarb, thawed and undrained
    Milk (optional)
    Sugar (optional)

1 Preheat oven to 375°. Let piecrusts stand at room temperature for 15 minutes as directed on package. Meanwhile, for filling, in a large bowl stir together the ¾ cup sugar, the flour, and cinnamon; stir in fresh rhubarb.

2 Line a 9-inch pie plate with 1 of the piecrusts; spoon in filling. Trim bottom pastry to edge of pie plate. Cut slits in remaining piecrust; place on filling and seal. Crimp edge as desired. If desired, brush with milk and sprinkle with sugar. To prevent overbrowning, cover edge of pie with foil.

3 Bake in preheated oven for 25 minutes. Remove foil. Bake for 20 to 30 minutes more or until filling is bubbly in center and pastry is golden. Cool on a wire rack.

Nutrition Facts per serving: 365 cal., 13 g total fat (5 g sat. fat), 12 mg chol., 129 mg sodium, 58 g carbo., 24 g fiber, 4 g pro.

SWEET GLAZED CHERRY PIE

Prep: 20 minutes
Bake: 80 minutes

. . . .

Oven: 375°F
Makes: 8 servings

½	cup granulated sugar
3	tablespoons cornstarch
1	16-ounce package frozen unsweetened pitted dark sweet cherries
½	teaspoon vanilla
1	15-ounce package folded refrigerated unbaked piecrust (2 crusts)
¾	cup sliced almonds, toasted
1	21-ounce can cherry pie filling
¼	cup sifted powdered sugar
1	to 1½ teaspoons milk

1 In a bowl stir together granulated sugar and cornstarch. Add frozen cherries and vanilla; toss. Let stand at room temperature about 1 hour or until a syrup forms; stir occasionally. Meanwhile, let piecrusts stand at room temperature for 15 minutes as directed on package.

2 Preheat oven to 375°. Line a 9-inch pie plate with 1 of the piecrusts. Place ½ cup of the almonds in bottom of pastry-lined pie plate. Stir cherry mixture; spoon on top of almonds. Spoon pie filling over cherry mixture, spreading evenly.

3 Cut slits in remaining piecrust; place on filling and seal. Crimp edge as desired. To prevent overbrowning, cover edge of pie with foil.

4 Bake in preheated oven for 50 minutes. Remove foil. Bake about 30 minutes more or until top is golden and filling is bubbly. Cool completely on a wire rack.

5 Before serving, in a small bowl stir together powdered sugar and enough of the milk to make of drizzling consistency. Drizzle over pie. Sprinkle remaining ¼ cup almonds on top of pie.

Nutrition Facts per serving: 507 cal., 21 g total fat (7 g sat. fat), 10 mg chol., 211 mg sodium, 76 g carbo., 3 g fiber, 5 g pro.

LAYERED APPLE-CRANBERRY PIE

Prep: 10 minutes
Bake: 40 minutes

. . . .

Oven: 375°F
Makes: 8 servings

1	15-ounce package folded refrigerated unbaked piecrust (2 crusts)
1	21-ounce can apple pie filling
½	of a 16-ounce can whole cranberry sauce
	Granulated or coarse sugar (optional)

1 Preheat oven to 375°. Let piecrusts stand at room temperature for 15 minutes as directed on package.

2 Line a 9-inch pie plate with 1 of the piecrusts; spoon in apple pie filling. Spoon the cranberry sauce over pie filling.

3 Cut slits in the remaining piecrust; place on filling and seal. Crimp edge as desired. If desired, sprinkle with sugar.

4 To prevent overbrowning, cover edge of pie with foil. Bake in preheated oven for 25 minutes. Remove foil. Bake for 15 to 20 minutes more or until top is golden. Cool on wire rack.

Nutrition Facts per serving: 356 cal., 14 g total fat (6 g sat. fat), 10 mg chol., 224 mg sodium, 56 g carbo., 1 g fiber, 1 g pro.

DOUBLE BERRY VANILLA CREAM PIE

Prep: 30 minutes

Chill: 1 hour + **2** to **24** hours

Makes: 8 servings

1   4-serving-size package cook-and-serve vanilla pudding mix

1³⁄₄   cups milk

½   cup dairy sour cream

1   9-inch baked pastry shell*

1   10-ounce package frozen strawberries in syrup, thawed

1   tablespoon cornstarch

5   cups fresh strawberries, hulled

1   cup fresh blueberries

    Sweetened whipped cream (optional)

1 For cream filling, cook pudding mix according to package directions, except use the 1³⁄₄ cups milk for the liquid. Cool pudding for 10 minutes. Fold in the sour cream. Spread into bottom of the baked pastry shell. Cover with plastic wrap; chill about 1 hour or until firm.

2 For glaze, place thawed strawberries in a blender container; cover and blend until nearly smooth. In a small saucepan stir strawberry puree into cornstarch. Cook and stir until thickened and bubbly. Cook and stir for 2 minutes more. Remove from heat. Cover surface with plastic wrap. Cool to room temperature.

3 To assemble pie, arrange half of the fresh strawberries, stem ends down, over sour cream layer in pastry shell. Sprinkle with half of the blueberries. Drizzle one-third of the glaze over the blueberries and strawberries.

4 Arrange the remaining strawberries and blueberries over the first layer. Drizzle remaining glaze over berries. Cover and chill for at least 2 hours or up to 24 hours. Serve immediately. If desired, top with whipped cream.

***Note:** For a baked pastry shell, bake one 9-inch frozen unbaked deep-dish pastry shell according to package directions. Or let one-half of a 15-ounce package folded refrigerated unbaked piecrust (1 crust) stand at room temperature for 15 minutes as directed on package; line a 9-inch pie plate with piecrust and bake according to package directions.

Nutrition Facts per serving: 306 cal., 13 g total fat (4 g sat. fat), 10 mg chol., 176 mg sodium, 45 g carbo., 4 g fiber, 5 g pro.

EXTREME CHOCOLATE PIE

Prep: 25 minutes
Cool: 1 hour
Chill: 4 to **24** hours

Oven: 350°F
Makes: 10 servings

1   8-ounce package brownie mix

1   cup sugar

³/₄ cup butter

6   ounces unsweetened chocolate, melted and cooled

1   teaspoon vanilla

³/₄ cup refrigerated or frozen egg product, thawed, or ³/₄ cup pasteurized eggs

1   1.45-ounce bar dark sweet chocolate, coarsely chopped

1   recipe Chocolate Whipped Cream (optional)

1 Preheat oven to 350°. Grease a 9-inch pie plate; set aside. For crust, prepare brownie mix according to package directions. Spread in the bottom of prepared pie plate. Bake in preheated oven for 20 to 25 minutes or until toothpick comes out clean. Cool on wire rack for 1 hour.

2 For filling, in a medium mixing bowl beat sugar and butter with an electric mixer on medium speed about 4 minutes or until fluffy. Stir in the melted and cooled chocolate and the vanilla. Gradually add egg product, beating on low speed until combined. Beat on medium to high speed about 1 minute or until light and fluffy, scraping side of bowl constantly.

3 Spoon filling over baked brownie in pie plate. Cover and chill for at least 4 hours or up to 24 hours.

4 To serve, sprinkle with chopped chocolate bar. If desired, serve with Chocolate Whipped Cream.

Chocolate Whipped Cream: In a chilled small mixing bowl combine ¹/₂ cup whipping cream, 1 tablespoon sugar, and 1¹/₂ teaspoons unsweetened cocoa powder. Beat with chilled beaters of an electric mixer (or a rotary beater) on medium speed until soft peaks form (tips curl).

Nutrition Facts per serving: 428 cal., 29 g total fat (16 g sat. fat), 61 mg chol., 285 mg sodium, 45 g carbo., 3 g fiber, 5 g pro

LEMON CREAM TART

Prep: **30** minutes
Bake: **35** minutes

Oven: 350°F
Makes: 12 to 16 servings

1	16½-ounce package lemon bar mix
½	cup finely chopped macadamia nuts
1	8-ounce package cream cheese, softened
½	teaspoon vanilla
1	teaspoon finely shredded lemon peel
1	8-ounce carton dairy sour cream
1	tablespoon sugar
½	teaspoon vanilla
1½	to 2 cups fresh berries (such as blueberries, raspberries, and/or blackberries)
	Fresh mint leaves, cut into long thin strips (optional)

1 Preheat oven to 350°. Prepare lemon filling mixture according to package directions for lemon bar mix; set aside. Press packaged crust mixture into the bottom of a 10-inch springform pan or a 9×9×2-inch baking pan. Sprinkle macadamia nuts evenly over crust; press gently into crust. Bake in preheated oven about 10 minutes or until lightly browned. Set aside to cool.

2 Meanwhile, in a medium mixing bowl combine cream cheese and ½ teaspoon vanilla; beat with an electric mixer on medium to high speed until smooth. Add lemon filling mixture; beat until combined. Stir in lemon peel. Pour cream cheese mixture evenly over the crust in the pan. Bake about 25 minutes more or until set. Cool on wire rack for 1 hour. Cover and chill for at least 2 hours or up to 24 hours.

3 Just before serving, in a small bowl stir together sour cream, sugar, and ½ teaspoon vanilla. Spread sour cream mixture over tart. Sprinkle fresh berries and mint leaf strips (if desired) evenly over tart.

Nutrition Facts per serving: 190 cal., 16 g total fat (8 g sat. fat), 82 mg chol., 109 mg sodium, 7 g carbo., 5 g fiber, 4 g pro.

STRAWBERRY-BANANA CHEESECAKE TART

Prep: 20 minutes
Bake: 25 minutes

Oven: 325°F
Makes: 10 servings

1	package 1-layer-size chocolate cake mix
1	egg yolk
2	tablespoons butter, melted
1	8-ounce package cream cheese, softened
2	tablespoons sugar
2	small bananas
1	egg
1	egg white
1	cup small fresh strawberries, halved
¼	cup fudge ice cream topping

1 Preheat oven to 325°. Grease a 9-inch tart pan with a removable bottom or a quiche dish; set aside. Set aside ⅓ cup of the dry cake mix. For crust, pour remaining dry cake mix into a small bowl. Add egg yolk and melted butter to dry cake mix in bowl; mix with a fork to form coarse crumbs. Pat crumbs into bottom and halfway up side of prepared pan. Set aside.

2 In a large mixing bowl combine cream cheese and sugar; beat with an electric mixer on medium speed until fluffy. Mash 1 of the bananas (about ⅓ cup mashed); beat into cream cheese mixture along with the reserved ⅓ cup dry cake mix. Stir in whole egg and egg white; pour into prepared crust.

3 Bake in preheated oven about 25 minutes or until center is set when gently shaken. Cool in pan for 1 hour on wire rack. Cover and chill for at least 2 hours or up to 24 hours.

4 Just before serving, slice remaining banana. Arrange banana slices and strawberry halves on the tart. Remove side of tart pan. Heat fudge topping just enough so that it can be drizzled; drizzle over the fruit. Serve immediately.

Nutrition Facts per serving: 277 cal., 14 g total fat (7 g sat. fat), 74 mg chol., 337 mg sodium, 35 g carbo., 1 g fiber, 4 g pro.

STRAWBERRY ICE CREAM TART

Prep: 30 minutes
Bake: 20 minutes

....

Oven: 350°F
Makes: 12 servings

Strawberry and/or vanilla ice cream (about 2 pints)
Nonstick cooking spray
1   18-ounce roll refrigerated sugar cookie dough
⅓   cup sliced almonds
1   tablespoon sugar
¼   teaspoon ground cinnamon
4   cups fresh strawberries
¼   cup strawberry ice cream topping
Coconut, toasted (optional)

1 Use an ice cream scoop to form 12 ice cream balls. Place ice cream balls on a large cold plate; store in the freezer.

2 Preheat oven to 350°. Line an 11×7×1½-inch baking pan with foil. Lightly coat foil with cooking spray. With fingers, press the cookie dough evenly in prepared pan. Sprinkle almonds over dough, pressing lightly into dough. In a small bowl stir together sugar and cinnamon. Sprinkle mixture evenly over dough. Bake in preheated oven about 20 minutes or until top is golden. Cool in pan for 1 hour.

3 Place strawberries in bowl, cutting large strawberries in half. Cover and chill.

4 To assemble tart, stir topping into strawberries. Gently lift crust from pan; carefully peel off foil. Place crust on serving tray. Quickly transfer ice cream scoops from freezer to crust. Spoon some of the strawberry mixture on top. If desired, sprinkle with coconut. Cut tart into 12 pieces. Serve immediately. Pass remaining strawberry mixture to spoon on each serving.

Nutrition Facts per serving: 324 cal., 14 g total fat (5 g sat. fat), 25 mg chol., 206 mg sodium, 47 g carbo., 2 g fiber, 4 g pro.

Banana Split Ice Cream Tart: Prepare tart as directed, except use vanilla, chocolate, and strawberry ice creams (2 pints total). Substitute 1 large banana, sliced, for half of the strawberries. If desired, top with whipped cream and maraschino cherries.

Nutrition Facts per serving: 344 cal., 16 g total fat (6 g sat fat), 38 mg chol., 226 mg sodium, 47 g carbo., 2 dietary fiber, 4 g pro.

PEANUT BUTTER S'MORE TARTS

Prep: 15 minutes

Makes: 6 tarts

1   cup semisweet chocolate pieces (6 ounces)

$\frac{1}{2}$ cup peanut butter

$1\frac{1}{2}$ cups tiny marshmallows

$\frac{1}{2}$ cup chopped peanuts

1   4-ounce package graham cracker tart shells (6)

1 In a small saucepan melt the chocolate pieces over low heat, stirring constantly. Remove from heat. Stir in peanut butter until smooth. Stir in marshmallows and peanuts. Spoon into tart shells. Cover and chill for at least 2 hours or up to 24 hours. Let stand at room temperature for 30 minutes before serving.

Nutrition Facts per tart: 505 cal., 31 g total fat (8 g sat. fat), 0 mg chol., 257 mg sodium, 42 g carbo., 7 g fiber, 10 g pro.

FAST & FRUITY BANANA SPLIT TARTS

Start to Finish:

10 minutes

. . . .

Makes: 15 tarts

1   8-ounce tub cream cheese with pineapple

¼   cup strawberry preserves

1   2.1-ounce package (15) baked miniature phyllo shells

1   banana, thinly sliced

⅓   cup chocolate ice cream topping

1 For filling, in a small mixing bowl beat the cream cheese and preserves with an electric mixer on low to medium speed until light and fluffy. Spoon filling into phyllo shells.

2 To serve, divide banana slices among phyllo shells. Drizzle with ice cream topping. Serve immediately.

Make-Ahead Directions: Prepare as directed in step 1. Cover and refrigerate tarts up to 4 hours. Just before serving, add banana slices and drizzle tarts with ice cream topping.

Nutrition Facts per tart: 115 cal., 6 g total fat (3 g sat. fat), 13 mg chol., 63 mg sodium, 14 g carbo., 0 g fiber, 1 g pro.

FRUIT-TOPPED PHYLLO TARTS

Start to Finish:

15 minutes

. . . .

Makes: 15 tarts

3   tablespoons apple jelly

½   of an 8-ounce package cream cheese, softened

1   2.1-ounce package (15) baked miniature phyllo shells

15   red and/or green seedless grape halves, strawberry halves, or small pieces of mango

1 In a small saucepan heat and stir the apple jelly over medium-low heat until melted. Stir 2 tablespoons of the jelly into the cream cheese until smooth. Divide cream cheese mixture among tart shells.

2 In a small bowl combine fruit and the remaining 1 tablespoon jelly; stir gently to coat. Spoon a piece of fruit on top of each tart. Serve immediately or chill up to 4 hours before serving.

Nutrition Facts per tart: 62 cal., 4 g total fat (2 g sat. fat), 8 mg chol., 33 mg sodium, 6 g carbo., 0 g fiber, 1 g pro.

LIKE-A-LINZER TORTE

Prep: 25 minutes
Bake: 45 minutes

Oven: 325°F
Makes: 12 servings

1	18-ounce roll refrigerated sugar cookie dough
½	of a 12-ounce can apricot cake and pastry filling
¼	cup sliced almonds, toasted
2	tablespoons all-purpose flour
1	egg yolk
1	tablespoon water

1 Preheat oven to 325°. Grease a 9- to 10-inch tart pan with a removable bottom. Pat two-thirds of the cookie dough into the bottom of the prepared pan. Spread with apricot filling and sprinkle with toasted almonds.

2 On a lightly floured surface, knead the flour into the remaining cookie dough. Roll to a 9- or 10-inch circle; cut into ½-inch-wide strips. Lay strips across the filling to form a lattice pattern. In a small bowl stir together egg yolk and the water; brush over dough strips.

3 Bake in the preheated oven for 45 to 50 minutes or until golden. Cool on a wire rack.

Nutrition Facts per serving: 239 cal., 11 g total fat (2 g sat. fat), 30 mg chol., 188 mg sodium, 33 g carbo., 1 g fiber, 3 g pro.

SALTED PEANUT BARS

Prep: 25 minutes

Chill: 1 hour

· · · · · · · · · · · · · · · · · · · ·

Makes: 60 pieces

Nonstick cooking spray

4   cups dry-roasted or honey-roasted peanuts

1   10½-ounce package tiny marshmallows

½   cup butter

1   14-ounce can sweetened condensed milk (1⅓ cups)

1   10-ounce package peanut butter-flavored pieces

½   cup creamy peanut butter

1 Line a 13×9×2-inch baking pan with heavy foil. Coat foil with cooking spray. Evenly spread 2 cups of the peanuts in prepared baking pan.

2 In a 3-quart saucepan combine marshmallows and butter; heat and stir over medium-low heat until melted. Stir in sweetened condensed milk, peanut butter pieces, and peanut butter until smooth. Quickly pour peanut butter mixture over peanuts in pan. Sprinkle remaining peanuts on top. Gently press remaining 2 cups peanuts into peanut butter mixture.

3 Chill about 1 hour or until firm; cut into pieces. Store, covered, in refrigerator.

Nutrition Facts per piece: 144 cal., 10 g total fat (3 g sat. fat), 7 mg chol., 128 mg sodium, 12 g carbo., 1 g fiber, 4 g pro.

EASY GINGERBREAD BARS

Prep: 10 minutes
Bake: 20 minutes

· · · · · · · · · · · · · · · · ·

Oven: 350°F
Makes: 24 bars

1	14½-ounce package gingerbread mix
¾	cup water
1	egg
1	7-ounce package tropical blend mixed dried fruit bits
1	cup chopped pecans
1	cup sifted powdered sugar
⅛	teaspoon ground ginger
3	to 4 teaspoons milk

1 Preheat oven to 350°. Grease a 13×9×2-inch baking pan; set aside. In a medium bowl stir together gingerbread mix, the water, egg, fruit bits, and pecans. Spread batter in prepared baking pan.

2 Bake in preheated oven for 20 to 25 minutes or until a toothpick inserted near the center comes out clean. Cool in pan on a wire rack.

3 For glaze, in a small bowl stir together the powdered sugar and ginger; stir in enough of the milk to make a drizzling consistency. Drizzle glaze over gingerbread. Cut into bars.

Nutrition Facts per bar: 148 cal., 6 g total fat (1 g sat. fat), 9 mg chol., 123 mg sodium, 24 g carbo., 0 g fiber, 2 g pro.

CHOCOLATE CARAMEL-NUT BARS

Prep: 20 minutes
Bake: 30 minutes

. . . .

Oven: 350°F
Makes: 24 bars

Nonstick cooking spray
1   package 2-layer-size white cake mix
1   cup quick-cooking rolled oats
½   cup peanut butter
1   egg
2   tablespoons milk
1   8-ounce package reduced-fat cream cheese (Neufchâtel)
1   12¼-ounce jar caramel ice cream topping
1   11½-ounce package milk chocolate pieces
1   cup cocktail peanuts

1 Preheat oven to 350°. Coat a 13×9×2-inch baking pan with cooking spray. Set aside.

2 For crumb mixture, in a large bowl combine cake mix and oats. Using a pastry blender, cut in peanut butter until mixture resembles fine crumbs. In a small bowl beat egg and milk with a fork; add to peanut butter mixture, stirring until well mixed. Set aside ¾ cup of the crumb mixture. Press remaining crumb mixture into bottom of prepared baking pan.

3 For filling, in a medium mixing bowl beat cream cheese with an electric mixer on medium speed until smooth. Add caramel topping; beat until mixed. Spread on top of crumb mixture in baking pan. Sprinkle chocolate pieces on top; sprinkle with peanuts. Sprinkle evenly with reserved crumb mixture.

4 Bake in preheated oven for 30 minutes. Cool completely on a wire rack. Cut into 24 bars. Store, covered, in the refrigerator.

Nutrition Facts per bar: 311 cal., 14 g total fat (5 g sat. fat), 16 mg chol., 273 mg sodium, 41 g carbo., 1 g fiber, 7 g pro.

PUMPKIN SPICE WHOOPIES

Prep: 35 minutes

Bake: 15 minutes per batch

· · · · · · · · · · · · · · · · · · ·

Oven: 375°F

Makes: 15 cookie sandwiches

1	cup canned pumpkin
1/3	cup butter, softened
1	package 2-layer-size spice cake mix
2	eggs
1/2	cup milk
1	recipe Marshmallow-Spice Filling

1 Preheat oven to 375°. Line a cookie sheet with parchment paper or foil (grease foil, if using). In a large mixing bowl combine pumpkin and butter; beat with an electric mixer on medium speed until smooth. Add cake mix, eggs, and milk; beat on low speed until combined. Beat on medium speed for 1 minute.

2 Drop mounds of batter by heaping tablespoons 3 inches apart on prepared cookie sheet. Keep remaining batter chilled.

3 Bake in preheated oven about 15 minutes or until set and lightly browned around edges. Carefully remove from parchment or foil; cool on wire rack.

4 Repeat with remaining batter, lining cooled cookie sheets each time with new parchment or greased foil. (If desired, place cookies in a covered storage container with waxed paper between layers to prevent sticking. Store cookies at room temperature for up to 24 hours.)

5 Spread about 2½ tablespoons of the Marshmallow-Spice Filling on the flat side of a cookie; top with a second cookie. Repeat with remaining cookies and remaining Marshmallow-Spice Filling. Serve immediately or cover and chill up to 2 hours.

Marshmallow-Spice Filling: In a medium mixing bowl combine one 8-ounce package cream cheese, softened, and ½ cup butter, softened; beat with an electric mixer on medium speed until smooth. Add 2 cups sifted powdered sugar, ½ of a 7-ounce jar marshmallow creme, 1 teaspoon vanilla, ½ teaspoon ground cinnamon, and ½ teaspoon ground nutmeg. Beat until well mixed.

Nutrition Facts per cookie sandwich: 379 cal., 19 g total fat (11 g sat. fat), 75 mg chol., 387 mg sodium, 49 g carbo., 1 g fiber, 3 g pro.

EASY LEMON SUGAR SNAPS

Prep: 25 minutes
Bake: 9 minutes per batch

· ·

Oven: 375°F
Makes: about 3½ dozen cookies

³⁄₄ cup butter, softened

1 egg

1 package 2-layer-size lemon cake mix (with pudding in the mix)*

1 cup yellow cornmeal

2 tablespoons finely shredded lemon peel

Coarse sugar or granulated sugar

1 Preheat oven to 375°. In a large mixing bowl beat butter and egg with an electric mixer on medium to high speed for 30 seconds. Gradually beat in dry cake mix until combined; stir in cornmeal and lemon peel. If necessary, use your hands to knead in cornmeal until well mixed.

2 Using 1 tablespoon of the dough for each cookie, roll into 1-inch balls. Roll in sugar. Place 2 inches apart on ungreased cookie sheets.

3 Bake in preheated oven for 9 to 10 minutes or until bottoms are lightly browned. Cool on cookie sheet for 1 minute. Transfer to wire rack; cool.

*Note: It is very important that the cake mix be the type with "pudding in the mix." If it isn't, the mixture will be too dry to work.

Nutrition Facts per cookie: 99 cal., 5 g total fat (2 g sat. fat), 14 mg chol., 114 mg sodium, 14 g carbo., 0 g fiber, 1 g pro.

PEACH-RASPBERRY PASTRY STACKS

Prep: 35 minutes
Bake: 12 minutes

. . . .

Oven: 375°F
Makes: 12 servings

½ of a 17.3-ounce package frozen puff pastry (1 sheet), thawed

2 cups frozen unsweetened peach slices, thawed

1 cup whipping cream

½ cup purchased lemon curd

¼ cup seedless red raspberry preserves or strawberry jelly

Fresh raspberries (optional)

1 Preheat oven to 375°. Unfold puff pastry on a lightly floured surface. Cut puff pastry into 3 rectangles along the fold lines. Cut each rectangle in half; cut each rectangle half diagonally to form a total of 12 triangles. Place triangles 1 inch apart on an ungreased baking sheet.

2 Bake in preheated oven for 12 to 15 minutes or until golden. Transfer to a wire rack; cool. (If desired, place cooled baked pastry triangles in an airtight container; cover. Store at room temperature overnight.)

3 Coarsely chop peach slices; drain well in colander. Pat peaches dry with clean paper towels.

4 In a chilled large mixing bowl beat whipping cream with chilled beaters of an electric mixer on medium speed until soft peaks form (tips curl); fold in lemon curd. Fold in chopped peaches. If desired, cover and chill for up to 4 hours.

5 Spoon raspberry preserves into a small saucepan; heat over medium-low heat just until melted, stirring occasionally.

6 Split puff pastry triangles horizontally and place bottom halves on dessert plates; top with lemon curd mixture. Top with remaining puff pastry halves. Lightly drizzle with melted preserves. If desired, garnish with fresh raspberries.

Nutrition Facts per serving: 232 cal., 14 g total fat (5 g sat. fat), 37 mg chol., 96 mg sodium, 17 g carbo., 2 g fiber, 1 g pro.

PLUMP APPLE DUMPLINGS WITH CARAMEL SAUCE

Prep: 30 minutes
Bake: 35 minutes

Oven: 400°F
Makes: 4 servings

½	of a 17.3-ounce package frozen puff pastry (1 sheet), thawed
4	medium cooking apples (such as Golden Delicious or Jonathan)
1	tablespoon sugar
½	teaspoon ground cinnamon
1	egg
1	teaspoon water
½	cup caramel ice cream topping
⅓	cup chopped pecans, toasted

1 Unfold puff pastry on a lightly floured surface. Roll pastry into a 14-inch square. Using a fluted pastry cutter or table knife, cut pastry into four 7-inch squares. Set aside.

2 Preheat oven to 400°. Core apples; peel apples, if desired. If necessary, trim bottoms of apples so they stand upright. Place an apple in the center of each pastry square. In a small bowl combine sugar and cinnamon; spoon into centers of apples.

3 In another small bowl beat egg and the water with a fork. Moisten the edges of the pastry squares with egg mixture; fold corners to center over fruit. Pinch to seal, pleating and folding pastry along seams as necessary. Place dumplings in a 13×9×2-inch baking pan. Brush wrapped apples with egg mixture.

4 Bake dumplings in preheated oven about 35 minutes or until fruit is tender and pastry is brown.

5 Meanwhile, for sauce, in a microwave-safe 2-cup glass measure combine caramel topping and pecans. Microwave, uncovered, on 100% power (high) for 30 to 60 seconds or until heated through.

6 Serve dumplings warm with sauce.

Nutrition Facts per serving: 571 cal., 27 g total fat (1 g sat. fat), 53 mg chol., 355 mg sodium, 78 g carbo., 6 g fiber, 5 g pro.

CRANBERRY-PEAR COBBLER

Prep: 25 minutes
Bake: 15 minutes

Oven: 400°F
Makes: 8 servings

1	16-ounce can whole cranberry sauce
¼	cup sugar
2	tablespoons cornstarch
½	teaspoon finely shredded lemon peel (optional)
4	cups peeled, cored, and sliced pears
1	7.75-ounce package cinnamon swirl complete biscuit mix
½	cup chopped pecans, toasted
1	tablespoon butter or margarine, melted
1	tablespoon sugar
	Vanilla ice cream (optional)

1 Preheat oven to 400°. In a microwave-safe 2-quart rectangular baking dish* stir together cranberry sauce, the ¼ cup sugar, the cornstarch, and, if desired, lemon peel. Gently stir in pears. Cover with plastic wrap; microwave on 100% power (high) for 9 to 11 minutes or until mixture is bubbly and pears are just tender, stirring once halfway through cooking. Gently stir cranberry mixture again.

2 Meanwhile, prepare biscuit mix according to package directions. Stir in pecans. Drop mixture into 8 mounds on hot cranberry mixture. Drizzle with melted butter. Sprinkle with the 1 tablespoon sugar.

3 Bake in preheated oven for 15 to 18 minutes or until biscuits are golden. Cool for 30 minutes before serving.

4 To serve, spoon fruit and biscuits into dessert bowls. If desired, serve with ice cream.

*Note: If baking dish does not fit in microwave, place the fruit mixture in a large saucepan; bring to boiling over medium heat, stirring frequently. Transfer to the 2-quart rectangular baking dish and proceed as directed in step 2.

Nutrition Facts per serving: 346 cal., 10 g total fat (1 g sat. fat), 4 mg chol., 269 mg sodium, 65 g carbo., 3 g fiber, 2 g pro.

POLENTA-PECAN APPLE COBBLER

Prep: 15 minutes
Bake: 25 minutes

Oven: 375°F
Makes: 6 servings

½   cup all-purpose flour
⅓   cup quick-cooking polenta mix or yellow cornmeal
2   tablespoons granulated sugar
1   teaspoon baking powder
½   teaspoon salt
3   tablespoons butter
½   cup chopped pecans
2   tablespoons packed brown sugar
½   teaspoon ground cinnamon
2   21-ounce cans apple pie filling
⅓   cup half-and-half or light cream
    Half-and-half or light cream (optional)

1 Preheat oven to 375°. For topping, in a medium bowl stir together flour, polenta mix, granulated sugar, baking powder, and salt. Using a pastry blender, cut in butter until mixture resembles coarse crumbs; set aside. In a small bowl combine pecans, brown sugar, and cinnamon; set aside.

2 In a medium saucepan heat the apple pie filling until bubbly, stirring frequently. Cover and set aside to keep hot. Stir the ⅓ cup half-and-half into flour mixture, stirring just to moisten.

3 Transfer hot filling to a 2-quart square baking dish. Immediately drop topping by rounded teaspoons on top of filling. Sprinkle evenly with pecan mixture.

4 Bake in preheated oven about 25 minutes or until topping is lightly browned. Cool about 30 minutes before serving. If desired, serve with additional half-and-half.

Nutrition Facts per serving: 441 cal., 15 g total fat (6 g sat. fat), 22 mg chol., 498 mg sodium, 77 g carbo., 4 g fiber, 4 g pro.

HARVEST PUDDING

Prep: 25 minutes
Bake: 45 minutes

Oven: 350°F
Makes: 12 servings

⅓ cup quick-cooking rolled oats

¼ cup all-purpose flour

2 tablespoons packed brown sugar

⅛ teaspoon ground cinnamon

¼ cup butter

2 tablespoons chopped walnuts

1 package 2-layer-size sour cream white cake mix

3 eggs

Dairy sour cream

Pear nectar

2 medium pears, cored and finely chopped

1 medium cooking apple, cored and finely chopped

1 Preheat oven to 350°. Grease a 3-quart rectangular baking dish; set aside. For topping, in a small bowl combine oats, flour, brown sugar, and cinnamon. Using a pastry blender, cut in butter until pieces are pea-size. Stir in walnuts. Set aside.

2 Prepare cake mix according to package directions, except use 3 whole eggs instead of the egg whites, sour cream instead of the oil, use half of the water called for, and use pear nectar for the other half of the water called for. Stir in chopped pears and apple. Pour into prepared baking dish; spread evenly.

3 Bake in preheated oven for 20 minutes. Carefully pull oven rack out slightly; very carefully sprinkle topping over cake. Return to oven; bake pudding for 25 to 30 minutes more or until a toothpick inserted near the center comes out clean. Cool in pan on a wire rack for 30 minutes. Serve warm.

Nutrition Facts per serving: 333 cal., 12 g total fat (5 g sat. fat), 66 mg chol., 431 mg sodium, 53 g carbo., 1 g fiber, 5 g pro.

BERRIES 'N' BROWNIES

4	cups fresh red raspberries
4	to 5 tablespoons sugar
2	teaspoons finely shredded orange peel
2	cups whipping cream
$\frac{1}{4}$	cup raspberry liqueur (Chambord) (optional)
4	3-inch squares purchased brownies (such as milk chocolate, blond, or marbled brownies), cut into chunks

1 Set aside 8 to 10 of the raspberries. In a large bowl combine the remaining raspberries, the sugar, and orange peel. Spoon berry mixture into a 1- to 1½- quart compote dish or serving bowl.

2 In a chilled mixing bowl combine whipping cream and liqueur (if using); beat with chilled beaters of an electric mixer on medium speed until soft peaks form (tips curl). Spoon onto raspberry mixture. Top whipped cream with the brownie chunks and reserved raspberries.

Nutrition Facts per serving: 263 cal., 19 g total fat (10 g sat. fat), 69 mg chol., 63 mg sodium, 23 g carbo., 5 g fiber, 3 g pro.

BANANA SPLIT TRIFLES

Start to Finish:

15 minutes

. . . .

Makes: 4 servings

2   to 3 cups tin roof sundae, chocolate chunk, or vanilla ice cream

4   soft-style oatmeal or chocolate chip cookies (each about 3 inches in diameter), crumbled

⅔   cup hot fudge ice cream topping and/or strawberry preserves

½   cup whipped cream

2   small bananas, halved lengthwise and sliced into 1- to 2-inch pieces

1 In a medium bowl use a wooden spoon to stir ice cream until softened. In each of 4 parfait glasses or other tall glasses layer cookie crumbs, softened ice cream, and hot fudge topping, layering ingredients to the tops of the glasses.

2 Top trifles with whipped cream and banana slices. Serve immediately or cover and freeze until serving time or up to 1 hour.

Nutrition Facts per serving: 524 cal., 23 g total fat (12 g sat. fat), 48 mg chol., 161 mg sodium, 73 g carbo., 3 g fiber, 6 g pro.

GINGERBREAD-PEAR DESSERT

Prep: 30 minutes
Bake: 60 minutes

Oven: 375°F/325°F
Makes: 10 servings

½	cup sugar
2	tablespoons lemon juice
5	medium pears, peeled, cored, and sliced
⅓	cup seedless red raspberry jam
1	14½-ounce package gingerbread mix
½	cup butter, cut up
1	egg yolk
1	8-ounce package cream cheese, softened
⅓	cup sugar
3	eggs
½	teaspoon vanilla
1	teaspoon finely shredded lemon peel

1 In a large saucepan bring 2 cups water, the ½ cup sugar, and lemon juice to boiling. Add pears. Simmer, uncovered, for 5 minutes. Remove from heat. Stir in raspberry jam. Cool for 1 hour. (If desired, cover and chill for up to 6 hours.) Drain well.

2 Meanwhile, preheat oven to 375°. Place gingerbread mix in a large bowl. Using a pastry blender, cut butter into gingerbread mix until pieces are pea-size. Stir in egg yolk just until combined. Remove and discard ½ cup of the crumb mixture. Press remaining mixture onto bottom of a 10-inch springform pan. Bake in preheated oven for 25 minutes. Cool completely.

3 In a medium mixing bowl beat cream cheese with an electric mixer on medium to high speed for 30 seconds. Add the ⅓ cup sugar; beat until light and fluffy. Add eggs and vanilla; beat on medium speed until combined. Stir in lemon peel. Spoon half of cream cheese mixture into crust. Spoon drained pears evenly over cream cheese mixture in crust. Spoon remaining cream cheese mixture on the pears.

4 Reduce oven temperature to 325°. Bake for 35 to 40 minutes or until center is set. Cool in pan for 30 minutes. Loosen side of springform pan. Cover; chill at least 2 hours or up to 24 hours. Remove side of pan.

Nutrition Facts per serving: 424 cal., 22 g total fat (12 g sat. fat), 133 mg chol., 402 mg sodium, 52 g carbo., 2 g fiber, 6 g pro.

SHORTCUT NAPOLEONS

Prep: 30 minutes
Bake: 18 minutes

Oven: 400°F
Makes: 8 servings

½ of a 17.3-ounce package frozen puff pastry (1 sheet)
1 4-serving-size package instant vanilla or chocolate pudding mix
1¼ cups milk
1 8-ounce carton dairy sour cream
1 cup raspberries
1 cup sifted powdered sugar
3 to 4 teaspoons milk
1 tablespoon chocolate-flavored syrup

1 Let folded puff pastry stand at room temperature for 30 minutes to thaw. Preheat oven to 400°. On a lightly floured surface, unfold pastry and roll into a 10-inch square. Using a sharp knife, cut pastry into eight 5×2½-inch rectangles. Arrange pastry rectangles on an ungreased baking sheet. Prick several times with a fork.

2 Bake in preheated oven for 18 to 20 minutes or until golden. Transfer to a wire rack; cool. Split rectangles in half horizontally.

3 Meanwhile, prepare pudding mix according to package directions, except use the 1¼ cups milk and beat in sour cream along with the milk.

4 Spoon about ⅓ cup of the pudding mixture onto bottom half of each cooled pastry rectangle; top with raspberries and top halves of pastry rectangles.

5 In a small bowl combine powdered sugar and enough of the 3 to 4 teaspoons milk to make of drizzling consistency. Spoon over pastry rectangles to glaze. Drizzle chocolate-flavored syrup over glaze. If desired, gently draw a knife through the syrup in several places to make a pretty design. Serve immediately or chill up to 2 hours.

Nutrition Facts per serving: 323 cal., 16 g total fat (4 g sat. fat), 16 mg chol., 331 mg sodium, 41 g carbo., 1 g fiber, 4 g pro.

HARVEST PUMPKIN TRIFLE

Prep: 30 minutes
Chill: 2 to **24** hours

Makes: 8 servings

1   10³/₄-ounce package frozen pound cake, cut into ¹/₂-inch cubes
2   to 4 tablespoons cream sherry or orange juice
1   16-ounce can whole cranberry sauce
¹/₃   cup orange marmalade
1   15-ounce can pumpkin
1   cup milk
1   4-serving-size package instant vanilla pudding mix
1   teaspoon ground cinnamon
1   teaspoon ground ginger
1   cup whipping cream
2   tablespoons sugar
¹/₂   teaspoon vanilla
¹/₂   cup chopped walnuts, toasted

1 Divide the cake cubes evenly among eight 10- to 12-ounce glasses about 4 inches high. (Or layer all of the cake cubes in a 2¹/₂-quart clear serving bowl or soufflé dish.) Sprinkle cake cubes with sherry.

2 In a small bowl stir together cranberry sauce and orange marmalade. Spoon over cake cubes. In a large bowl stir together pumpkin, milk, pudding mix, cinnamon, and ginger. Spoon over cranberry layer.

3 In a chilled medium mixing bowl combine whipping cream, sugar, and vanilla. Beat with chilled beaters of an electric mixer on medium speed until soft peaks form (tips curl). Gently spread over pumpkin layer. Cover and chill for at least 2 hours or up to 24 hours. Sprinkle with walnuts before serving.

Nutrition Facts per serving: 532 cal., 25 g total fat (12 g sat. fat), 86 mg chol., 381 mg sodium, 73 g carbo., 3 g fiber, 5 g pro.

BANANAS SUZETTE OVER POUND CAKE

Start to Finish:

15 minutes

....

Makes: 4 servings

2   tablespoons butter or margarine

$\frac{1}{2}$ of a $10\frac{3}{4}$-ounce package frozen pound cake, thawed and cut into 4 slices

2   medium ripe, yet firm, bananas

3   tablespoons sugar

2   tablespoons orange-flavored liqueur or orange juice

2   tablespoons orange juice

$\frac{1}{8}$ teaspoon ground nutmeg

1   cup vanilla ice cream

1 In a medium skillet melt 1 tablespoon of the butter over medium heat. Add pound cake slices; cook for 1 to 2 minutes or until brown, turning once. Remove from skillet; set aside.

2 Peel bananas; bias-slice each banana into 8 pieces. In the same skillet combine sugar, liqueur, orange juice, and remaining 1 tablespoon butter. Heat about 1 minute or until butter melts and sugar begins to dissolve. Add the bananas; heat for 2 to 4 minutes more or just until the bananas are tender, stirring once. Stir in the nutmeg.

3 To serve, place a small scoop of vanilla ice cream on each pound cake slice. Spoon bananas and sauce over ice cream and pound cake slices.

Nutrition Facts per serving: 394 cal., 18 g total fat (11 g sat. fat), 74 mg chol., 229 mg sodium, 53 g carbo., 2 g fiber, 4 g pro.

PEANUT BUTTER PIZZAS

Prep: 20 minutes
Bake: 10 minutes

Oven: 375°F
Makes: 5 or 6 individual pizzas

1　10-ounce package refrigerated pizza dough (for 1 crust)
⅔　cup chunky peanut butter
2　cups assorted toppers (such as grape jelly or strawberry preserves, marshmallow creme, tiny marshmallows, chocolate-hazelnut spread, sliced fresh strawberries, peanuts, and/or sliced bananas)
　　Cinnamon sugar (optional)

1 Preheat oven to 375°. Lightly grease 2 baking sheets; set aside.

2 Divide dough into 5 or 6 pieces. Cover; let rest for 10 minutes. Roll each dough piece into a 6-inch circle. Place dough circles on prepared baking sheets. Prick dough circles generously with a fork (do not allow to rise).

3 Bake in preheated oven for 10 to 12 minutes or until lightly browned.

4 Remove from oven. While still warm, spread with peanut butter. Arrange on serving board or platter. Serve warm with assorted toppers. If desired, sprinkle with cinnamon sugar.

Nutrition Facts per pizza: 523 cal., 26 g total fat (4 g sat. fat), 0 mg chol., 490 mg sodium, 62 g carbo., 4 g fiber, 15 g pro.

TRIFLE-STYLE RASPBERRY PARFAITS

Prep: 25 minutes

Chill: 2 to **24** hours

. . . .

Makes: 4 to 6 servings

2	cups fresh or frozen raspberries
³⁄₄	cup sugar
2	tablespoons quick-cooking tapioca
1	tablespoon raspberry liqueur (Chambord) (optional)
1	cup whipping cream
1	tablespoon sugar
¹⁄₂	of a 10³⁄₄-ounce package frozen pound cake, thawed, cut into ¹⁄₂-inch cubes, and toasted* (about 3 cups)
¹⁄₂	cup grated bittersweet chocolate (3 ounces)

1 Thaw the frozen raspberries, if using; do not drain. In a medium saucepan stir together the ³⁄₄ cup sugar and the tapioca. Stir in the berries. Mash slightly. Let stand for 10 minutes. Bring mixture to boiling; reduce heat. Boil gently for 1 minute, stirring constantly. Remove from heat. If desired, stir in raspberry liqueur. Cool slightly. Transfer raspberry mixture to a medium bowl. Cover and chill for at least 2 hours or up to 24 hours.

2 Before serving, in a chilled medium mixing bowl combine whipping cream and the 1 tablespoon sugar; beat with chilled beaters of an electric mixer on medium speed until stiff peaks form (tips stand straight). Spoon half of the raspberry mixture in the bottoms of 4 to 6 parfait glasses or other tall glasses. Top with half of the pound cake cubes and half of the chocolate. Top with half of the whipped cream mixture. Repeat layers. Serve immediately or cover and chill for up to 1 hour.

*Note: To toast pound cake cubes, preheat oven to 350°. Spread cubes in a single layer in a shallow baking pan. Bake in preheated oven about 10 minutes or until lightly golden.

Nutrition Facts per serving: 674 cal., 37 g total fat (22 g sat. fat), 125 mg chol., 163 mg sodium, 84 g carbo., 6 g fiber, 5 g pro.

COOKIES & CREAM

Start to Finish:

15 minutes

. . . .

Makes: 8 servings

½   cup whipping cream

2   tablespoons honey

½   cup dairy sour cream

24 purchased large soft cookies (such as ginger or oatmeal)

    Honey

1 In a small chilled mixing bowl combine whipping cream and the 2 tablespoons honey; beat with chilled beaters of an electric mixer on medium speed until soft peaks form (tips curl). Fold in sour cream.

2 To serve, lay a cookie on each of 8 dessert plates. Top each serving with a spoonful of the whipped cream mixture. Top with another cookie and another spoonful of the whipped cream mixture. Top each serving with a third cookie and more whipped cream mixture. Drizzle with additional honey.

Nutrition Facts per serving: 456 cal., 21 g total fat (10 g sat. fat), 43 mg chol., 310 mg sodium, 61 g carbo., 2 g fiber, 5 g pro.

BERRY PATCH ICE CREAM DESSERT

Prep: 30 minutes
Bake: 25 minutes

Oven: 325°F
Makes: 10 servings

1 19- to 22-ounce package fudge brownie mix
1 quart vanilla ice cream
2½ cups fresh or frozen berries (such as raspberries, blueberries, and halved strawberries)
¼ cup chocolate ice cream topping or raspberry syrup

1 Preheat oven to 325°. Lightly grease two 8×1½-inch round baking pans; line bottom of each pan with waxed paper. Grease waxed paper; set pans aside. Prepare brownie mix according to package directions; divide batter evenly between prepared pans.

2 Bake in preheated oven for 25 minutes. Cool in pans on wire racks for 10 minutes. Loosen edges, invert, and carefully remove brownie rounds from pans. Peel off waxed paper. Cool completely on wire racks. Wrap each of the brownie rounds in plastic wrap. Place 1 of the brownie rounds in an airtight freezer container and freeze for up to 2 months (use this layer to make another Berry Patch Ice Cream Dessert). Store remaining brownie round at room temperature for several hours or overnight while berry-ice cream layer is being frozen.

3 For berry-ice cream layer, line an 8×1½-inch round pan with plastic wrap, allowing excess to extend over edge; set aside. In a large bowl use a wooden spoon to stir ice cream just until softened. Carefully fold in 1 cup of the berries. Spread berry-ice cream mixture evenly in prepared pan. Cover and freeze for at least 4 hours or up to 24 hours.

4 To serve, place the brownie round on a serving plate. Invert berry-ice cream layer onto brownie; peel off plastic wrap. Top with the remaining 1½ cups berries. Drizzle with chocolate topping. Let stand for 15 minutes before serving.

Nutrition Facts per serving: 350 cal., 19 g total fat (8 g sat. fat), 58 mg chol., 141 mg sodium, 44 g carbo., 3 g fiber, 4 g pro.

HAZELNUT CREAM CASSATA

Prep: 30 minutes
Bake: 15 minutes

. . . .

Oven: 350°F
Makes: 12 servings

1	package 2-layer-size white cake mix or lemon-flavored cake mix
1	tablespoon finely shredded lemon peel (only if using white cake mix)
1/3	cup chocolate-hazelnut spread
1/3	cup ricotta cheese
1/3	cup seedless red raspberry jam
1 1/2	cups whipping cream
2	tablespoons sifted powdered sugar
	Halved hazelnuts, toasted

1 Preheat oven to 350°. Grease and flour three 9×1 1/2-inch round cake pans; set aside. Prepare cake mix according to package directions. (If using white cake mix, stir in the finely shredded lemon peel.) Divide batter among prepared pans. (If you have only two 9-inch cake pans, cover and chill one-third of the batter and bake it after the other layers are out of the pans.)

2 Bake in preheated oven about 15 minutes or until a toothpick inserted near the centers comes out clean. Let cakes cool in pans on a wire rack for 10 minutes. Remove cakes from pans; cool completely on wire racks.

3 For filling, in a small bowl stir together chocolate-hazelnut spread and ricotta cheese. Place one layer of the cake on a serving platter; spread top with half of the jam. Spread half of the ricotta mixture over jam. Top with another layer of cake. Spread with remaining jam and remaining ricotta mixture. Top with remaining layer of cake.

4 In a chilled large mixing bowl combine whipping cream and powdered sugar; beat with chilled beaters of an electric mixer on medium speed just until stiff peaks form (tips stand straight). Spread whipped cream over top and side of cake. Top with hazelnuts. Serve immediately or store, covered, in refrigerator for up to 24 hours.

Nutrition Facts per serving: 413 cal., 23 g total fat (10 g sat. fat), 45 mg chol., 310 mg sodium, 47 g carbo., 1 g fiber, 5 g pro.

INDEX

A

METRIC INFORMATION

The charts on this page provide a guide for converting measurements from the U.S. customary system, which is used throughout this book, to the metric system.

Product Differences

Most of the ingredients called for in the recipes in this book are available in most countries. However, some are known by different names. Here are some common American ingredients and their possible counterparts:

> Sugar (white) is granulated, fine granulated, or castor sugar.

> Powdered sugar is icing sugar.

> All-purpose flour is enriched, bleached or unbleached white household flour. When self-rising flour is used in place of all-purpose flour in a recipe that calls for leavening, omit the leavening agent (baking soda or baking powder) and salt.

> Light-colored corn syrup is golden syrup.

> Cornstarch is cornflour.

> Baking soda is bicarbonate of soda.

> Vanilla or vanilla extract is vanilla essence.

> Green, red, or yellow sweet peppers are capsicums or bell peppers.

> Golden raisins are sultanas.

Volume and Weight

The United States traditionally uses cup measures for liquid and solid ingredients. The chart below shows the approximate imperial and metric equivalents. If you are accustomed to weighing solid ingredients, the following approximate equivalents will be helpful.

> 1 cup butter, castor sugar, or rice = 8 ounces = ½ pound = 250 grams

> 1 cup flour = 4 ounces = ¼ pound = 125 grams

> 1 cup icing sugar = 5 ounces = 150 grams

Canadian and U.S. volume for a cup measure is 8 fluid ounces (237 ml), but the standard metric equivalent is 250 ml. 1 British imperial cup is 10 fluid ounces.

In Australia, 1 tablespoon equals 20 ml, and there are 4 teaspoons in the Australian tablespoon.

Spoon measures are used for smaller amounts of ingredients. Although the size of the tablespoon varies slightly in different countries, for practical purposes and for recipes in this book, a straight substitution is all that's necessary. Measurements made using cups or spoons always should be level unless stated otherwise.

Common Weight Range Replacements

Imperial / U.S.	Metric
½ ounce	15 g
1 ounce	25 g or 30 g
4 ounces (¼ pound)	115 g or 125 g
8 ounces (½ pound)	225 g or 250 g
16 ounces (1 pound)	450 g or 500 g
1¼ pounds	625 g
1½ pounds	750 g
2 pounds or 2¼ pounds	1,000 g or 1 Kg

Oven Temperature Equivalents

Fahrenheit Setting	Celsius Setting*	Gas Setting
300°F	150°C Gas	Mark 2 (very low)
325°F	160°C Gas	Mark 3 (low)
350°F	180°C Gas	Mark 4 (moderate)
375°F	190°C Gas	Mark 5 (moderate)
400°F	200°C Gas	Mark 6 (hot)
425°F	220°C Gas	Mark 7 (hot)
450°F	230°C Gas	Mark 8 (very hot)
475°F	240°C Gas	Mark 9 (very hot)
500°F	260°C Gas	Mark 10 (extremely hot)
Broil	Broil	Grill

*Electric and gas ovens may be calibrated using celsius. However, for an electric oven, increase celsius setting 10 to 20 degrees when cooking above 160°C. For convection or forced air ovens (gas or electric) lower the temperature setting 25°F/10°C when cooking at all heat levels.

Baking Pan Sizes

Imperial / U.S.	Metric
9x1½-inch round cake pan	22- or 23x4-cm (1.5 L)
9x1½-inch pie plate	22- or 23x4-cm (1 L)
8x8x2-inch square cake pan	20x5-cm (2 L)
9x9x2-inch square cake pan	22- or 23x4.5-cm (2.5 L)
11x7x1½-inch baking pan	28x17x4-cm (2 L)
2-quart rectangular baking pan	30x19x4.5-cm (3 L)
13x9x2-inch baking pan	34x22x4.5-cm (3.5 L)
15x10x1-inch jelly roll pan	40x25x2-cm
9x5x3-inch loaf pan	23x13x8-cm (2 L)
2-quart casserole	2 L

U.S. / Standard	Metric Equivalents
⅛ teaspoon =	0.5 ml
¼ teaspoon =	1 ml
½ teaspoon =	2 ml
1 teaspoon =	5 ml
1 tablespoon =	15 ml
2 tablespoons =	25 ml
¼ cup =	2 fluid ounces = 50 ml
⅓ cup =	3 fluid ounces = 75 ml
½ cup =	4 fluid ounces = 125 ml
⅔ cup =	5 fluid ounces = 150 ml
¾ cup =	6 fluid ounces = 175 ml
1 cup =	8 fluid ounces = 250 ml
2 cups =	1 pint = 500 ml
1 quart =	1 litre